STRATEGY AND GLOBAL MANAGEMENT:
Global Market Opportunities and Challenges

STRATEGY AND GLOBAL MANAGEMENT:

Global Market Opportunities and Challenges

DR. JABIR KHALIL

PENTAGON PRESS

STRATEGY AND GLOBAL MANAGEMENT:
Global Market Opportunities and Challenges

First Published 2006

ISBN 81-8274-200-5

Published by

PENTAGON PRESS
A-38, Hauz Khas, New Delhi-110016 (India)
Phones: 011-41656996/7/8, 41517091
Telefax: 011-41656997
email: pentagonpress@touchtelindia.net

Sales Office:
Flat # 105-106, 4262, St. # 3
Ansari Road, Darya Ganj, New Delhi-110002
Phones: 011-41563901/2, 23287705
Website: www.pentagon-press.com

Printed by New Elegant Printers, New Delhi.

Contents

Preface

The global economy is undergoing dramatic economic changes. The removal of technical, trade, and monetary barriers and the liberalisation of the world economies, including those of the transitional economies and emerging nations, create challenges and opportunities from the standpoint of investment and financial transactions.

The privatisation of state-owned enterprises and the development of shareholder capitalism acquired great importance in the recent past and constitute a *nova terra* that needs further exploration and research. Private ownership, through titles or stocks, stimulates work incentives and increases productivity, whereas common ownership means common neglect, as Aristotle had predicted some twenty-five centuries ago.

With the drastic reforms in emerging and other nations—the deregulations in industrial countries, the globalisation of business, and the growing number of shareholders worldwide, international finance is expected to play a vital role in matters of foreign exchange, cross-border capital flows, joint ventures, and economic growth.

This book weaves together a theoretical framework of international markets supported by the latest empirical research and related applications. It provides a comprehensive analysis of traditional and modern theories of international market systems, problems of globalisation, and exchange rates, as well as related adjustment and stabilisation policies for industrialised and emerging nations. In addition to brief historical review, the book deals with advanced theories of international trade and finance, as well as the related real world performance. the problems of emerging markets, the international capital movements and banking activities, market capitalisation, as well as investment movements and cross-border management, economic and financial integration, related effects of macroeconomic policies in open economies, and challenges of global expansion.

The book is of great theoretical and practical importance to business leaders with a wide range of interests in international finance and business development. It is also useful to people interested in the growing number of jobs in the field, particularly the young urban professionals. It can be used as a guide for "International Finance" and as a supplement in "International Economics" and "Economics of Emerging Nations."

Introduction

To stay competitive, every company will need to serve the international market, And to truly compete on the global scene, companies must be localized—which goes beyond translating languages to adapting all contents to meet cultural standards.

Business concepts come and go. One concept, which seems to have come to stay, is **culture**. It looks like one of those grand concepts. It emerged on the intellectual landscape of business in the early 1980s, and has captured the interests of academics, journalists and businesspeople alike. In fact, the concept has a rich ancestry in business. It can be traced back at least as far as the writings of Mayo and Barnard in the United States in the 1930s.

People can have many theories about why the culture concept was able to catch their interest so thoroughly at this time; perhaps the time was ripe. Maybe the reason was people's growing international interest or maybe it was an increase in the interest of human beings. One thing is clear, however, the cultural idea has led people to 're-evaluate the attributes of organisational success which are not part and parcel of the 'orthodox' rationalist paradigm (Green, 1988, p. 121).

Culture can be used for many different types of analysis. It can provide the foundation or the background for various kinds of understanding. One way to formulate the basic question of this study could be: How do business leaders think as a result of their national culture, and what are the consequences for how business leadership is exercised? Also, how do business followers think as a result of their national culture, and what are the consequences of how business leadership **can** or **should** be exercised?

However, it appears that it is related to human values one way or the other and, like culture, interest in human values dates back many years (Lewin, 1935: Allport, 1937 ; Bruner and Goodman, 1947: Kluckhohn and Strodtbeck, 1961). The term 'value' is used in all social science subjects (for example, Anthropology, Psychology, Sociology, Business Management, Political Science and Economics). Each of them provides it with a different though not completely unrelated meaning. 'Value' is very much an interdisciplinary term, like 'system' or 'leadership'. Maybe as a forerunner to the interest in culture, management researchers have, during the past 30 years or so, begun to recognize the importance of personal values in understanding business behaviour. According to Davis and Rasool (1988), the impetus to this area of inquiry was given by Guth and Tagiuri (1965), who illustrated ways in which personal values influence the choice of corporate strategy. The literature has since been replete with a majority suggesting a strong relationship between a manager's personal values and his or her decision-making (Haire et al., 1966; Senger, 1970; Sikula, 1971; Pezeshkpur, 1975; Hughes et al., 1976; Bennis and Nanus, 1985; Peters and Austin, 1985; Deal and Kennedy. 1988). So, the inquiry in this study into the relation between values (culture) and management behaviour (leadership) rests on a solid background.

Culture is the intersubjective aspect of life. It is learnt, much of it at a very young age, and it is reinforced through social pressure. The result is that culture belongs to a whole group, not to its individuals, and we cannot avoid it. It paramountly determines our behavior and at the same time it gives us an anchoring point, an identity, a social place and a world view. Because of the human need for order and consistency, our basic assumptions about humankind, nature and social activities become patterned into what may be called 'cultural paradigms'; these assumptions form a coherent pattern. This pattern or framework is used to structure experience, to give meaning to thoughts and actions. It is transmitted in many ways, including long-standing and often unwritten rules, shared standards and even prejudices. Within this general understanding of what culture means, it can be defined as being slightly different from one situation to another. Every such definition becomes, at least partly, a theory, a model or an interpretation (depending on your basic attitude to what research is for), and it suits a purpose.

My purpose is to discuss business leadership in the light of national cultures. In order to gain an analytical focus and edge, I have chosen to separate culture (as norms, values assumptions, beliefs and so on) from the way it expresses itself in the form of behaviour, language, organisations, institutions, artifacts and so on. This is also consistent with a common understanding, whether culture is broadly or narrowly defined and includes basic norms, values and assumptions of a human group, organisation or nation. My choice of delimiting the content of culture means, among other things, that I understand language to be a mirror of culture, not a part of culture itself. Another dimension of culture is to clarify how deep-seated its shared qualities are (Kilmann et al., 1986, p. 89). Values, for instance, can appear or be hidden at various levels of depth. At the conscious level, or close to it, they may appear as behavioral norms. Such norms are either written or unwritten rules of the game. Examples of such norms are:

- To be on time at meetings.
- To wear dark business suits to work.
- Not to share information with other groups.

Globalisation has a strong cultural dimension since it brings together in an unprecedented way the values, ideas, lifestyles, and views of the world whose differences appear the more important as they become commonly perceptible. It changes the representations of the world.

CHAPTER 1

Global Opportunities and Challenges

Privatisation and Globalisation: A Perspective

The transfer of state-held assets into private hands, now commonly referred to as privatisation, is a relatively new economic concept. Because this process offers substantial benefits to divesting governments, as well as the new owners and the general citizenry of a country, it is acquiring increased acceptance throughout the world. As a result, the privatisation phenomenon is producing thousands of new, privately held companies in over 100 different countries in both the industrialized and developing worlds. These companies, with their unique operating cultures and characteristics, constitute a formidable market force in the expanding global economy.

The transition from long-term state control to newly formed private governance, however, is a complex and sometimes confusing process. The manner in which the enterprise makes this operational transformation will often determine its ultimate viability and establish the firm's capacity to function as a valued customer or as an effective strategic partner for an American company.

Depending on definition, the privatisation of state-held assets is traceable to countries in Asia that began to privatise some of their state-owned businesses in the 1960s. Later, in the mid-1970s, the military government of Chile attempted to divest several of the country's larger loss-producing enterprises by offering them for sale to private investors.

The early attempts at privatisation were not particularly successful. However, the efforts did provide a counterbalance to the prevailing trend of nationalisation that was in economic vogue during the years following World War II. In Great Britain during the 1940s, for example, over 20 per cent of the country's workforce was employed by nationalised industries. These and other large European organisations at that time were responsible for creating thousands of new jobs and were instrumental in the rebuilding of the war-ravaged infrastructure.

As the economies of Europe improved, the state-owned companies became increasingly susceptible to political pressure for unwarranted job creation. This led to greater operating inefficiencies, accompanied by a broadening divergence from prevailing market forces. The lack of a profit-motivated management structure also contributed substantially to expanding financial losses that could be curtailed only through the process of privatisation.

The globalisation of markets, the increased need for working capital, and new technology, combined with an improved investment environment, are contributing to the acceleration in the rate of new privatisation. This rapid rate of expansion had a tsunami-like effect on many nationalized industries, leaving literally tens of thousands of formerly state-owned enterprises in its wake. The surviving firms are now attempting to become cost conscious, profit driven, and market focused by adopting operating philosophies that are in major conflict with their prior centrally planned operating techniques.

The ability to achieve improved productivity and increased operating efficiency throughout a country's industrial infrastructure is one of the principal reasons why many governments resort to privatisation. With increased globalisation, it is imperative that a nation's commercial organisations be able to compete effectively with major corporations throughout the world. Under state ownership, companies are unable to be both politically benevolent and competitively productive simultaneously. Without a strong incentive to improve, productivity suffers and innovation falters. On the other hand, the effect of privatisation, often accompanied by radical restructuring, will result in improved operating efficiency and increased worker productivity that enable the company to become more price competitive in its local and foreign markets. Increased globalisation is in fact forcing many governments to privatise their commercial holdings as a way of improving the competitiveness of its industrial base. Under the auspices of the state, a company has no incentive to improve its ability to compete because of the assured support and financial subsidisation of the parent. Frequently, this also includes protective regulations that are instituted by the government to insulate the enterprise from external competitive forces. With the continuation of state control, these business units are unable to adjust to increased competition should it arise. This lack of competitiveness becomes even more pronounced when the enterprise attempts to enter into cross border commercial transactions.

If we asked an ordinary person on the streets of London, New York, Bangkok, or Rio de Janeiro about the essence of globalisation, the answer would probably involve some reference to growing forms of political and economic interdependence fuelled by 'new technologies' like personal computers, the Internet, cellular phones, pagers, fax, palm pilots, digital cameras, high-definition televisions, satellites, jet planes, space shuttles, and supertankers. As subsequent chapters will show, however, technology provides only a partial explanation for the existence of contemporary forms of globalisation. Yet, it would be foolish to deny that these new innovations have played a crucial role in the creation, multiplication, expansion, and intensification of global social interconnections and exchanges. The Internet, in particular, has assumed a pivotal function in facilitating globalisation through the creation of the World Wide Web that connects billions of individuals, private associations, and governments. Since most of these technologies have been around for less than three decades, it seems to make sense to agree with those commentators who claim that globalisation is, indeed, a new phenomenon.

The dynamic nature of the phenomenon, the enhancement of worldwide interdependence and the general growth of awareness of deepening global connections are gradual processes with deep historical roots. For example, the engineers who developed laptop and supersonic jet planes stand on the shoulders of earlier innovators who created the steam engine, the cotton gin, the telegraph, the phonograph, the telephone, the typewriter, the internal-combustion engine, and electrical appliances. These products, in turn, owe their existence to much earlier technological inventions such as the telescope, the compass, water wheels, windmills, gunpowder, the printing press, and oceangoing ships. In order to acknowledge the full historical record, we reach back even further to such momentous technological and social achievements as the production of paper, the development of writing, the invention of the wheel, the domestication of wild plants and animals, the emergence of language, and, finally, the slow outward migration of our African ancestors at the dawn of human evolution.

Changes in the way in which people undertake economic production and organise the exchange of commodities represent one obvious aspect of the great transformation of our age. Economic globalisation refers to the intensification and expansion of economic interrelations across the globe. Gigantic flows of capital and technology have stimulated trade in goods and services. Markets have extended their reach around the world, in the process creating new linkages among national economies. Huge transnational corporations, powerful international economic institutions, and large regional trading systems have emerged as the major building blocks of the 21st century's global economic order.

Contemporary economic globalisation can be traced back to the gradual emergence of a new international economic order assembled at an economic conference held towards the end of World War II in the sleepy New England town of Bretton Woods. Under the leadership of the United States of America and Great Britain, the major economic powers of the global North reversed their protectionist policies of the interwar period (1918-39). In addition to arriving at a firm commitment to expand international trade, the participants of the conference also agreed to establish binding rules on international economic activities. Moreover, they resolved to create a more stable money exchange system in which the value of each country's currency was pegged to a fixed gold value of the US dollar. Within these prescribed limits, individual nations were free to control the permeability of their borders. This allowed states to set their own political and economic agendas.

The Bretton Woods Conference also set the institutional foundations for the establishment of three new international economic organisations. The **International Monetary Fund** (IMF) was created to administer the international monetary system. The **International Bank for Reconstruction and Development**, later known as the **World Bank**, was initially designed to provide loans for Europe's postwar reconstruction. During the 1950s, however, its purpose was expanded to fund various industrial projects in developing countries around the world. Finally, the General Agreement on Tariffs and Trade (GATT) was established in 1947 as a global trade organisation charged with fashioning and enforcing multilateral trade agreements. In 1995, the **World Trade Organisation** (WTO) was founded as the successor organisation to GATT. The WTO became the focal point of intense public controversy over the design and the effects of economic globalisation.

An ideology can be defined as a system of widely shared ideas, patterned beliefs, guiding norms and values, and ideals accepted as truth by a particular group of people. Ideologies offer individuals a more or less coherent picture of the world not only as it is, but also as it ought to be. In doing so, they help organise the complex human experience into fairly simple, but frequently distorted, images that serve as guide and compass for social and political action. These simplified but distorted ideas are often employed to legitimise certain political interests or to defend dominant power structures. Seeking to imbue society with their preferred norms and values, ideologists present the public with a circumscribed agenda of things to discuss, claims to make, and questions to ask. They speak to their audience in stories and narratives that persuade, praise, condemn, distinguish 'truths' from 'falsehoods', and separate the 'good' from the 'bad'. Thus, ideology connects theory and practice by orienting and organising human action in accordance with generalised claims, and codes of conduct. Like all social processes, globalisation contains an ideological dimension filled with a range of norms, claims, beliefs, and narratives about the phenomenon itself. For example, the heated public debate over whether globalisation represents a 'good' or a 'bad' aspect occurs in the arena of ideology. Hence, before exploring the ideological dimension of globalisation we should make an important analytical distinction between **globalisation**—social processes of intensifying global interdependence that have been described by various commentators in different, often contradictory ways—and **globalism**—an ideology that endows the concept of globalisation with neoliberal values and meanings.

Managing Global Operations

Many business books begin with a perfunctory statement similar to "In these turbulent, dynamic, complex, days of global management . . ." We believe that firms doing business across the globe have communications tools that make global management infinitely easier in the 2000s than in prior decades. Fax machines, email, satellite communications, cellular telephones, and computer local area networks are tools that enable managers to communicate at speeds few could have imagined a short time ago. We have never had it easier. Certainly there has been much political turmoil in the 2000s:

the crumbling of the Eastern bloc, wars in the Middle East and Bosnia, racial strife in South Africa—but such turbulence is not peculiar to modern times. What we do have today is the ability to spot political trends faster. Through satellite communications, we receive vital news reports and coverage at unimaginable speed.

Those who insist that the management of the global firm is more difficult in 1996 are correct for the decisions must be made faster, and operations must quickly change directions in order to survive. Business trends shift as quickly in the 2000s as the technologies that tell us about the shifts.

The operations function is the very soul of the organisation. The function is made up of men and women who are responsible for production. Because of their intimacy with the product, the people of production know more than anyone else in the organisation about what goes into that product.

Road Map to Global Operations

The initial decision to globalise an organisation requires a great deal of planning and consideration. Which country in that region should the company make its first overtures to? Which city in the country has the best location? What form of global operations should the company adopt? These are some of the big questions that any company intending to globalise its operations must answer. At the initial deliberation stage, other operational factors such as location, capacity, human resources, materials management, and technology come into play.

From a macro perspective, the foreign country's political climate, legal effect systems, government regulations, and economic status will inevitably impact the business environment. At the micro level, local tax treaties, availability of skilled labour, infrastructure of the city, transportation, proximity to raw materials, wage structure, and quality of life will affect the day-to-day 'operations. Multifactors such as culture, religion, customs, natural resources, attitude of local people towards foreign investment, and openness of the community all have a significant bearing on shaping the future success of the global operations.

Factors for Global Operations

Sheth and Eshghi (1992) offer four factors that motivate companies to contemplate the use of global operations: cost competitiveness, competitive markets, manufacturing processes, and government policy.

Cost Competitiveness

Two popular generic strategies are cost leadership and differentiation. The cost leadership strategy seeks to achieve and maintain a competitive advantage through realising lower unit costs of production and distribution. The differentiation strategy attempts to achieve a competitive advantage through providing features that differentiate the product or service.

Competitive Markets

Time-based competition mandates that the faster the company reacts to market changes, the quicker it brings its products to the market, the more likely the company is to survive and succeed. Advantages derive from being close to the local market: The company is quick to bring its products to the local market—some products have a short shelf life and shipping via air is usually too costly; consumers are more sophisticated in choosing products and services, and tastes change rapidly—being close to the local market not only enables the company to customise its products to local flavours but also allows it to be more responsive to market changes.

When the domestic market shows signs of approaching maturity, expanding to an overseas market can be a significant step toward seeking continued growth. When Nike decided to open a plant in China, important considerations included not only the cheap labour and material costs but also the enormous market potential that China presents. The prospect of capturing one per cent of China's total population of 1.2 billion people would translate into over ten million pairs of shoes for Nike.

However, it does not take long before an untapped market is flooded with competition.

Manufacturing Competency

Flexible manufacturing, JIT, CAD, and CAM make globalising operations feasible. The increasing use of information technology in manufacturing and services improves global networks, reduces long-distance barriers, and shortens the communication time. Several U.S. credit-card companies and banks own data processing facilities in Latin American and Asian countries to take advantage of the low labour costs. This way, outcomes from on-the-spot processing are communicated back through information networks almost instantaneously. Without jeopardizing the quality of service and responsiveness to customers, they are able to reduce data-processing costs.

An important factor in manufacturing competency is the **exchange of technology** across national boundaries. To compete on a global basis, Ford not only transfers technology to foreign countries but also tries to learn from locals. The exchange...includes such issues as the technical standards in each country, government regulations, special characteristics of local markets, and international transportation costs.

Global Operation Strategy

An organisation with a customer focus concentrates on exceeding the customer's expectations. These expectations must be well understood by management and in line with company strategy. The product or service should do more for the customer than the customer has a right to expect.

A restaurant that advertises that it features an "all-you-can-eat food bar for only $3.99," will meet the customers' expectations if customers have to let their belts out a notch at the end of a meal. Customers may be somewhat pleased that they must rely on antacids the rest of the evening, for they have achieved what they intended—stuffing themselves silly for a low price. Another restaurant may charge its customers $50 for a meal. In this case, the customer expects the waiter or waitress to anticipate their wants and needs. Yet, if you were to stand outside both restaurants and ask customers, "On a scale of 1 to 5, 5 being best, how satisfied were you with your dining experience?" You might be surprised to discover that the 'all-you-can-eat' place scored as high as the expensive restaurant. It is because the cheaper restaurant is able to meet customer expectations as well as the fancier establishment.

A customer focus has been well enunciated in the early 1990s. Companies should similarly strive to exceed the expectations of their employees. This can be accomplished through pay, promotions, benefits, or just plain surprises. "Because of your outstanding performance last month, every one will get an extra vacation day this year!" It may be difficult to imagine a company exceeding expectations during lean times, but allegiance to the employees during hard periods is critical to long-term success. Bonuses should never be awarded to senior managers who achieve cost savings by laying off workers. The size of the workforce often grows too large in the first place from years of poor planning, and managers should not reward themselves for later recognizing the error of their ways. Operations were not viewed as a strategic area of the firm until the Japanese demonstrated to the world how truly strategic operations can be.

Emerging Markets

Emerging markets—that is, markets of developing and transitional economies—deal primarily with stocks and bonds. Out of thirty-one emerging markets in the world, ten are in Asia, seven in Europe, seven in Latin America, and seven in the Middle East/Africa. Asia had the largest number of stocks (758 out of a total of 1,424 for all emerging markets) traded in the last week of January 1998, followed by Latin America (270), Middle East/Africa (236), and Europe (160).

From the Asian emerging markets, South Korea has the largest number of stocks, followed by Malaysia, Taiwan, India, Thailand, Indonesia, Philippines, China, Pakistan, and Sri Lanka.

In the European emerging markets, Greece has the largest number of stocks, followed by Russia, Poland, Portugal, Hungary, the Czech Republic, Slovakia, and the Balkan countries.

Although the emerging markets of Latin America are growing, they are still limited in number and size. There are some 1,200 public companies in the major markets of Latin America with a combined market capitalisation of about $300 billion, with Brazil having the largest number of stocks traded, followed by Mexico, Chile, Argentina, Peru, Colombia, and Venezuela.

In the Middle East or African markets, South Africa has the largest number of stocks traded. In the 1980s, the entry of Greece, Portugal, and Spain into the European Union, as well as the high economic growth of Hong Kong, South Korea, Singapore, and Taiwan (the four Asian 'tigers') stimulated the growth of their stock markets. However, the recent financial crisis in Asia reduced the performance of the stock markets, mainly in Asia, Russia, and Latin America, but growth started again after the financial crisis was over.

As a result of the drop in commodity prices of the Latin American and other developing countries, it became difficult for them to service the loans they took, mainly in the 1980s, from international banks. Although there were some debt-to-equity swaps, where loans were exchanged for equity investment in developing countries, the banks were mostly dissatisfied and hesitated to give new loans. In order to avoid an international crisis in financial markets, negotiations were enacted between the creditor banks, which formed the Paris Club in 1756, and the emerging nations to reschedule non-performing debt with a steep discount.

As a result, the Brady bonds, from the name of the United States Secretary of the Treasury, were introduced in the 1990s, which replaced existing government debt with a market value less than the par value of the initial debt. After the emerging nations initiated reforms, approved and funded mainly by the IMF and the World Bank, sovereign debt was transformed into tradable Brady bonds, with guarantees (principal or interest collateral) by the United States Treasury, but at a reduced value. About twenty countries have issued such bonds, including Argentina, Brazil, Venezuela, and other Latin American countries. Bulgaria, Nigeria, the Philippines, and Poland also replaced government debt with bonds with a market value less than the par value of the initial debt. The total capitalisation of the Brady bonds is about $100 billion, in addition to the Eurobonds and the domestic bonds of far more value emerging nations are periodically issuing.

The total capitalisation of the bond markets in the world is more than $16 trillion, about half of which are denominated by U.S. bonds, more than one fourth by European currency bonds, and around 20 per cent by Japanese yen bonds.

Table 1.1

	2000	*2001*
Bond Issues		
Emerging markets	7,789	101,926
Africa	0	1,648
Asia	2,604	43,144
Europe	2,335	7,408
Middle East	0	2,570
Western Hemisphere	2,850	47,157
Equity Issues		
Emerging markets	1,166	16,414
Africa	0	781
Asia	900	9,789
Europe	97	1,289
Middle East	70	894
Western Hemisphere	98	3,661
Syndicated Loan Commitments		
Emerging markets	28,377	79,737
Africa	2,127	2,658
Asia	12,541	49,488

(Contd.)

	2000	2001
Europe	9,139	11,457
Middle East	1,089	5,836
Western Hemisphere	3,480	10,297
Short-term Commitments		
Emerging markets	4,423	30,458
Africa	83	3,701
Asia	3,116	20,374
Europe	775	3,136
Middle East	350	0
Western Hemisphere	100	3,248
Total		
Emerging markets	41,755	228,535
Africa	2,210	8,788
Asia	19,161	122,795
Europe	12,346	23,290
Middle East	1,509	9,300
Western Hemisphere	6,528	64,363

Source: IMF, *International Capital Market, 2003, 77.*

Commercial paper, certificates of deposit, revolving credits, and trade markets have the largest amounts of equity issues and syndicated loan commitments while Western Hemisphere and European emerging markets have the largest amounts of bond issues. However, Middle East and African emerging markets have small amounts of such financial instruments.

According to the World Bank classification, developing nations are the ones with a low or middle level of per capita income as compared to developed nations with high per capita income. Emerging stock markets include the financial markets of developing countries and those growing in size, turnover, and sophistication. The capitalisation of all emerging stock markets, which is growing rapidly, accounts for about 12 per cent of the total world market capitalisation in which developed or advanced markets are included. There is not much concentration in the emerging markets, as a large number of firms are traded in each national market. However, privatisation of large state enterprises leads to more concentration and inequality. Although such markets are volatile and risky, the high growth potential, the diversification, and the relatively high return they offer make them attractive.

Table 1.2 shows population, per capita income, inflation, and market capitalisation for major emerging markets in Asia, Europe, Middle East/Africa, and Latin America. Before the turmoil in the Asian financial markets, particularly in Indonesia, Malaysia, South Korea, and Thailand, these markets were booming. In Europe, Greece and Portugal try to adjust their markets to those of the European Union, as the Eastern European countries and Russia do, although at a lower pace.

From all emerging markets, Brazil has the largest stock market capitalisation (more than $250 billion), followed by South Africa, China, Mexico, India, and Russia.

African and Asian Emerging Markets

An important group of Middle East/Africa emerging markets includes the countries of South Africa, Turkey, UAE, Egypt, Morocco, Jordan, and Zimbabwe.

South Africa's monetary policy was such that part of the increase in money supply was counterbalanced by the decline in the velocity of money. As a result of stabilisation measures, the stock market is going up and more foreign investment is flowing into the country.

In the Middle East, UAE has a relatively high growth of money supply, but a declining velocity of money, as Table 1.2 shows, so that stable prices can be achieved.

From the other Middle East countries, Turkey has the highest stock market value, followed by UAE, Egypt, and Morocco. Turkey's market capitalisation is around 30 per cent of GDP, compared to 40 per cent for Morocco, 30 per cent for Egypt, and as high as 120 per cent for the United States. Some 45 per cent of the Turkish stock market value is under foreign ownership, 16 per cent for Egypt, and only 3 per cent for Morocco, whereas the average daily volume is around $200 million, $31 million, and $6 million, respectively.

Table 1.2: Major International Emerging Markets: Population; GDP per Capita (US$); Inflation (GDP Deflator, Average Annual per cent Growth, 1997-2002); Market Capitalisation (Billions of US$), 2001

Economy	*Population (millions)*	*GDP Per Capita*	*Inflation Rate*	*Market Capitalisation*
ASIA				
China	1,227	860	13.6	206.4
India	961	390	9.4	128.5
Indonesia	200	1,110	8.5	29.1
Korea, Rep.	46	10,550	5.3	41.9
Malaysia	21	4,680	4.4	93.6
Pakistan	137	490	11.4	11.0
Philippines	73	1,220	8.7	31.4
Sri Lanka	18	800	9.9	2.1
EUROPE				
Czech Rep.	10	5,200	17.7	12.8
Greece	11	12,010	11.3	34.2
Hungary	10	4,430	22.5	15.0
Poland	39	3,590	29.5	12.1
Portugal	10	10,450	6.3	39.0
Russian Fed.	147	2,740	394.0	128.2
Slovakia	5	3,700	12.7	1.8
MIDDLE EAST AND AFRICA				
Egypt	60	1,180	10.5	20.8
UAE	6	15,810	12.2	45.3
Jordan	4	1,570	3.9	5.4
Morocco	28	1,250	3.7	12.2
South Africa	38	3,400	10.1	232.1
Turkey	64	3,130	78.2	61.1
Zimbabwe	11	750	22.6	2.0

(*Contd. . . .*)

(Contd. . . .)

Economy	*Population (millions)*	*GDP Per Capita*	*Inflation Rate*	*Market Capitalisation*
LATIN AMERICA				
Argentina	36	8,570	13.0	59.3
Brazil	164	4,720	475.2	255.5
Chile	15	5,020	13.6	72.0
Colombia	38	2,280	26.1	19.5
Mexico	95	3,680	18.5	156.6
Peru	25	2,460	288.8	17.6
Venezuela	23	3,450	46.7	14.6

Note: In some cases, earlier years' data were available.

Source: World Bank, World Development Report; IMF, International Financial Statistics, both various issues; *The Economist*: Pocket World in Figures, 1998, 34; and Bruno Solnik, International Investment, 3rd Edition (New York: Addison-Wesley, 1996), 255.

The government of Turkey, following a policy of privatisation, recently sold 132.4 million shares or 12.3 per cent stake in Turkiy Is Bankasi A.S. for $12.2 billion. Salomon Smith Barney managed the sale of the firm, 55 per cent of which was sold to foreign investors and 45 per cent to Turkish investors. Moreover, Turkcell, a Turkish phone company 41 per cent of which is owned by Sonera company of Finland and 50.3 per cent by Cukurova, a Turkish financial and industrial big firm, decided to proceed with a big Initial Public Offering (IPO). The IPO stock would be sold domestically and overseas with a partial listing in the New York Stock Exchange or in the London Stock Exchange. The total equity value of Turkcell is estimated at $16 billion

Although Turkey adopted the EU's common tariff on most industrial products, reducing the average tariff from 27 per cent to 13 per cent, further reforms are needed, especially in agriculture, which employs about half the work force, and financial and other services. According to the WTO, more privatisation is needed, mainly in telecommunications banking, and airlines, as well as fiscal discipline and closer budget controls to stabilise the economy and improve the stock market. More or less, similar reforms are needed by other Asian and African emerging nations.

UAE, with a population of 6 million and a per capita income of more than $15,000, has a stock market capitalisation of more than $45 billion. The reforms of the Egyptian markets, which are gradually linked to global markets, are improving slowly. However, privatisation of banks stimulated the Egyptian Stock Exchange, which has a market capitalisation of more than $20 billion. Nevertheless, Egypt, with a population of 60 million, a foreign debt close to $30 billion and direct investment about $1 billion a year, needs further fiscal and monetary reforms.

The Asian financial crisis in 1997 and later has swept the region and hung over the world economies as a dark cloud. The Asian Miracle seems to have faded away, and the emerging markets in the area, primarily South Korea, Malaysia, India, Indonesia, Thailand, China, and even the advanced market of Japan, came under financial turmoil. However, after a period of adjustment, these markets reached stability and eventually regained high growth rate. A similar problem occurred in Mexico, which devalued its peso in late 1994, affecting other countries, including Brazil and Argentina; but with an aid package by the International Monetary Fund (IMF) and the United States, it managed to avoid a further currency crisis.

The Japanese economy also came under a severe financial crisis recently, which was due mainly to huge bad loans by the Japanese banks. Another reason was what John Maynard Keynes called **liquidity trap**, resulting from a falling demand for goods and services short of the country's production, regardless of how low interest rates are, a phenomenon similar to that of the Great Depression. Presently, though, consumer spending in Japan, as well as in almost all other countries, is high, and the global economy is not expected to face the problem of defective demand or overproduction in the near future.

The IMF and other institutions agreed to a huge bailout for East Asian nations, providing $55 billion for South Korea, which is higher than that of $48 billion for Mexico in 1994. Some $20 billion of that amount came from the IMF, $15 billion from the World Bank, and the rest from the United States and Japan. Also, Thailand received $17 billion, and Indonesia was promised $43 billion.

China's and India's Emerging Markets

China, with a population of 1.3 billion, which switched from the Maoist revolution of 1949 and the communist doctrines to denationalisation and other reforms, achieved high rates of economic growth in the last fifteen years. Nevertheless, as the Chinese economy is gradually opening to international trade, it is more and more exposed to financial turmoil. Although China's $134 billion foreign exchange reserves put its currency out of the prospect of devaluation, the $119 billion foreign debt and the reliance of the country on foreign investment may delay the liberalisation of the financial sector and other reforms in the economy.

In order to stop paying huge subsidies to inefficient state enterprises, the Communist Party Congress in September 1997 decided to privatise some 3,000 inefficient state enterprises, out of about 300,000 in China, mainly through public sale of shares or transferring control to the managers and workers in the enterprises. The shares, for which each worker pays up to $500 (about three times the average monthly salary), cannot be sold, except to another employee, and have a value in line with the company's assets.

Although only about 700 companies have permission to trade shares in China's young stock markets, mainly in Shanghai and Shenzhen, expectations are that many more companies will have shares in the rapidly growing Chinese stock markets domestically and eventually internationally. Already Nasdaq of the United States and the Shanghai Stock Exchange are doing cross-training and are forging closer ties toward a dual listing agreement.

Emerging Markets of Europe

After the fall of the Soviet Union in 1989 and especially after President Boris Yeltsin defeated Communist hard-liners by shelling the Parliament in 1993, Russia's privatisation programme proceeded rapidly. Shares in thousands of government companies were sold in auctions or given to managers and workers. Many workers, though, quickly sold the offered shares, leaving stocks in relatively few hands. Foreign investors from Wall Street, London, and elsewhere put huge amounts of money in Russian stocks, whereas mutual funds, pension funds, and institutional investors moved rapidly into the wild Russian markets. (*Source:* IMF, *International Financial Statistics,* various issues.)

Because of the mess in the domestic market, equity valuations of Russian companies are in deep discounts. Thus, the market value of Gazprom's reserves was only at $0.20 per barrel of oil equivalent, compared to $11.00 for Exxon's reserves and $8.00 for Amoco's. The reserves of Gazprom, which has sold gas to Western Europe for thirty years, are estimated at 33 trillion cubic metres of gas and 15 billion barrels of oil. About 10 million barrels is the production of oil equivalent per day, which is more than the production of any other company in the world. Gazprom's American Depository Receipts (ADR) were recently priced in Wall Street at $19.90 and its market capitalisation is $47 billion.

Moreover, Gazprom decided to place over $3 billion in convertible bonds and Eurobonds in addition to $4 billion in loans. Also there are some twelve additional Russian companies with ADRs, including Lukoil, with market capitalisation of $21 billion, and other oil, electricity, telecom, and metal firms, whereas the number of Russian companies entering the American stock markets is growing rapidly.

The stock market of Russia is expected to improve also as Russian companies are acquiring foreign firms. Thus, Lukoil Europe, a subsidiary of the Russian oil giant, bought 51 per cent of oil refinery from the State Ownership Fund of Romania for $300 million with the hope to make Romania a key route of oil from the Caspian Sea. Other Russian entrepreneurs also bought Vega, a smaller refinery, whereas Lukoil plans to expand into Yugoslavia.

Russia, the biggest market in Eastern Europe, remains an attractive place for equity investors. With a stock market capitalisation of around $130 billion, roughly on a par with India, Russia's dollar-adjusted equity indices went up 130 per cent in 1996 and 175 per cent in 1997. Although Russia is facing a possible downgrading of its credit rating by Moody Investors Service (mainly in its $6 billion international bonds), political stability and reforms, as well as massive natural resources, would make Russian equities attractive in the near future. As a result of the good expectations of the Russian economy, the IMF relaxed the $10.1 billion loan terms, although required tax revenue targets were not achieved and the value of the rouble and the stock market of Moscow declined

All the stock markets of Eastern European and the Balkan countries present good opportunities for foreign investment. Hungary, with an index growth in equity market of 350 per cent in 1996 and 130 per cent in 1997, as well as a volume 50 per cent higher in 1997 compared to 1996, is in the forefront, followed by Romania, with more than quadrupled and Estonia with more than doubled growth in equity markets in 1997.

Poland, with a low price-earning ratio, and the Czech Republic are expected to recover and show a strong position in their stock markets, as the other Eastern European countries.

The Warsaw Stock Exchange of Poland, with a market value of about $12 billion, is rapidly growing in size mainly because of privatisation of state-owned enterprises. Recently, Schroders, the London-based investment bank, in competition with Goldman Sachs and Credit Suisse First Boston, arranged the flotation of Telecomunikacja Polska (TPSA), which has a market capitalisation of around $10 billion. Schroders, which also coordinated the flotation of Bank Hadlowy of Poland, first arranged the sale of 15 per cent of TPSA's equity and the promotion of a new share issue.

Since the end of communism in 1989, Poland has attracted more than $20 billion foreign direct investment. Among other investors, Motorola Inc. agreed to establish a software centre in Krakow to make cellular phones and computers worth about $110 billion. The Jagiellonian University in Krakow would provide some 500 well-educated staff in high-tech research and development.

Bulgaria, with a population of around 8.5 million people, initiated the first joint stock companies in 1989, which resulted from the privatisation of state-owned enterprises. The Sofia Stock Exchange (SSE) started its first trading sessions in April 1992. The Securities and Stock Exchange Commission controls and regulates the Bulgarian stock market. The mass privatisation of 1996-97 later contributed to the revitalisation of the SSE. Some forty-six investment intermediaries have been licensed to facilitate securities transactions. In 1991, the IMF supported the liberalisation programme of Bulgaria, after price and foreign trade liberalisation programmes were enacted.

The official exchange rate was fixed at the level of 1,000 levs per German mark, or about 0.5 euros.

In the Former Yugoslavian Republic of Macedonia (FYROM), with a population of around 2 million, a commodity market with agricultural products, established in 1992, has limited activities, if at all. The first stock market of FYROM was created in 1992. Some 240 stock companies, transformed in the process of privatisation, participate in the Stock Exchange of FYROM Inc. in Skopje, which provides regular information for the trading and the quoted companies. However, this highly regulated market is at a low level of development.

Romania, with a population of about 23 million, followed the French model and created the first stock exchanges in Bucharest, Braila, and Galatzi in 1881. However, because of wars and other changes, the normal function of the stock market started after the reforms of 1989. In order to facilitate transactions, ninety-six brokerage companies have already been licensed. In 1997, there were eleven companies with a large number of high-priced shares quoted in the Bucharest

Stock Exchange in the first category, and fifty-two smaller companies in the second category. From May 1992, the foreign exchange regime is based on a floating rate of the national currency.

In Yugoslavia, the Belgrade Stock Exchange operated successfully from 1894 to 1941 with its securities listed in the big European financial centres. It resumed its operations in 1990, but the economic sanctions imposed by NATO, because of the conflict over Bosnia, mainly in 1992-1993, and currently over Kosovo, weakened this Balkan financial market.

Privatisation and Capital Market Development

Strategy to Promote Economic Growth

The prevalence of SOEs and the limited development of capital markets in developing countries have not come about by chance. They result from a strategy of government intervention in which SOEs are supposed to be the engines of growth. However, most SOEs perform poorly and are poor financial risks. Government intervention in finance often results in negative real interest rates and a disincentive to save. Finance cannot flow naturally to the SOEs under these conditions. Therefore, governments have nationalised banks and created DFIs to channel finance to SOEs and favoured projects. These measures have thwarted financial market development, limited access to capital by the private sector, limited productive investment, and constrained economic growth.

Working through different but complementary channels, privatisation and capital markets are key components of reform, and help to promote economic growth. However, although the fallacies and failures of the interventionist strategy are clear, for too many countries privatisation of SOEs has yet to seriously begin, and too many governments continue to dominate finance to the detriment of economic growth.

The implications of inefficient SOEs and distorted financial markets for governments are straightforward. Policy dialogue must be stepped up to explain to governments why the failure to privatise reduces the efficiency, productivity, and growth of the economy and hinders the development of more efficient capital markets, which further constrains economic growth. Privatisation needs to expand in scope and increase in intensity.

Governments must also take steps to support capital market development. Public-awareness programmes are needed to explain the benefits of capital markets and privatisation. A regulatory framework is necessary for the public to have confidence in capital market instruments. Governments must become aware of the synergies between capital market development and privatisation so that both programmes will benefit. Privatising the process of privatisation will enable capital markets infrastructure and agents to develop.

The type of privatisation chosen will have important implications for developing capital markets. Two of the most significant forms of privatisation are also among the best for promoting capital markets. Governments must transfer remaining SOEs to the private sector using the combined techniques of broad-based share sales of the best, blue-chip SOEs, and mass privatisation by vouchers for the remaining medium and large enterprises.

These two techniques are also politically astute. Broad based share sales and mass privatisation by vouchers have the particular advantage of making the population a part of the newly emerging capital markets immediately. Economic adjustment, whether in the United Kingdom, Jamaica, or Moldova, involves some difficult changes for the population. Making citizens shareholders, however, enables them to share in the benefits of reform. Broad based equity ownership encourages the population to use the services of institutional investors, such as mutual funds, insurance companies, and private sector pension funds.

Additional areas of the economy, especially economic infrastructure (telecommunications, power, transportation, and municipal services), must be opened to the private sector through BOT and related techniques. The privatisation of potential institutional investors, including social security, must be pursued. With the drive to privatise and develop capital markets, significant sums of money will flow to the now privatised pension funds. The pension funds will become a force in the secondary markets, providing professionalism and stability. In addition, these funds will provide a source of finance to be tapped by private sector companies wishing to sell their shares on the market. The development of large pools of investment funds managed by private sector institutional investors allows large infrastructure projects to be increasingly financed from domestic sources.

The effort to expand the scope of privatisation will increase the breadth, depth and efficiency of capital markets. The parallel streams and cross-cutting currents of privatisation and capital market development will contribute to overall economic growth.

Privatisation and capital markets development should be among the easier planks of economic reform for governments to implement. Privatisations can be structured to provide benefits to virtually all citizens. Workers and managers of SOEs can also benefit through preferential access to shares. Governments which privatise successfully tend to fare well politically, as citizens realise that economic reform promotes growth and higher incomes. Privatisation and capital market development will not solve all problems by themselves, but they are required steps on the road to growth and development.

CHAPTER 2

Doing Business in Newly Privatised Markets, Global Opportunities and Challenges

The increasing numbers of newly privatised companies provide a powerful force in the global economy for many U.S. firms. These former state organisations, recently exposed to competitive realities, can offer significant opportunities for private sector expansion. A firm that wants to take advantage of these possibilities must first decide on a dynamic strategy that is appropriate for its organisation and is consistent with the company's resources and business objectives.

The strategic direction that is ultimately selected will depend on an evaluation of influencing factors that are both internal and external to the organisation. The weight that the company decides to allocate to each factor will depend on the fundamental characteristics of the individual company involved.

The principal elements that require consideration in the strategic selection process include an analysis of market factors, the type of product or service involved, and the method that is chosen to reach the newly privatised enterprises. This decision-making process, and its conclusions, will profoundly influence a firm's ability to achieve and sustain its competitive advantage in the markets that it selects.

Underlying each consideration are the amount of risk associated with each option and the effect this risk will have on the company's resources. The level of acceptable risk will depend on the size of the company that is making the decision and the amount of resources that it is willing to commit to the developmental process. The implementation of a strategy that could be instrumental to the long-term success of a company may justify a significant commitment of financial and management resources to some form of structured alliance with a large newly privatised partner.

On the other hand, if a proposed strategy is confined to a more limited activity, with less of an impact on the entire company, the resource allocation can be substantially less. This may lead to a business approach that might involve a more informal relationship than would normally be associated with a long-term alliance and could then involve the use of marketing intermediaries such as sales agents or distributors.

The growth of privatisation is causing many U.S. companies to re-evaluate their traditional methods of operations and to consider more seriously new opportunities in foreign markets. A good example of the reprioritisation of markets is the American communications companies such as AT&T which previously concentrated their efforts on U.S. markets and are now forming alliances with denationalised foreign carriers.

The emergence of new telephone companies through privatisation is also causing American communications equipment makers to look to foreign markets as well. Lucent Technologies, for example, had previously marketed only to domestic carriers. The company is now reaching out to a variety of newly privatised companies that operate overseas. In a recent financial report, Lucent attributed 49 per cent of its financial growth to the development of foreign markets through marketing contracts with over 75 new service providers in Europe.

There is an implicit commitment to either a long- or short-term relationship in whichever method of interfirm association a company selects as its strategy. The duration of the commitment can be as important to a company's success as its strategic direction. If a company is unwilling to place its resources at risk over an extended period of time, an association that is less demanding than a strategic alliance is desirable. If, on the other hand, a long-term commitment is beneficial for a company's future competitive position, a well designed alliance will provide a favourable strategic direction and will warrant a long-term commitment necessary to realise its full economic potential.

Once a company forms any type of association it should provide sufficient flexibility to accommodate changing economic conditions. It should also contain a mechanism for monitoring its progression and the implementation of operational adjustments that will allow the relationship to grow according to the prevailing circumstances.

The benefit of such operational flexibility is evident in Fiat's $840 million association with Russia's former state-owned automobile manufacturer, Gaz. Fiat's original plan was to produce 150,000 "world cars" annually at a new greenfield factory alongside the existing Gaz light van and car plant at Nizhny Novgorod. The plan was prepared before Russia's economic crisis.

Since the economic problems began, there has been a considerable devaluation of the ruble against the dollar. This forced Fiat to renegotiate the alliance. The bulk of the company's investment will now occur at the end of the five year period instead of its beginning, while Fiat's total commitment remains the same. The initial investment is now limited to a smaller assembly operation that will produce approximately 20,000 cars a year.

Th Fiat/Gaz Joint Venture is financed in part by the European Bank for Reconstruction and Development (EBRD), which owns a 20 per cent interest in the venture. For its 40 per cent share, Fiat is contributing know-how and machine tools and equipment that are made primarily by other Fiat subsidiaries.

The Russian partner, Gorky Automobilny Zavod, is contributing land, infrastructure, and labour, as well as its existing distribution network.

In adjusting its operations to conform to current economic conditions instead of withdrawing from the country, Fiat is relying on a long-term strategy based on its considerable emerging market experience. The company believes that when the Russian economy eventually improves it will be able to benefit from this strategy. It will then have a much stronger competitive position in the large Russian auto market than it would have if it had to start over.

Size is also apparent in most of the Latin American privatisations and in many of the West European countries as well. These large newly privatised companies provide a more feasible strategic target for similarly sized private sector companies. Large firms usually possess a sufficiently large supply of available investment capital that allows them to entertain an alliance with equally large state companies.

Many of the former nationally owned companies also require considerable restructuring before they can function satisfactorily in a competitive environment. Only similarly sized organisations have the operational ability and fiscal tolerance to embark on a long-range, large-scale restructuring process.

There are ways, however, for a smaller organisation to participate in higher risk countries. One of these ways is to consider carefully the creditworthiness of the potential partner's enterprise. Another is to establish a method of payment that will ensure receipt of any revenue that might be owed. Confirmed letters of credit will guarantee the receipt of payment and reduce the possibility of financial loss. Another approach is to take a conservative investment approach that will be able to better withstand economic fluctuations and minimise the effect of possible loss by the private sector partner.

In the Fiat example, the Italian company's principal investment vehicle was equipment and know-how. This method of limiting direct financial risk is common in ventures with former state-owned companies that badly need this type of assistance but are located in relatively high-risk areas. Investment substitution is also an approach that other companies may take when they are merely unable, or unwilling, to invest their more critical financial reserves.

There are also other forms of strategic relationships that companies use which do not require actual financial investment. One of these is the transfer of technology. This strategy requires a minimum level of investment and is an effective method of market development. Technology transfers also provide an excellent foundation for a future expanded relationship that is based on actual operating experience. This improved knowledge of a partner's capabilities will considerably reduce the element of investment risk if the later formation of a strategic alliance is desired.

Direct marketing by exporting to privatised companies is another strategy that entails relatively low levels of financial risk. This approach will also give a company the opportunity to become more familiar with a particular market area before it makes a larger or longer-term financial commitment.

A company's size, its available resources, and its propensity for risk are important factors in its strategic decision-making process. These will significantly influence the company's decision if it prefers to be a partner with a former state owned company, a purveyor of know-how, or a seller of product. Other important elements in the selection of a particular strategy will include an evaluation of the composition of the new market and potential competitive forces, and the type of products that the company intends to direct toward the new market area.

Strategic Business Alternatives

The increasing numbers of newly privatised companies provide a powerful force in the global economy for many U.S.

firms. These former state organisations, recently exposed to competitive realities, can offer significant opportunities for private sector expansion. A firm that wants to take advantage of these possibilities must first decide on a dynamic strategy that is appropriate for its organisation and is consistent with the company's resources and business objectives.

The strategic direction that is ultimately selected will depend on an evaluation of influencing factors that are both internal and external to the organisation. The weight that the company decides to allocate to each factor will depend on the fundamental characteristics of the individual company involved.

The principal elements that require consideration in the strategic selection process include an analysis of market factors, the type of product or service involved, and the method that is chosen to reach the newly privatised enterprises. This decision-making process, and its conclusions, will profoundly influence a firm's ability to achieve and sustain its competitive advantage in the markets that it selects.

Underlying each consideration is the amount of risk associated with each option and the effect this risk will have on the company's resources. The level of acceptable risk depends on the size of the company that is making the decision and the amount of resources that it is willing to commit to the developmental process. The implementation of a strategy that could be instrumental to the long-term success of a company may justify a significant commitment of financial and management resources to some form of structured alliance with a large newly privatised partner.

On the other hand, if a proposed strategy is confined to a more limited activity, with less of an impact on the entire company, the resource allocation can be substantially less. This may lead to a business approach that might involve a more informal relationship than would normally be associated with a long-term alliance and could then involve the use of marketing intermediaries such as sales agents or distributors.

There is an implicit commitment to either a long-term or short-term relationship in whichever method of interfirm association a company selects as its strategy. The duration of the commitment can be as important to a company's success as its strategic direction. If a company is unwilling to place its resources at risk over an extended period of time, an association that is less demanding than a strategic alliance is desirable. If, on the other hand, a long-term commitment is beneficial for a company's future competitive position, a well designed alliance will provide a favourable strategic direction and will warrant a long-term commitment necessary to realise its full economic potential.

Market Evaluation

The characteristics of the U.S. market and its relative level of economic stability are well known to participating companies. This is not necessarily true in dealing with newly privatised enterprises in foreign countries. Even when there is market proximity, in Mexico or Canada, for example, intrinsic country or cultural characteristics may preclude participation by individual U.S. companies. These inherent market qualities can be even more formidable as the distance and differences between markets increase. Even in the developed and mature economies of Western Europe there are often significant language, social, political, and commercial barriers that may limit American companies from full participation. The necessity of realistically evaluating the new market arena becomes more critical when the newly privatised enterprise is located in a developing economy. The opportunity for future market expansion in the area served by the newly privatised enterprise will provide an important consideration in the formation of a market strategy by the private sector company. The determination of future potential will depend on factors that are most influential to the company and will vary considerably between product types. However, certain basic demographic factors are influential in most assessments of growth potential. These usually include:

1. Population size and growth rates
2. Education levels and literacy rates
3. Life expectancy
4. Population dispersion.

Relevant indicators of potential economic growth can also bear heavily on a company's strategic decision. These are:

1. GDP rates—historical and projected
2. Share of GDP distribution, agricultural vs. industry, import vs. export, and so on
3. Individual income levels and relative size of income distribution
4. Consumer price inflation rates
5. Unemployment rates
6. Personal savings rates
7. Hourly labour rates
8. Company-specific indicators (telephone ownership per 100 population for communication carriers).

Political Stability

The irrational replacement of industry by government structures has diminished considerably with market liberalisation and increasing emphasis on globalisation. No where in the world is serious consideration being given to a discontinuance of privatisation programmes or in other words a renationalisation of critical industries and commercial enterprises. The benefits of privatisation programmes have been too compelling and too widely accepted to be abandoned.

The more recent changes in political direction are resulting primarily from a revision in macroeconomic policies brought about by democratically elected governments and are directed toward further market liberalisation. Even the abandonment of command or planned economies was actually more evolutionary than revolutionary. The political changes that took place in China and the Soviet Union have effectively opened markets that were previously closed to generations of international traders. This increased liberalisation is also generating thousands of newly privatised companies that are hungry for new products, private partners, and advanced technology.

The greatest prospect of political instability remains in some of the depressed economies, and this consideration is bound to influence some companies' business strategies. One of the most prominent examples of this is post-Yeltsin Russia. This country's commitment to democratic principles remains ambivalent. A large segment of the population is more economically disadvantaged than they were under the communist regime, and many of the country's critical industrial and financial institutions are governed by an economic oligarchy. These conflicting elements will pose a considerable challenge to Vladimir Putin's government.

The ineffectiveness of the political forces in solving the country's economic problems has produced serious consequences for existing and potential private sector companies. Many of the companies that entered the Russian market are withdrawing completely or are significantly reducing their level of business activity. Other companies that were preparing strategic entry plans were forced to revise or postpone their anticipated activities. Even in Russia, however, many companies are committed to the country's long-term potential and remain economically active.

While the threat of political disruption around the world has diminished, a company needs to give serious consideration to the potential continuity of a country's political stability when it is formulating its operating strategy.

Market Infrastructure

The type of infrastructure that can affect a company's strategy regarding market entry can be both physical and social. Physical considerations include the ability to move products from one location to another. The national rail and road system, and the frequency and reliability of air transportation to and from the country and within its borders are important considerations and must be kept in mind. The adequacy and maintenance of a nation's ports and harbour system must also be considered when a company is contemplating the frequent shipment of raw materials or finished products as part of its business development plans.

The presence or lack of a communications system that can adequately support planned commercial activities is critical to the direction taken by the strategic plan. In many developing areas there is a lack of communication facilities to support existing business activities. As the economy expands, this deficiency becomes increasingly critical and can severely constrain future growth. The absence of state-of-the-art telecommunications networks can also impede the growth of many commercial enterprises that rely on the type of facility for commercial expansion. On the other hand, the lack of such facilities would be beneficial to a company interested in an alliance with a recently privatised communications company since it affords ample opportunity for future business expansion.

Adequate power-generating systems are another critical aspect of a country's infrastructure. The lack of the necessary physical framework for adequate power generation and distribution is almost endemic to the developing economies where many newly privatised companies reside. The cost of electrical power is an important element in the profit-making ability of many companies that are involved in manufacturing or resource extraction. In some countries in Central Asia, the cost of electrical power is so high and service is so unreliable that many companies decide against forming an alliance with state-owned mining companies for this reason. Since mineral extraction is a significant component of these countries' GDP, expensive electrical power severely limits the prospects of privatisation.

A company must also evaluate the social infrastructure of a country before forming a strategic alliance or other forms of business venture with privatised companies. One of the most important factors is the quality of a nation's legal system. Many of the new economies were part of a centrally planned system for many years. In a command economy, there is no need for a well-defined and codified system of laws since the government handles all disputes within the existing political framework.

The absence of an effective legal infrastructure is also one of the principal reasons that countries are unsuccessful in attracting foreign participation. Governments that show evidence of political instability and lack a defined legal system as well present almost insurmountable barriers to foreign business ventures with their privatised companies.

The integrity of a country's financial infrastructure is yet another important consideration in a company's decision to enter a new market. A country's ability to control inflationary pressures and avoid a devaluation of its currency can be very important in evaluating a particular economic area. Inflationary pressures have been prevalent in some recent privatisation markets, particularly those of Russia, Brazil, and Ukraine. This has severely weakened the commercial vitality of many of the newly privatised companies and discourages foreign participation.

Strategic Alliances

The formation of a strategic alliance is proving to be one of the dominant market mechanisms that private sector companies use to expand their business relationships with newly or partially privatised firms. This approach, when properly utilised, can provide substantial advantages to all participants in the alliance. Because of the reciprocal benefits, host governments are increasingly viewing an alliance with a foreign investor as a preferred method of transforming a former state-owned enterprise into a more vigorous market-oriented firm. As a result, foreign direct investments in the form of strategic alliances are profoundly altering the commercial profile of many countries.

The competition for such associations is increasing as governments become more aware of the advantages that new foreign capital will provide. Much of the competition for capital centres on factors that are important to new investors such as market size, availability of labour, openness to trade, level of natural resources, condition of internal infrastructure, and proximity and accessibility of regional markets.

The increasing demand for new funding, driven to a large degree by the increased emphasis on privatisation, is dynamically propelling the global growth of foreign direct investment. In spite of a decline in the global economy during 1997, FDI increased in all regions of the world and included investments in the developed and developing economies alike.

This form of financial commitment typically represents an investment that involves management control of a resident entity in one economy by an enterprise that is a resident of another economy. It is reflective of an investor's interest in a long-term commercial relationship with the foreign company. According to the United Nations Conference on Trade and Development (UNCTAD), the overall world inflow of invested capital amounted to almost $400 billion in 1997 alone. This was nearly twice the level of foreign direct investment in 1980.

A substantial portion of this investment growth was for new privatisations resulting from the denationalisation of former state-controlled sectors such as communications and electrical utilities.

After announcing a series of austerity measures, Brazil has become one of the principal recipients of cross-border foreign direct investment directed toward investment in new privatisations. Direct investment flowing to Brazil during 1998 was estimated at approximately $22 billion. This represents a $6 billion increase over the 1997 level of $16.3 billion and a doubling of the activity in the country during 1996.

A major contributor to the expanded level of investment during 1998 was the midyear privatisation of the giant Brazilian-owned communications company Brasileiras SA, or Telebras. This divestment, accompanied by the government's decision to privatise numerous other state-owned companies, is providing numerous opportunities for foreign companies to enter the Brazilian market through acquisitions and strategic alliances.

Transnational Corporations (TNCs) are particularly active in generating new investments. In 1998 they provided 19 per cent of the world inflow of invested capital and 27 per cent of the outwardly directed capital flow. The outflow of foreign direct investment funds from the United States alone rose by 53 per cent to $115 billion in 1997.

In addition to merger and acquisition activity, the TNCs are strategically repositioning themselves through cross-border interfirm agreements that center on improving the technological abilities of foreign firms. These technology transfer agreements among newly privatised firms, as well as the more mature private sector entities, increased from an annual average of less than 300 agreements in the early 1980s to over 600 in the mid-1990s. This heightened activity in technology transfer agreements is resulting in the growth of royalty payments approaching double-digit rates. In 1999, U.S. exports in the form of royalties and licensing revenues exceeded $37 billion.

Technology Transfer Arrangements

The need to improve technology is symptomatic of state-owned companies. Under government control, there is little reward for new achievements, and innovation is eventually discouraged. Without technical innovation, processes remain the same and new product introductions languish. State organisations are often insulated from global competition by trade barriers and their internal monopolistic position. The lack of competitive technology becomes critical when the company is privatised and leaves the state protection.

This technology gap can present a formidable barrier to the economic advancement of many newly privatised companies. The lack of technology can also pose significant economic problems for nations that traditionally rely on state enterprises for the majority of their industrial capacity or the maintenance of their national infrastructure. A country's sometimes unrelenting reliance on indigenous technology, without the normal stimulus provided by competition, can severely limit its ability to advance economically in a competitive global society.

This critical deficiency can create an excellent opportunity for U.S. companies which wish to take additional advantage of their existing technological accomplishments. A technology transfer agreement can provide an effective market entry vehicle for those companies unwilling to assume the level of organisational commitment that a strategic alliance requires. Such an arrangement requires relatively little or no financial investment on the part of the licensor and provides the company with an important additional source of operating revenue. Since little investment is required, there is also minimum risk. This type of arrangement also enables the licensing company to more easily extricate itself from a foreign market if there is a declining economy or if the country begins to evidence signs of political instability.

Because technology transfers provide limited risk exposure, they are often used by smaller single-technology companies interested in a business relationship with newly privatised companies. This type of company is less tolerant of financial loss and may lack the financial resources required by other methods of new market development. These companies may, however, still have access to advanced technologies that can be of value to many newly privatised organisations that wish to become more technically competent and market competitive.

The types of technology that newly privatised companies need span a broad spectrum of expertise that includes the diverse fields of electronics, oil exploration, pharmaceuticals, agricultural products and equipment, consumables, and, often, national defence. Requirements also exist for a variety of new or advanced techniques, including methods of marketing, medical treatment, replication of computer and entertainment software, and franchising of consumer services such as fast-food delivery systems.

The present wide acceptance of technology transfers is driven by the success achieved in the past by other emerging economies. Most notable of these is the Japanese paradigm of acquiring foreign technology to advance an industrial base devastated by World War II. Japan was extremely effective in acquiring, and eventually refining, advanced technologies obtained from American companies. Companies in South Korea subsequently followed this pattern when they had to rebuild in the mid-1950s following the conflict with their northern neighbours. By judiciously acquiring new technology, both of these Asian countries were able to rapidly achieve advanced technical and economic levels.

When China finally decided to enter the industrialised world, it also relied on new technology purchased from more advanced Western countries. Many U.S. companies took advantage of the opportunity by establishing technical arrangements with state-owned Chinese companies. This type of relationship was particularly favoured by American companies that were often precluded by the Chinese government from establishing wholly owned subsidiaries or significant strategic alliances. As privatisation advanced in Europe, Latin America, and the former Soviet countries, one of the principal modalities of achieving technical parity was through the vehicle of technology transfers with Western private sector companies.

The most basic form of technical agreement is the acquisition of contractual permission to use a specific brand or trademark or the authorised use of a specified process or production technique in a prescribed geographic area for a defined time period. In return for this permission, the technology provider receives a fee, commonly referred to as a royalty, for allowing use of the technology. A common adjunct to the process involves a continuing level of technical support to the licensee, along with the basic technology, to ensure the proper implementation of the acquired technology.

The broader agreement is most often employed by companies in developing countries that find it difficult to make use of the new technology. . . It normally takes a considerable amount of time for any company to independently develop and implement a new technology. The actual time required depends on how close the new technology is to existing areas of expertise within the organisation. There are varying levels of technical expertise within state companies. In west European companies the level can be quite high, while in China or the former Soviet states it can be far behind most of their more technocratic competitors. One of the principal advantages of technology transfers is the potential for accelerating the development cycle necessary for introducing new products or services. The importance of this advantage is inversely related to the prevailing level of technology within the company that is considering purchase. If the existing level of technical competence is low, the importance of accelerating the development of new products is great. If the technical gap between the newly privatised enterprise and its competitors is less severe, then the need to quickly bridge the gap through external sources becomes less critical.

Whichever the case, the purchase of new technology can achieve almost immediate technical parity with its international competitors for the privatised company. The company can avoid years of development effort through the vehicle of licensing. It can also realise the financial benefits that result from marketing the technically enhanced products far more quickly than if it depended on its own resources.

Increasing globalisation also results in decreasing product life cycles. This provides added impetus to the purchase of technology that is readily available. Without outside support, companies that find themselves behind the technical curve may be unable to take adequate advantage of their own developments before they become internationally obsolete.

The ability to avoid the consequence of failure is another substantial benefit available to the newly privatised company through the purchase of technology. Investments in R&D usually contain greater risk than alternative channels of investment, and newly privatised companies are less able to accommodate risk. In any company, a percentage of research efforts never materialise in marketable products. Many of the projects are unable to make it to the factory floor as economically replicable products. Others that are reproducible are not always accepted by a demanding marketplace. One of the principal cost components of new product development is the necessary write-off of R&D programmes that are unable to achieve programme targets. The privatised company can effectively avoid the cost of failure through the purchase of previously proven technology embodied in products that have already demonstrated a level of customer acceptance. For a privatised company that allows its technical level to lapse, the returns associated with the transfer of technology are usually greater than the returns from undertaking original research and development

Marketing and Sales Strategies

As privatisation expands, it is producing thousands of companies that were previously unavailable to U.S. commercial organisations. These new enterprises include manufacturing companies, utilities, retail establishments, agricultural units, and financial institutions. Their increased accessibility is presenting significant opportunities for increased sales volumes. In command economies, all of these businesses were formerly supplied by state-owned distribution channels. The products made available through this system were typically inferior in quality and aesthetically unappealing. When the countries abandoned the socialist system and converted to private ownership, the demand for improved products was substantial. This demand was accompanied by the establishment of new independently owned and operated businesses that function alongside the enterprises previously operated by the state.

Nowhere has the growth in new businesses been more dramatic than in Central and Eastern Europe. This area is providing an excellent example of rising entrepreneurship and is serving as an effective incubator for new private businesses. Within six years after the fall of the Berlin Wall, over 3.4 million nonagricultural businesses were established in the Central Eastern and Southern Europe (CEE) area, according to Eurostat, the statistical arm of the European Union. Most of these firms were established after communism fell, although in Poland and Hungary some small private businesses existed prior to the transition.

Of the CEE countries, Poland had the largest number of registered businesses by 1995, with over 1 million enterprises in operation. In absolute figures, the Czech Republic and Hungary established fewer firms, but in relation to the population, both had a higher rate of relative business concentration, with 68.4 and 50.7 enterprises per 1,000 population compared to Poland's 27.6. In relative terms, both the Czech Republic and Hungary exceeded the EU average of 43 establishments per 1,000 people. This concentration of new private businesses in an area previously populated by only state-owned establishments provides considerable new business opportunities for U.S companies.

Table 2.1: Number of Enterprises Established in September 1995

Country	*Approximate Number of Enterprises Established*	*Enterprises per 1,000 People*
Poland	1.100M	27.6
Czech Republic	.780	68.4
Hungary	.590	50.7
Romania	.390	16.0
Bulgaria	.320	34.3
Slovakia	.200	35.0
Lithuania	.100	36.3
Albania	.080	12.1
Estonia	.070	19.7
Latvia	.060	9.9

Source: Eurostart, The Economist, November 9, 1996, p. 124.

The new firms and their related business activity in the former Eastern Bloc are rapidly beginning to resemble the markets of the European Union. The EU, however, still has a larger proportion of service companies, while traditional industry is marginally more important in Eastern Europe. Also in the East, distribution companies are providing a larger and faster growing sector than in the more mature European economies. At the same time, East European entrepreneurs tend to be somewhat younger, with an average age of 38. Less than 40 per cent of their firms are managed by someone over 45 years old. All of these factors tend to make it easier to form new business relationships in Eastern Bloc countries than in the more established markets of Western Europe.

As these new East European organisations make the transition from command to market economies, one area of commonality among them and their commercial counterparts is emerging from state ownership in other regions of the world: a universal lack of understanding of how marketing is accomplished and the impact that competitive pressures have on a developing organisation. This lack of market knowledge is the most singular deficiency that multilateral development agencies ignore in their effort to transform public companies into privately productive competitive business units. The absence of market competency seriously constrains former state enterprises in their production of marketable products in economies where almost any imaginable product is in demand. The lack of marketing awareness also significantly impairs the ability of many newly privatised enterprises to generate increased levels of employment within their own organisations.

This lack of marketing skills persists among even those newly privatised companies that operate in clearly defined market structures in the more mature economies. These new organisations frequently find it difficult to reorient their operational direction from a producer mentality to the recognition of consumer directed demand. However, in the markets of the United States, EU, and Latin America, the newly privatised firm has the distinct advantage of observing the marketing policies and practices of other private sector firms that operate in their local economy. They are then better able to pattern themselves after other successful organisations that possess a more mature market orientation.

Exporting to the Newly Privatised Enterprise

With a reduction in transportation costs and the continuing removal of trade barriers, it is becoming much easier to serve foreign markets through exports instead of establishing foreign factories or forming strategic alliances. Between 1930 and 1990, average revenue per mile in air transport fell from 68 cents to 11 cents in U.S. dollars. Between the early 1980s and 1996, the unit cost of sea freight fell 70 per cent in real terms. The decline in freight costs was accompanied by reductions in other costs that influence companies' ability to export. The cost of a three-minute telephone call between New York and London fell precipitously from $244.65 to $3.32 between 1960 and 1990. At the same time, the cost of a unit of computing power fell 99 per cent.

These reductions in export cost components achieved by technological and logistical advance makes it more feasible for a company to branch out to foreign markets. At the same time, market liberalisation allows companies more latitude in their choice of areas served. Tariffs in developing countries also declined between 1970 and 1997, while concurrently the number of countries eliminating exchange controls on the purchase of imported goods and services increased from 35 to 137. This made it much easier for customers in foreign countries to import and subsequently pay for U.S. products. These improved conditions are propelling a substantial increase in exports from American producers. By 1998, U.S. exports approached $1 trillion, up approximately 25 per cent from 1995. They were also responsible for generating over 10 per cent of all American jobs.

The volume of trade that U.S. companies made with Russia in 1998 evidences the value of exports to newly privatised markets. During this troubled economic period, total U.S. exports grew by 8.8 per cent and reached a total of $3.58 billion. This was up from $3.29 billion during the previous year. Manufactured goods and consumer foodstuffs dominated the volume, with aircraft, meat products, machinery, and electrical equipment being the leading categories. Exports of commercial aircraft were the leading product category and amounted to approximately $840 million. The Russian government's granting of tariff waivers for the purchase of foreign aircraft by Russian airlines substantially contributed to this sales volume and resulted in the purchase of ten Boeing 737s by Aeroflot. This transaction was the first time a Russian airline was permitted to make an outright purchase of non-Russian aircraft.

U.S. medical and pharmaceutical exports also made a significant contribution to export totals in 1998. This product category declined in 1999 as Russian consumers turned to less expensive pharmaceutical products from India and Eastern Europe as the full impact of the declining rouble took its toll. Other significant export categories included preserved food, combine harvesters, and heavy machinery such as bulldozers and excavating equipment.

Individual company policies that contribute to an increased emphasis on export markets usually include domestic market saturation and a desire for economies of scale that provide an enhanced competitive pricing ability. In many industries, firms become more efficient by growing larger and producing higher volumes. Most companies expect that the result will be lower unit costs. Many companies also believe that when domestic markets become saturated, one of the best ways of achieving increased volume is to develop export marketing ability.

Economies of scale have helped the transnational corporations to become even larger by developing their export capacity. Sales of multinational firms outside of the home countries are growing 20 to 30 per cent faster than exports as a whole. It is the large corporations that first became aware of the benefits, and later the necessity, of foreign exports sales. Economies of scale are more important to larger companies. Smaller organisations must wage a constant battle for scarce resources such as financial capital and managerial talent, which makes it more difficult for them to deal with the demands of distributing and servicing their products overseas. They also have considerably less experience in developing new markets and less exposure to the problems that confront former state organisations following privatisation.

Particular types of small companies, however, can compete effectively by exporting to newly privatised enterprises in foreign markets. These are the companies that market highly technical content and that can provide a flexible response to their customer requirements. As the costs of new market entry continue to drop, the number of small companies that meet these criteria is increasing. In addition, as product

Table 2.2: Top Countries for Exporters

Region	*First Priority*	*Second Priority*
Central Europe and former Soviet Union	Hungary Czech Republic Poland	Slovakia Slovenia Russia Estonia
North Africa and the Middle East	Saudi Arabia	Tunisia Morocco Turkey Iran Egypt United Arab Emirates Kuwait Bahrain
Sub-Saharan Africa		South Africa Mauritius
Latin America	Chile	Mexico Colombia Brazil Argentina
Southeast Asia	Singapore Taiwan China Hong Kong India South Korea Malaysia	Thailand Philippines Indonesia

Source: Coface/Financial Times, January 4, 1998, p. 30.

life cycles decrease as a result of intensified advances in technology, the smaller company can succeed by being better equipped to respond to change than the larger, more unwieldy corporations. The competitive advantage in overseas markets is gradually shifting toward the smaller firm that possesses unique knowledge and quick response capabilities. Even the growth of the Internet is assisting small high-tech companies to export effectively to overseas markets by providing an economical means of reaching large numbers of widely dispersed customer organisations. To be effective, however, the smaller company must be selective in choosing a compatible business strategy and in carefully singling out the markets in which it decides to participate. This process is more critical to the smaller company since a financial loss can be more harmful to them than a comparable reversal would be to medium or large-scale corporations.

Since the majority of destinations contained in the table are privatisation intensive, it should be of special interest to companies looking to this type of market for foreign trade expansion.

After a company determines which markets contain the greatest export potential for its type of products, it must then consider the pricing implications of its export strategy.

Export Product Pricing

Potential demand level is a major determinant of a company's strategy for products exported to newly privatised companies in developing markets.

The vast majority of newly privatised companies have limited financial resources, which results in diminished ability to buy. This is especially true when these companies are compared with more mature organisations of the same type in advanced economies.

One advantage of marketing to a developing economy with a large number of recently privatised firms is the lack of a formidable local competitor in this type of business environment. Similarly, foreign companies frequently have been unable to establish a strong presence in this type of market environment. This provides the exporter with greater pricing latitude than might be possible in more mature foreign market areas with more entrenched competition.

Table 2.3: Sample Calculation of Cost-Plus Method

	Domestic Sale	*Export Sale*
Factory price	$7.50	$7.50
Domestic freight	.70	.70
	8.20	8.20
Export documentation		.50
		8.70
Ocean freight and insurance		1.20
		9.90
Import duty (12 % of landed cost)		1.19
		11.09
Wholesaler markup (15%)		1.23
	9.43	
Importer/distributor markup (22%)		2.44
		13.53
Retail markup (50%)	4.72	6.77
Final consumer price	$14.15	$20.30

Source: *Business America* (U.S. Department of Commerce), October 1993.

Marginal cost pricing is a more competitive method of pricing products for export. This approach considers the direct out-of-pocket expenses of producing and selling products for export as a floor beneath which prices cannot be set without incurring a loss. For example, export products may have to be modified for the export market to accommodate customer appearance preferences, different sizes, electrical systems, labels, or regulatory standards. These changes usually increase costs and reduce margins if the price remains unadjusted. On the other hand, the export product may be a stripped-down version of the domestic product and therefore cost less. Sometimes additional products can be produced without an increase in fixed costs. If this is possible, the incremental cost of producing additional products for export should be lower than the earlier average production cost for the domestic market.

In addition to production costs, overheads and research and development, other costs should be allocated to domestic and export products in proportion to the benefits derived from those expenditures. Other additional costs often associated with export sales include:

- Market research and credit checks
- Business travel
- International postage, cable, and telephone rates
- Translation costs
- Commissions, training charges, and other costs involving representation
- Product modification and special packaging requirements

After the company calculates the actual cost of the exported product, it should formulate an approximate consumer price for the new market.

CHAPTER 3

Organisational Innovation in Multinational Corporations

In the early years of the post-war development of the modern international corporation, organisational structures evolved slowly in response to geographical and market diversity. It was possible for corporate management to change organisation structure incrementally, beginning with an international division to handle the foreign activities of the company, shifting over time to a product-based or geographic divisional structure. The main determining variables were the importance of international business relative to the company's total business, on the one hand, and the diversity of products sold abroad, on the other (Stopford and Wells, 1972). However, today it is clear that the adoption of global strategies by many corporations has been accompanied by a significant increase in environmental complexity in response, organisational structures are changing more rapidly and there is an increase in the degree of experimentation with innovative structures and processes.

Given the fluidity of organisational structures and management processes within multinational corporations, the Carnegie Bosch Institute decided in 1994 to commission studies on 'International network corporations'. These were viewed as international corporations in which there was an emphasis on the autonomy of subsidiaries, lateral communication flows and the cross-border generation and transmission of knowledge.

Nohria and Ghoshal view the modern international corporation as evolving toward a network of related affiliates, rather than a hierarchical structure. They take a contingency perspective, emphasising the importance of *fit* between the structure of the corporation, its strategy and the environmental forces it faces. Fit between the environmental demands and the choice of corporate structure should have a strong impact on firm performance. This is a complex question, because the typical multinational corporation operates in a variety of industries and business environments, in addition to the diversity of its geographic spread.

Impact of Knowledge Flows within the Multinational Corporation

Given the need to transfer knowledge within the MNE, management systems allow the flow of knowledge to take place across different types of strategic contexts. Management systems and policies are designed to channel inter-unit knowledge flows and to regulate the relationships between the units of the MNE and their different strategic contexts. Obviously, the effectiveness of these organizational mechanisms varies. Not all coordination mechanisms are equally effective, nor can all types of knowledge be transferred through the same type of mechanisms. Therefore, the extent of knowledge transfer is partially determined by the choice of management systems and their actual effectiveness. Without the appropriate channels of communication, only casual knowledge flows can occur.

Gupta and Becerra argue that the effectiveness of an internal market for innovation depends on creating the impetus among units to learn from each other; a willingness to share knowledge; mechanisms for subsidiaries to learn about and contact each other; and mechanisms for the actual transfer of knowledge. Success in this endeavour depends primarily on trust.

Though transfer of knowledge is critical for MNEs, not every unit needs to exchange a similar amount of knowledge with all others. There are systematic differences within the MNE with regard to which units possess what type of knowledge and how they exchange it with the rest of the organisation. These differences underlie the strategic role of the units within the MNE. For instance, Gupta and Govindarajan (1991) have classified subsidiaries on a two-by-two matrix in terms of how much knowledge they contributed to the MNE and how much knowledge they obtain from it. This classification results in four strategic roles that the subsidiaries may take within the MNE: global innovator, integrated player, local innovator, and such as exporting and licensing, that would either have higher costs or higher risks, including the risk that leakage of knowledge may end up generating a strong foreign competitor.

Once they become global, MNEs enjoy the benefits of the worldwide generation, storage, and rapid deployment of relevant knowledge in markets with different needs and characteristics. This constitutes a substantial advantage over domestic firms with more limited locally derived knowledge (Ghoshal, 1987). For instance, engineering and consulting MNEs have this clear advantage over domestic competitors, which have a smaller pool of knowledge with less varied customer base. The internal strategic context and management systems within the MNE can be designed to allow different types of knowledge to flow throughout the organisation as needed. Transfer of knowledge is therefore a critical activity within the MNE. Until recently, the analysis of knowledge flows has relied on the study of the strategic context within the organisation, such as structure, management systems, unit goals, and policies. In one of the most influential books on organisation theory, Thompson (1967) analysed how workflow interdependence determines different types of departmentalisation and coordination, such as standardisation, planning, and mutual adjustment. Units that need each other for their daily routines within the MNE have greater co-ordination and continuous transfer of information between them. Different mechanisms of co-ordination can be designed to process the information flow among these units, including reports, teams, liaisons, and coordination through hierarchical supervisors (Galbraith, 1973).

However, simple information and data are only part of the knowledge base of any organisation. Such "declarative knowledge" is relatively easy to codify and transfer. Organisational arrangements can be used to manage and even guarantee that the necessary transfer of this type of knowledge will take place within the organisation rapidly and without overloads and bottlenecks. In contrast, "procedural knowledge" that deals with skills and competencies is usually tactic, often impossible to codify, and much more difficult to transfer. It frequently involves different managers and/or units interconnected through complex processes and procedures. It is this type of knowledge that may be the source of competitive advantage and which constitutes the core competence of an organisation. Interestingly, to remain competitive, organisations have the need to facilitate this transfer of knowledge inside the organisation, while making the process difficult to replicate outside the organisation (Kogut and Zander, 1992).

The transfer of procedural knowledge presents a much more important challenge for the MNE. Certainly, management systems can be designed to facilitate this type of transfer of knowledge, but their effectiveness is more limited in comparison to their effectiveness in transferring simple information. In addition, since this knowledge constitutes the essence of competitive advantage, its transfer entails some risk. Even within the organisation, the transfer of strategic resources from one unit to another may have important consequences for the functioning and future of these units, of which their managers are fully aware. In certain cases, some units may be reluctant to transfer strategic knowledge elsewhere within the organisation, when there is some risk involved in it from the unit's point of view. The problem becomes significant when, given the type of knowledge, its actual transfer cannot be forced by organisational policies. In these situations when the units perceive some risk, trust is essential for fluid transfer of knowledge to take place.

Trust has been defined as the willingness to become vulnerable to the actions of another party (Mayer, Davis, and Schoorman, 1995). In general, when individuals and organisations have trust in their partners, they become willing to engage in collaborative action with them despite the presence of risk that is contingent on the other party's less than fully controllable behaviour. The need for risk-taking and trust is central to all business activities. Since there is always some level of risk in any business relationship, a certain amount of trust is necessary for the economic system to function (Arrow, 1974). After all, we are willing to accept some degree of economic and even physical vulnerability when we buy a TV, toothpaste or anything else. Thus, it is not surprising that the concept of trust has a central role in management theory.

According to **transaction-costs economics**, the possibility of a partner's opportunistic behaviour (and the impossibility to write a contract that fully avoids such behaviour in all unpredictable future scenarios) induces exchange partners to form a combined organisation (Williamson, 1985). In that newly created organisation, common interests should prevail over selfish opportunism of the previously independent partners. In terms of trust, managers place greater trust in other units or managers within their own organisation than in those of other organisations, particularly if they are competitors. They are willing to accept much more vulnerability in their exchanges with other managers within their organisation than in any interaction with other organisations. Trust is a traditional element of business relations that becomes critical when risk is high. Only if there were sufficient trust would managers voluntarily engage in exchanges with risk and vulnerability.

Managing International Innovation Projects

In recent discussions of the modern multinational corporation (MNC), the increased competence of foreign subsidiaries and the need for close and increasingly sophisticated collaboration between units in the global corporate network are emphasised. The international dispersion of research and development (R&D) units is integral to this development, often reinforced by the dominance of acquisitions as a global expansion strategy. In this view of the MNC the effective management of an international network of innovative, or potentially innovative, units within a firm becomes an important determinant of competitiveness. Representative contributions in academic research are Doz (1986), Hedlund (1986), Bartlett and Ghoshal (1989), and White and Poynter (1990). However, few of these more speculative contributions have investigated in depth how these transnational or heterarchical processes work and the difficulties involved. Thus, there is a call for studies with a more explicit focus on a phenomenon that captures real action rather than a dream potential of the international network. The IIP can be regarded as a prime vehicle in leveraging knowledge assets across borders, and in creating competitive advantages by combining internationally dispersed needs and resources. Without a doubt, global innovation presents many challenges. In these processes, product development is no longer only a question of integrating and coordinating activities across functions and over time, a task demanding in itself, but also across geographical and cultural borders. An additional problem is that structures and systems at an organisational level often interfere with the intentions and actions of the people in the projects. Time after time in our research, we witnessed IIP managers not getting the obvious things right because the overall organisational architecture of the company suppressed rather than supported global knowledge-creation processes.

Management of Joint Ventures within International Business Networks

Diversified multinational corporations (MNCs) have to manage a high level of complexity which, as Doz and Prahalad (1993) have argued, stems from a combination of heterogeneity and multidimensionality. Heterogeneity results primarily from the particular trade-offs between businesses, countries, functions, and tasks that best suit the economic and political circumstances of different countries. Multidimensionality reflects the range of products or services, geographical regions, and supporting functions which diversified MNCs encompass. The need to articulate forms of organisation that can cope with growing MNC complexity has been increasingly recognised in recent years (cf. Bartlett *et al*, 1990; Ghoshal and Westney, 1993), and the 'network' form is a possible response.

In view of these complications, the question arises as to whether to treat China as just another country or to give it greater than usual prominence within an MNC's organization, thereby adding to heterogeneity. There are several considerations which favour the latter view. For instance, China is a huge potential market, sustaining a high rate of growth. It is, at the same time, a developing country in which joint ventures will normally be dependent upon their foreign parents for substantial technology transfer, managerial inputs, and assistance in supplier and market development in attaining international standards. The particular characteristics of China as a business environment also impinge on the product, regional, and functional aspects of MNC multidimensionality in three ways. First, there is a need to assist and monitor technology transfer for which the relevant expertise is likely to be located within an MNC's product groups or businesses. Second, an MNC has to view China as consisting of several internal markets because of its scale, infrastructural limitations, and regional differences in economic development. This requires a regional organisation with the sensitivity to manage the differentiation and heterogeneity of its markets. Because of the country's size and regional diversity, many MNCs now have multiple joint ventures in China. They may have to co-ordinate the relations between these joint ventures and the central authorities, as well as exploiting marketing and supply economies among them. Third, there is a need to provide functional support which is not always available from local partners, in areas such as finance and accounting, HRM, and legal affairs. China is therefore a unique business environment, creating complications for MNCs that attempt to integrate local operations into wider organisational systems. The problem is heightened by the fact that Chinese partners often supply the bulk of the ventures' managers and staff, who are normally not used to, and will not necessarily identify with, the norms and procedures of the MNC without foreign managerial guidance. Joint ventures in China may require an unusually heavy managerial investment by foreign partners, at least in the early years of their life, drawing heavily on the different dimensions of MNC organisational expertise. This chapter first addresses the ways in which nine prominent American MNCs have linked the management of their China joint ventures into their global structures. These structures have provided the multidimensional frameworks for intra-organisational managerial networking, concerned with decision-making and information exchange (Boyer, 1989). For such networking to extend effectively to joint ventures in China, it has been essential for US parent companies to exercise effective control and influence over management. The question then arises of where to locate decisions relevant to the joint ventures within the overall managerial network, bearing in mind the problem of reconciling the conflicting criteria of global integration and local differentiation. These three issues—**linkage, control, and decision levels**—are the main subjects of this chapter. The chapter poses a number of important questions which, while focused on China, also have a much wider relevance within global management:

1. How do MNCs link the management of China ventures into their corporate structures?
2. How do MNCs exercise and sustain control over these ventures?
3. How do MNCs locate decision-making relevant to their China business?

The full investigation from which it draws also examined certain processual aspects of the corporate networks operating within the structures. Indeed, a number of senior MNC managers both at corporate and regional levels emphasised that structure alone would not provide an adequate understanding of how their management systems operate with respect to, for example, the integrative functions performed by information exchange and the fostering of shared norms and values. This supports the view advanced by Doz and Prahalad (1993:26) that, for diversified MNCs, "one needs a theory that transcends the structural dimensions and focuses on underlying processes." Nonetheless, as the theory of "structuration" would suggest (Giddens, 1984), action and structure have a symbiotic relationship in organisations such that, while action can modify structure, it is also shaped and constrained by it. The structural dimensions do constitute a significant design challenge for MNC managers, and need to be considered.

Scope and Method of the Inquiry

The investigation from which this chapter draws, covers nine multinational enterprises whose headquarters are located in the United States. The companies are situated in the non-consumer electronics and fast-moving consumer goods (FMCG) sectors—four in the former and five in the latter. The non-consumer electronics companies manufactured telecommunication, process control, and office equipment. The FMCG companies produced branded foods, beverages, and household products. The choice of these two sectors was informed by the desire to contrast companies possessing a strong technological core competence in product design (electronics) with those possessing a strong consumer marketing core competence linked to the promotion of international brands (FMCG). Technological competence is likely to favour a logic of organisation by product group, whereas a strong marketing orientation is likely to favour a logic according to geography.

Nine joint ventures were visited in order to collect information on their internal management and links with parent companies—that is, one joint venture established by each US corporation in China, expatriate general managers, and in one case the American head of operations. Interviews were subsequently conducted in the USA with 12 senior corporate executives who had responsibility for China or who were otherwise closely involved with the corporation's policy toward its China ventures. A further six persons in the Hong Kong regional offices of five of the companies, who had a responsibility for their China ventures, were also interviewed. The procedure adopted for each interview was to ask open-ended questions based on standardised checklists. All the corporate and regional level interviews were tape-recorded, as were some in the joint ventures, depending on the acceptability of this procedure to the interviewee. In the following text and tables, the electronics companies are identified by the prefix "E" and FMCG companies by the prefix "F".

It is useful to distinguish between the *transactional* (input/output) and *managerial* links of the China joint ventures into their foreign parents' multinational networks. They were, in fact, considerably less integrated into global transactional networks than they were into the foreign parents' international management systems.

Only one of the joint ventures was selling any outputs to its MNC parent. The exception was Corporation E4, which had allocated the worldwide production of an older electronic process control system to its China joint venture. This corporation was therefore selling 25 per cent of its output value to other parts of its MNC parent's network. Rather more joint ventures were integrated with their MNC parents on the supply side. Three of the four electronics joint ventures purchased components from their MNCs. E3 took 80 per cent by value, E4 took 45 per cent, while E2 took 30 per cent. Among the fast-moving consumer goods joint ventures, only F2 received an appreciable amount of its process inputs from its MNC parent, at 40 per cent by value. The other FMCG joint ventures received under 5 per cent of their inputs from the American parents.

This low level of transactional integration is explained largely by the fact that all the MNCs had the establishment of a strategic position vis-a-vis competitors and access to the market as their over-riding priorities for establishing joint ventures in China. They were not primarily motivated by supply-side factors such as the availability of low-cost materials or labour. Their intention, at least initially, was to produce for the Chinese market rather than to integrate China into their international production networks.

The relatively limited transactional integration of these China joint ventures justifies focusing on managerial integration. The points at which China joint ventures are linked into the wider corporate structure of MNCs depends on how the issue of multidimensionality is resolved. This is clearly easier in the case of a single joint venture producing one product than that of several joint ventures producing different products, possibly destined for different segments of the Chinese market. In the former case, a straightforward product divisional line linkage down to the China joint venture, through one or more regional levels and supported by functional services, will be appropriate (Stopford and Wells, 1972). In the latter case, with diversified product categories, the regional and/or China level office has coordinating and representative roles to play, and probably responsibility for new business development in China as well.

Meier, Perez, and Woetzel (1995) note that many MNCs have established "China corporate centres" to assist business development and corporate positioning in China by coordinating and supporting business units in negotiating and establishing new ventures. They distinguish two main ways in which these centres can achieve effective co-ordination between product businesses or divisions active in China. One is the "team approach" where "the China centre comprises senior representatives or heads of the local business units, plus a senior country representative" (1995:25). It can, however, be difficult to achieve collaboration in this way between the business managers and the country manager. An alternative approach is therefore to have "focused leadership" with the China centre "led by a China CEO with country P&L responsibility to whom the China business units report" (ibid.).

A further consideration which bears on the role performed by the regional or country office is the operational status given to the China joint venture(s). There are several options relating to the level of local initiative that is favoured. Joint ventures can, for example, be defined as business units, with their own technological and functional resources and the autonomy to undertake their own commercial initiatives. Another option is to locate the formation of their strategy and most of their support at a Chinese country or Asia-Pacific regional level, and to run the joint ventures primarily as manufacturing and sales branch units with perhaps the additional responsibility for relations with local governmental authorities. The issue of how much decentralisation is accorded to the joint ventures is thus bound up with the role that is given to the country or regional office. It is a part of the wider issue of how decision-making autonomy for China is distributed through the MNC structure and how responsibilities are allocated to different levels and groups within that structure.

The nine corporations investigated attached great importance to the design of their global structures. These corporations found the question of how such design should map onto their joint ventures in China a significant challenge. Two important design decisions concerned the main lines of control and coordination relating to the joint ventures, and the autonomy they were accorded within the MNC framework. Five of the companies were actively experimenting with their structures for China. All were continuing to explore issues of balance and co-ordination between vertically and horizontally differentiated units within the overall matrix. As one corporate FMCG senior director commented on proposals to reorganise within China into business units: "This calls the China structure into question again. We've argued the functional structure versus the autonomous business unit structure ad infinitum . . . It has been the most difficult challenge that we have had [in the corporation globally] and it has been ugly, it really has been ugly." **(Corporation F3)**

The corporate strategy director of an electronics corporation indicated that his company faced similar uncertainties over appropriate reporting lines for its China joint ventures:

That's switched back and forth a few times: whether it's a solid line into the product divisions, which figure out the products the market needs during engineering, design and delivery, and dotted line into the geographic structure—or solid into the geographic and dotted into the divisions. **(Corporation E2)**

Table 3.1 summarizes how the nine MNCs were structured globally, the roles of their regional and China offices, the number of joint ventures they had in China, and how these formally linked into their structures. Four of the nine corporations were organised on the basis of global product businesses:

The businesses normally had worldwide responsibility for R&D, manufacturing and, in some cases, marketing. They carried profit responsibility and were the main investment arms of their corporations. Their regional offices had responsibilities primarily for business development, market co-ordination, and functional support. One electronics corporation (E3) operated a balanced matrix of product and geographical units. The remaining four FMCG corporations were organised primarily on a geographical basis. As expected, the product dimension tended to be more prominent in the electronics sector and the geographical dimension in the FMCG sector.

Multiple-product business MNCs faced a greater challenge in how to organise for China than those which had all their products falling within the same category, especially when, at the same time, there are potential synergies in China between the product groups. The status and role of the unit dealing with China varies between the six MNCs (El, E2, E3, Fl, F2, and F4) with diversified products. The organisation of their China centres varied from few links between product

Table 3.1: The Location of China Joint Ventures in MNE Structures

Company	*Global structure*	*Role of regional office*	*Role of China company*	*Number of JVs, reporting to*
El	Product based	Primary role is as regional offices for product divisions. Also new territory development; functional support including IT and legal; government relations.	*Holding company (limited team approach).* Government relations; profit consolidation; secure potential inter-JV synergies; functional support including quality.	6 JVs, reporting to region-based product division managers.
E2	Product based	Product marketing, sales and service; functional support. Also regional offices of product divisions.	*Team approach.* Consolidating China market strategy; co-ordinating JVs and field operations; functional support.	3 JVs, reporting primarily to CEOs.
E3	Matrix	Business development; marketing; functional support.	*Focused leadership. Reports directly to corporate CEO.* Government relations; co-ordinate business units in China for market advantage; functional support, including operations and legal.	9 JVs, reporting to CEO of China company.

(*Contd.*)

Company	*Global structure*	*Role of regional office*	*Role of China company*	*Number of JVs, reporting to*
E4	Product based	Assist business units (JVs, subsidiaries) in market development, coordination of marketing and technology transfer.	*No China company.*	1 JV, reporting to regional manager.
Fl	Product based	Policy and consolidation for regional group of countries within product business; functional support.	*China office for each product business. Line responsibility for JVs.* Central government relations; functional support, (including marketing and operations).	13 JVs in main product sector, reporting to VP Sales Operations in China Office.
F2	Geographical	*Limited team approach at this level.* Overseeing businesses in Asia-Pacific region with functional support. Also product category officers to disseminate and oversee product strategy.	*Line responsibility forJVs.* Central Asia office with Country Manager overseeing China businesses; functional support (including marketing, government relations, China information).	4 JVs, reporting to Country Manager, China.

(*Contd.*)

Company	*Global structure*	*Role of regional office*	*Role of China company*	*Number of JVs, reporting to*
F3	Geographical	Overseeing country units; functional support.	*Line responsibility for China businesses* especially marketing; functional support (including R&D).	3 JVs, reporting to Managing Director for China.
F4	Geographical	Overseeing country units; functional support (HR is at this level). Also product category managers.	*Primarily line responsibility for JVs with limited team approach.* Functional support (including marketing).	3 JVs (plus 3 wholly-owned subsidiaries) reporting to Regional VP for China.
F5	Geographical	General overseeing of geographical divisions within regional groups; functional support.	*Line responsibility for JVs.* functional support, (including legal, marketing, IS, PR).	17 JVs, reporting to Executive VP in China company.

personnel at the China level (Fl), through a limited team approach, to a highly focused leadership. The organisation of China activities was more uniform and straightforward in the remaining MNCs that had products with relatively homogeneous technologies and markets. Every corporation, except for E4, however, had a China company or office, and each one had recently created or was developing the role of a China CEO.

Those companies which pursued a dominant dimensional logic nonetheless endeavoured to build in other dimensions in a complementary manner. As is well appreciated from experience with multidimensional structures (cf. Davis and

Lawrence, 1977; Knight, 1977), this is liable to generate friction, and several of the MNCs had experienced resistance over attempts to reinforce non-dominant structural dimensions. It is therefore instructive to examine some examples of corporate-joint venture structures in more detail, with particular reference to the role of the regional and China levels. These are the three electronics MNCs with multiple product operations in China, and one of the geographical-line organisations which was highly diversified into different categories of food and beverages.

Example: E1 was organised on the basis of global, vertical, product businesses which had worldwide responsibility for R&D, manufacturing, marketing, and sales. Its six joint ventures in China were integrated into the worldwide organisation of their respective product lines, with products assigned to each as a result of global planning by one of the product businesses. Their general managers reported to business managers located at the Asia-Pacific level.

The geographical arm of the organisation subdivided below the corporate level into three regions, of which one was Asia-Pacific. The Asia-Pacific region had, in turn, a Chinese general manager reporting to it. The Asia-Pacific regional office provided what it termed "the horizontal infrastructure" for the businesses, and this involved a complete range of functions such as financial, accounting, corporate treasury, information systems, human resources, legal, and facilities. The role of the geographical dimension was, according to its Senior Vice-President:

> To do with delivering common shared corporate services in support of the [vertical] businesses. It also includes things like government and public affairs, new market development and new territory development—not necessarily what a business might do once we, in a sense, create a presence in that particular territory.

Its geographical organisation was also intended to present a unified corporate face, both internally to its employees, administering, for instance, a common benefits policy, and externally to customer and governments. To quote the same SVP:

> We have very focused, aggressive businesses that can basically compete with any niche competitor, yet have the ability to look and act like one extremely large corporation when we want to.

The corporation had recently extended its geographical dimension within China with the establishment of a holding company as an umbrella over all the corporation's joint ventures in that country. In addition to the taxation and foreign exchange management advantages this offered, the major organisational benefit was seen to be better positioning for the corporation vis-a-vis the central government. Relationships with ministries relevant to its various products were vital for the continued development of its business, as were those with the municipal government of Shanghai, where three of its joint ventures are located. Nonetheless, the corporation saw its China holding company as performing a supportive role to the product-based businesses that remained the focus of its organisation. This exemplifies a relatively weak team approach. In fact, the regional CEO described it as "really more like a paper corporation."

Example: E2 had recently enhanced its China company and was intending this to operate in a stronger team mode. It had felt the need to develop a comprehensive strategy for China which was not forthcoming from the previous arrangement whereby self-contained joint ventures, with their own engineering, manufacturing, selling, and service facilities, reported to separate business divisions. There had indeed been considerable conflict between the joint ventures and the China office, which tried to co-ordinate the product divisions and to orient them more toward the market. According to the CEO of the China company:

> Instead of worrying about the customer or competition, there were a lot of inter-murals going on and because of that . . . we really have not invested what we feel now is

> necessary to go into the market . . . When I came here, one of the jobs that I was given was to get ourselves into a dominant position in the market, and to try to get some better focus on the customer. That clearly requires a distribution system and a field system that is more coordinated among all of the divisions than we had.

The corporation had reorganised its China company to contain four business division directors, a consolidated marketing function in charge of China field operations, and an executive in charge of the joint ventures which it intended to expand beyond the existing number of three. While all of these key positions reported to the CEO of the China company, the intention was to generate a team approach rather than one of focused leadership. That is, to bring strategic and market development perspectives alongside those of product "push" which were already influential. To quote the China CEO again:

> The intention really is to try to get a more focused strategy on China, and not necessarily just from the products that we make over there but from the strength that the corporation can bring to the market because it clearly has a lot of strength that we have not capitalised on for this market. To try to get a strategy put together is probably one of the biggest issues we had in that ours was a product, dealer-driven strategy rather than what the end-customers may need ... not to worry too much about what you can make right now, but trying to judge a little bit as to which way the market will go.

Example: E3 is pursuing business opportunities in China on the basis of a Memorandum of Understanding (MOU) with the central government. Subsequent to the Memorandum, the corporation established a China company intended to present a single face to the Chinese government and to co-ordinate the hitherto separate initiatives of its product businesses. It exemplified the focused approach and has been regarded by some as pioneering a new structure for China. The China CEO enjoyed considerable personal respect within the corporation, and unusual status, since he was the only country head to report directly to the corporate CEO alongside the heads of the five global product groups and four regions. He claimed that this arrangement signified the first time his corporation had applied a combined global and local strategy.

The corporation's international operations were organised as a balanced matrix. Its "shared accountability model" stated that product groups and regions share responsibility for its business in China. The product groups had responsibility for the products that were available, the kinds of services the corporation was willing to offer, linkages to other (telecommunications) operations, and the sourcing of products that were not built locally. The regions had the main say on decisions which were customer-facing in terms of sales and project-bidding. However, the China company constituted something of an exception to this balance. It shared responsibility with the product groups for the China income statement and it jointly signed up the plans that were drawn up for China along with the product groups. The China company did, however, co-ordinate the various product groups in order to offer complete solutions to Chinese customers, and it showed the corporation's face to the Chinese government. It is also reported to have taken the lead in formulating the corporation's strategy for China. According to the VP of Strategic Planning for the China company who, significantly, was located at corporate head office:

> Increasingly, it will be speaking with a voice of its own. It says that it has a strategy and the groups have to bring themselves into conformity with that strategy as they operate in China. That's developing as time goes on.

An example of this developing role concerned a major initiative with the Chinese civil aeronautics administration. The project was not sufficiently attractive to win the enthusiasm of any individual product group, but taken as a whole it could do a great deal to enhance the reputation of the corporation in China as a total solutions vendor in the information technology field. The CEO of the China company pushed the project through, even though none of the product groups thought it was worth their time.

Example: F2 had four China joint ventures which were responsible for different products that, collectively, fell into its three main food processing categories. While organised on the basis of geographic line responsibilities, F2 has addressed the question of how to build into its structure the specific strategic considerations of each product category. In addition to its geographical structure, it had established a "category management system" at the global and regional levels of its organisation. Each of the corporation's three main product categories had a manager located at the Asia-Pacific regional office. This arrangement was intended to ensure that the relevant joint ventures in China were sufficiently briefed on corporate thinking for the product category. In the regional office, which physically contained subsidiary area office for China, Hong Kong, and Taiwan, the corporation pursued a limited team approach:

> The regional manager might be lending help to Japan or Australia or Singapore, but would also be providing similar assistance to the PRC joint ventures. For example, joint venture A would be getting the latest thinking on our coffee strategy and our coffee label ... So there is a pan-Asia category manager system that works with the marketing and development lady who is in charge of PRC. **(Corporate President F2)**

At a corporate level, the global product categories were linked together through "worldwide category councils" which met to review progress and strategy. Although the issue had been debated within the corporation, and remained highly sensitive, the regional organisation retained the line responsibility and was the stronger dimension. This was illustrated by its regional and country level organisation. Each of the corporation's four joint ventures in China reported to a country manager for China who also had two other managers under him with responsibilities for PRC sales and marketing/ strategy across all three product categories. The sub-regional Area Office for Central Asia (PRC, Hong Kong, and Taiwan), to which the country manager reported, had no product category representatives either. It provided functional support in the areas of finance, human resources, technical, PRC information, and government relations areas. The product category managers were located at the next level up, namely Asia-Pacific, from which they performed the largely advisory roles already mentioned.

In short, senior executives in each of the MNCs were exploring how best to locate China joint ventures within their global structures. This was a significant issue within the wider problem of how best to organise the management of worldwide activities. When their structures reflected the primacy of one dimension, such as differentiated product businesses, they endeavoured to incorporate other complementary dimensions. China's huge size, and the unusual significance in increasing international competition creates more complex environments for managers to deal with. The diversity of countries, customer behaviour, and management styles requires local adaptations combined with a global strategy. New organisational structures and administrative mechanisms are designed to cope with this increased diversity. Multinational corporations have adapted various solutions, such as decentralisation, divisionalisation, and matrix structures to reduce the strategic variety that top managers have to cope with at the corporate level, but they are not sufficient. Top managers have to develop a "world view" or "mind-set." Bartlett and Ghoshal (1989) argued that "the task is not to build a sophisticated structure, but to create a matrix in the minds of managers." Moreover the executives in the top management team have the particular function to integrate strategies across business sectors and geographical zones. Consequently, the complexity of top managers' mental maps of their competition should match the complexity of their international strategic systems. Even in companies focused on their national markets, executives cannot neglect the turbulence created by new entrants coming from foreign countries. Organisational learning becomes a priority in order to counteract ethnocentric biases: that is, the tendency to focus on and prefer one's own social group and country. Ethnocentric bias leads to strategic myopia in a global economy. Catching up with globalisation trends becomes extremely difficult for late movers unless they can create substantial competitive advantages. Ethnocentrism is a form of cognitive rigidity. It reduces the scope of events considered by managers and freezes the strategies learned in the home market. As a consequence, decision makers fail to adapt to different rules of the game. At the organisational level, international competition should stimulate knowledge flows across borders. At the individual level, international competition should stimulate managerial learning by:

- Making explicit one's own schema of the competition.
- Allowing comparison with others in order to elicit ethnocentric biases.
- Preparing and improving the strategic debate within the firm and with external experts.
- Developing one's own schema before being forced to do so by a major crisis.

It is commonly argued that the creation and sharing of knowledge are critical strengths of successful international corporations. Sharing a variety of conceptions amongst top managers on critical issues is one of the processes that strengthens a firm's competitive potential.

Strategy is thinking, preparing, and interpreting action; thus, cognitive analysis methods should help managers to analyse their international environments and formulate international strategies. Some managers' biases are conscious, some are unconscious; the purpose of cognitive analysis (the analysis of knowledge) is to raise awareness and to stimulate the learning process.

This chapter demonstrates the ethnocentric biases of top managers toward international competition. Methods for mapping strategic thinking are presented and applied to the world car manufacturing industry and the European brewing industry. We discuss how managers can learn from the comparison of their cognitive maps with those of other experts, how they can improve strategic debates and strengthen scenario planning. It will be argued that such methods are helpful in developing managers' cognitive complexity in order to match the complexity of international competition.

In recent years it has become evident that traditional organisational forms may no longer be sufficient for achieving or maintaining competitive advantage on a worldwide basis. Nowhere is this more evident than in the case of the multinational enterprise (MNE) operating in a global industry environment. Competing in a global industry requires extensive strategic coordination among the various subsidiaries of the MNE, resulting in a high level of interdependence between subsidiaries. This has led multinational firms to develop and implement strategies, structures, organisational processes, and systems that enable the firm to capitalise on the advantages of interdependencies that exist among its various sub-units, most clearly in differentiated network organisations.

Although a great deal of attention has been paid to the organisational structure issues involved in implementing international strategies (Egelhoff, 1982; Stopford and Wells, 1972) it has become apparent that there is a need to focus on subsidiary managers and their role in the implementation process. This shift in focus has occurred because it is increasingly recognised that lower levels in the organisation, such as the profit centre or business unit, are the sites of strategic renewal. Entrepreneurial processes at these levels operationally define the firm's competitive advantage. Extended to the foreign subsidiary or business unit, competitive advantage must be defined in such a manner that managers of these units respond simultaneously to local market conditions and act in accordance with a globally integrated corporate strategy (Bartlett and Ghoshal, 1989).

Prior to the recent dramatic globalisation of many industries, the primary concern of the subsidiary manager was the performance of the subsidiary in the local market. Industry globalisation has resulted in a redefined role for the subsidiary manager, wherein he or she is increasingly accountable for the contribution made by the subsidiary to the competitive position of the corporation as a whole. This is particularly true in multinational firms that exhibit an international network structure, in which the activities of any particular foreign subsidiary are highly interdependent with those of subsidiaries in other countries. In such international network corporations, managerial decisions and actions that take place in one location can have important ramifications for the operations and performance of other sub-units throughout the firm. Because of this major change, it has become increasingly important to focus on internal processes and human resources policies at the level of the foreign subsidiary.

If managers at the foreign subsidiary level are expected to contribute to the achievement of corporate level goals, then it is important for the MNE to have organisational systems and processes that encourage and facilitate subsidiary manager decisions that are consistent with such goals. One aspect of organisational design through which headquarters can greatly affect the subsidiary manager's perception and performance of his or her role is that of international human resources management practices (Edstrom and Galbraith, 1977; Kobrin, 1994; Rosenzweig and Nohria, 1994). In particular, it is increasingly recognised that the compensation and reward system is a key factor in the implementation of an organisation's strategy and the accomplishment of its strategic objectives (Galbraith and Kazanjian, 1986; Schuler and MacMillan, 1984). Compensation and reward systems can be used to encourage the top management actions and behaviors necessary to meet the firm's objectives (Finkelstein and Hambrick, 1989). In the case of the foreign subsidiary manager, the compensation and reward system can be used to elicit or support those behaviours and decisions that are in accordance with the global strategic goals of the MNE as opposed to those that address only local market performance.

We will also discuss the results of a recent research study undertaken to better understand the role of compensation and reward systems in the implementation of different types of international strategies. First, we will examine the characteristics of foreign subsidiaries with two different strategic roles. The discussion will then focus on the elements of the compensation programmes used to manage foreign subsidiaries with one of these two distinct strategic roles. Finally, we will present some implications of this study for the management of foreign subsidiaries.

International Network Business

Re-engineering Corporations

Hammer and Champy (1993) define **Business Process Re-engineering** (BPR) as "the fundamental rethinking and radical redesign of business processes to achieve dramatic improvements in critical contemporary measures of performance, such as cost, quality, service, and speed." With the promise of quantum improvements in performance, many companies worldwide have embraced this new form of business transformation.

What are the basic ideas underlying BPR? A considerable literature emphasises that organisations have traditionally been organised hierarchically, with specialisation into functional areas. While this structure aids exception-based decision-making and the need for authority and control, it ignores the "white space" between the functional areas in the organisation (Rummler and Brache, 1990). In other words, the operations of each functional area may work well by themselves, but the links between these functional areas may be less than satisfactory. When that happens, the output from one functional area may not mesh well with the needs of other functional areas downstream. Furthermore, the wait time between functional areas for any transaction may be significantly longer than the actual processing time within an area. In short, because no one owns, manages, and co-ordinates the various functional areas in a hierarchical organisation, the co-ordination that yields smooth operations from beginning to end of the process is generally missing.

If co-ordination is important and challenging for corporations within a single nation, the stakes and difficulties are magnified in multinational companies. As Bartlett and Ghoshal (1989) point out, International Network Corporations (INCs) purposely establish distributed operations in various international locations to take advantage of the markets and specialised resources that each location offers. However, this distribution comes at a cost: an INC must reconcile the diversity of perspectives and interests it deliberately fosters, integrate the widespread assets and resources it deliberately disperses, and co-ordinate the roles and responsibilities it deliberately differentiates (Bartlett and Ghoshal, 1989). Furthermore, the strategies it uses to do so depend on whether what is to be coordinated are goods, resources, or information. Given these added complexities of transnational flows, having a good understanding of co-ordination becomes particularly critical for the successful operation and process and redesign of an international network corporation. To solve co-ordination problems, whether domestic or international, many BPR experts advocate a *process* rather than a *structural* view of an organisation. In a process orientation, the actions of many functional areas are coordinated to achieve the customer's goals. Problematic handoffs and communications between the traditional functional areas are eliminated or redesigned to allow those transitions to be done quickly and smoothly. Essentially, streamlining occurs by managing the "white space" that is ignored in traditional organisation charts. To that end, Hammer and Champy (1993) recommend several heuristics for BPR:

- Combine several jobs into one
- Let workers make decisions
- Refine processes into multiple versions

- Perform work where it makes the most sense
- Reduce checks and controls
- Minimise reconciliation.

These recommendations seem hard to argue with as techniques for creating lean, efficient organisations. And while BPR's annals do contain several glowing and oft-repeated success stories, these contrast sharply with reported failure rates of 40 to 70 per cent. Why have these failures occurred, and how can managers learn from them? According to some surveys, poor change management strategies and implementation are one major reason (Reynolds, 1994). Given the magnitude of BPR-induced change, employees' fears and their resistance to organisational change are not unexpected barriers.

We believe that two additional factors contribute to BPR failures. One is the danger of radical change. Despite some practitioners' recommendations that one redesign from scratch, companies' histories cannot be ignored; while critical resources, such as expertise and power, cannot easily be altered or shifted. The other major culprit is the failure to consider the human issues involved in re-engineering. That is, many re-engineering projects focus on the more accessible daily operations, ignoring the critical social and political elements that comprise the organisational context in which the process operates. These elements are particularly critical in multinational firms, where social and political systems vary across the firm's operating entities, adding a level of complexity to the BPR task.

Given this understanding, the main goal is to develop a methodology and tools for BPR that are particularly useful for international network corporations. The main argument is that social context, a missing element in most BPR models and methods, can and should be gainfully included in process redesign tools and techniques. While social context is useful in domestic process re-engineering, it is even more important in international network corporations. This heightened importance comes because social context varies across operating units of an INC, and must be made explicit more when co-ordinated for the corporation to work effectively and efficiently.

The chapter's central element and practical foundation is a manufacturing company's purchasing process. Using case study data from this process, as well as research on other existing BPR models, the chapter first assesses the limitations of existing models, noting problems that might be altered by an international setting. Using the purchasing process, the chapter then develops a framework for BPR that addresses the shortcomings of existing models. Key elements of this new framework are deep and surface structures. It also describes three specific deep structure elements—expertise, goal conflict, and accountability—and illustrates their importance to the process through examples from the case study. The subsequent section provides a more formal representation of deep and surface structures by developing the Goal-Exception-Dependency (GED) model of organisational processes, with heuristics for process redesign that use the model's elements. Again, examples of the model and its heuristics draw on the case study. Having established a model of BPR for single-nation processes, the final section extends this model to international firms. The chapter details the particular differences between single nation and international BPR, and describes the utility of the GED model and accountability for understanding and redesigning processes in international network corporations.

Limitations of Current Methodologies

Why do the limitations of BPR methodologies exist, especially the relative ignorance of social context? Some deficits can be understood by tracing the history of re-engineering. That is, many common concepts and practices of re-engineering grew out of process analysis methods and tools used in computer science and systems analysis. Because they came from the "hard" sciences, these process models are good at capturing the visible or clearly described interactions between parts of the system. They help us to manage process logistics by identifying bottlenecks, communication breakdowns, and inefficiencies, often enabling the use of information technology to solve these problems. Because social context is not an issue in modelling a computer system, no means for looking beneath the surface of a process at its supporting context was ever developed. However, social context is clearly important in understanding organisations and redesigning processes, so that when these limited models are applied in organisational settings, the results are not always satisfactory. Therein, perhaps, lie some of the seeds of BPR failure. The following section details elements of this fundamental limitation in most BPR modelling and redesign methodologies. These limitations are:

1. Focus on surface-level activities only
2. Focus on a single operational routine only
3. Failure to show missing resource and information flows
4. Failure to capture process emergence
5. Reliance on quantitative methods
6. Lack of adequate heuristics for process redesign.

In recent years, multinational corporations (MNCs) have increasingly been conceived as multicentred organisational forms, with foreign subsidiaries playing different roles within a larger network structure. By adopting an internally differentiated form, rather than insisting on identical roles for each foreign subsidiary, MNCs can tap the distinctive capabilities of each subsidiary and optimise their worldwide operations. Such MNCs are also better positioned to benefit from network flexibility, as they can shift production and sourcing among subsidiaries as various external conditions—competitive, financial, or regulatory—change. The chapters in this volume, many of which explicitly refer to MNCs as 'networks', are testimony to the growing popularity of understanding MNCs in this way.

At one end of the spectrum of sustainability, some organisations stand out by relying on the specialised talents of skilled individuals, and they enjoy stable profitability over time. Software firms, book publishers, and consulting firms fit this description. Other profit-stable firms rely on long-term, complex relationships between themselves and their customers, as in defence, aerospace, accounting, and investment banking. In these businesses, organisational features and international strategy styles are dictated by specialised human processes or the highly specialised needs of a few customers implicitly views FDI as a result, or an end point—yet by definition foreign market entry is also a beginning, and indeed is the beginning of a critical phase of the MNC's life. Explaining initial market entry is important, but understanding the process of building a strong and successful subsidiary after initial entry surely has important consequences for firm performance, The post-entry phase of foreign direct investment can be understood by presenting the experience of the Sony Corporation

Sony, the Japanese-based electronics and entertainment firm, is by any measure a mature and complex MNC. The Sony brand name ranks along with Coca-Cola and McDonald's among the most recognised in the world. Its worldwide sales in 1993 of $34 billion were almost equally distributed among North America (30.4 per cent), Europe (26.0 per cent), and Japan (25.8 per cent). In the United States, Sony employed more than 20,000 people at many sites and in many distinct lines of business, including televisions, magnetic tape, semiconductors, and precision audio equipment. These lines of business varied widely in their importance and contribution to the corporation's worldwide activities: some performed only local manufacturing, others engaged in research and development, and others played a role of worldwide leadership.

Sony's activities in the United States are a vital part of its worldwide network, but they were not created overnight. Until 1972, Sony manufactured its products exclusively in Japan and exported them around the world. Its first direct investment in the United States was small, restricted to a single line of business—televisions—and a single operation—final assembly. Over the next 20 years, Sony's US activities evolved both in terms of the functions performed and in terms of the lines of business represented. A case study of Sony in the United States can therefore shed light on many aspects of post-entry management.

Of course, Sony's experience in the United States is not representative of all MNCs. Its evolution took place over many years, consisted of many discrete steps, and involved many separate entries in distinct lines of business. We make no claim that Sony's experience is typical. Yet it is precisely the lengthy, gradual process of evolution which makes Sony an effective prototype, allowing us to think clearly about the dynamics of MNC evolution, and thereby providing a benchmark against which the post-entry management in other firms can be examined.

This case study of Sony was conducted by gathering archival, documentary, and interview data. At first, we gathered and digested publicly available data, including company annual reports, press articles, books, and biographies. Once we had developed an understanding of the milestones in Sony's evolution in the United States, we conducted a series of interviews. First we met with senior managers at the Sony Engineering and Manufacturing America (SEMA) headquarters in New Jersey. We then visited Sony divisions in San Diego, California; Tijuana, Mexico; Pittsburgh, Pennsylvania; and San Antonio, Texas. A final series of interviews were conducted at SEMA headquarters in New Jersey and at the Sony Corporation headquarters in Tokyo.

In all, we interviewed more than 40 Sony managers, some more than once. They included a cross-section of managers: Americans and Japanese; senior executives, division managers, and technical professionals; and included functions including R&D, manufacturing, human resources, finance, and business planning.

It is critical to note, however, that multinational networks are not born; they evolve. Aside from the few firms that are truly born multinational—that, from their moment of founding, might source inputs in one country, design products in another, manufacture in yet another country, and raise funds in still another—most MNCs begin in one country and evolve over time to become differentiated networks. This process of evolution is hardly automatic, but requires deliberate managerial action, often sustained over many years. The great number of MNCs that, despite their age, have never evolved into differentiated networks makes plain that the passage of time is not a sufficient condition for evolution. Furthermore, as firms which are able to navigate this evolutionary process more swiftly, more fully, and more efficiently are likely to achieve a superior competitiveness. With the increase in US revenues, however, came concerns about vulnerability to trade disputes. In the early 1970s, US television makers charged their Japanese rivals with dumping, prompting a Department of Commerce investigation. Akio Morita, by now Sony's CEO, successfully fought the charges, but was so shaken by the allegations that he decided to set up a manufacturing site in the United States. In strict economic terms, manufacturing in the USA did not yet make sense—at 360 yen to the dollar, it was more efficient to produce in Japan and export to the USA —but finding ways to reduce dependence on exports was seen as vital.

In August 1972, Sony became the first Japanese firm to undertake direct investment in the United States, establishing a small manufacturing operation at the Rancho Bernardo Industrial Park, north of San Diego. Thirty Americans were hired, none of whom had experience in appliance manufacturing, so that Sony could train them from scratch. A team of Japanese expatriates supervised the fledgling venture, training the Americans and reproducing exactly the final television assembly layout in Japan.

At the outset, Sony's San Diego plant had a narrow focus: it performed final assembly for just one product—televisions. Strictly speaking, San Diego did not assemble televisions—it re-assembled televisions that had already been assembled, adjusted, then disassembled, in Japan. As one manager recalled, so concerned were Japanese managers about the quality of American workmanship that first they wanted to find out if Americans, working under the supervision of Japanese managers, could properly re-assemble a television. The quality of re-assembly at San Diego was carefully monitored by managers in Japan, and once they were satisfied that American workers could properly re-assemble televisions, prior assembly in Japan was discontinued.

Managing Transnational Network

After a decade of globalising markets, restructuring industries, transforming technologies, and intensifying competition, there must be few precious managers who have been unaffected by the subsequent waves of downsizing, delayering, restructuring, and re-engineering that have reconfigured the form and redefined the functioning of the modern transnational organisation. More important to the surviving managers is the impact that these transformational changes have had on their individual roles and responsibilities —and, by implication, on the personal competencies required of those who must implement the new management tasks.

In the wake of the explosion in global competition during the 1980s, most companies were forced to recognise that they could no longer succeed on the basis of their historic narrow sources of competitive advantage. In an earlier study, we showed that the most successful worldwide companies were those that had been able to build three potentially conflicting strategic capabilities: global-scale efficiency, local flexibility and responsiveness, and an integrated process of cross-border innovation and learning. It was the need to develop this multilayered strategic capability that led companies to build what we described as a truly transnational organisation with three distinctive characteristics:

Multidimensional Perspectives

To be able to sense and analyse the numerous and often conflicting opportunities, pressures, and demands it faces worldwide, the transnational organisation must be built around three strong management groups, each with access to the company's decision-making process. Capable national subsidiary management is needed to sense and represent the changing needs of local customers and the aspirations of host governments; influential global or regional business management is needed to track the strategy of cross-border competitors and to rationalise the company's assets, products, and strategies worldwide; and effective functional management is needed to enhance and consolidate corporate knowledge and expertise, and facilitate its transfer and use among dispersed national units.

Distributed, Interdependent Capabilities

Having sensed the diverse opportunities and demands it faces, the transnational company must then be able to respond to them in a timely and effective manner. To do so, the company neither centralises its capabilities in the home country nor fragments them on a local-for-local basis among different subsidiaries. Rather, it distributes its resources and capabilities around the world, typically building organisational assets in major markets, in key competitive centres, and in locations providing access to scarce expertise, such as technology. In any case, resources are specialised and linked regionally or globally to achieve economies of scale and skill. One major consequence of such a configuration of distributed, specialised capabilities is a high level of interdependence among worldwide units, The transnational company manages these interdependencies by creating processes and mechanisms for extensive cross-unit flow of resources, products, and knowledge. As a result, the transnational company builds a structure that can be described as an integrated network.

Flexible, Integrative Processes

Having established management groups representing multiple perspectives and a network of distributed and interdependent assets and capabilities, the transnational firm requires a management process that can resolve the diversity of interests and perspectives and integrate the dispersed responsibilities. This requires a sophisticated and subtle decision-making machinery based on three different but interdependent management mechanisms. The first is a supportive but constrained escalation process that allows top management to intervene directly in the content of certain decisions—a carefully managed form of centralisation. The second is to define individual roles and supportive systems to influence specific key decisions through formalisation. The third is socialisation, built through shared norms and values and relationships that create a context for delegated decisions. It is only by developing and selectively managing this portfolio of processes that a company can integrate the multidimensional management perspectives and co-ordinate the dispersed resources and capabilities that characterise the transnational organisation.

In the second stage of our research project, we observed numerous companies that were converging on this organisational model despite wide differences in their core business, national origin, and corporate histories. Some, like AT&T, Komatsu, ABB, and Corning, were forced to shed traditional authority-based hierarchies to adopt the newer form, while others, like 3M, Kao, ISS, and Intel, had built their organisations in networked form over many decades and, as a result, had avoided the worst pathologies of the classic bureaucracies. In many ways this latter group provided both the example and the inspiration for companies in the first group that were undergoing painful transformations to the integrated networked model.

As the understanding of the operations of this emerging corporate form got better, three additional characteristics common to companies making the transformational change were noticed. The first and most widespread trend observed was that companies were restructuring their old approach of dividing the organisation from the top-down into groups, sectors, and divisions. Instead, they were building from the bottom-up on a foundation of small front-line operating units. For example, the $30 billion Swiss-based electro-technical giant,

ABB, divided its operations into 1,300 local operating companies, each of which is structured as a separate legal entity with its own balance sheet and P&L responsibilities. 3M's $15 billion of sales are generated by a portfolio of over 60,000 products, managed by 3,900 profit centres that are at the heart of the company's entrepreneurial process. And ISS, the Danish-based cleaning services organisation attributes its growth into a $2 billion multinational corporation to its policy of forming not one national subsidiary, but four or five small autonomous businesses in each of the 17 countries it has expanded into, allowing each of them to grow by serving a particular client group.

The second common characteristic in the emerging organisation model is the portfolio of cross-unit integrative processes designed to break down the insulated vertically oriented relationships that have dominated the classic authority-based hierarchy. In ABB, the tensions embodied in the company's global matrix were resolved through a proliferation of business boards, functional councils, and project teams designed to play a primary role in ABB's management process at every level of the organisation. At 3M, the R&D community's carefully developed network of communications channels and decision-making forums became the model for similar relationships that were fostered to link marketing and manufacturing resources across the company's portfolio of innovative front-line units. And ISS made extensive use of both training and development as well as regional cross-unit meetings and committees to ensure that knowledge and expertise developed in one part of the company were rapidly transferred system-wide.

Finally, in the emerging organisation, these changes to the old structure and processes were supported by a strong commitment to genuine empowerment, a philosophy that represented a powerful challenge to the authority-based culture in most classic hierarchies. In ABB, CEO Percy Barnevik based the company's management practice on the twin principles of **radically decentralised responsibility** and **tightly held**

individual accountability. 3M was known for its core principles that espoused a commitment to entrepreneurship and a belief in the individual, and had long worked to translate those beliefs into a culture that "stimulates ordinary people to produce extraordinary performance." And in his 30 years at the head of ISS, Poul Andreassen had developed a set of guiding principles, central to which was a genuine respect for his workers and a delegation of responsibility as close to the individual contract as possible.

This radically decentralised yet horizontally linked network organisational model with a strong culture of empowerment required companies to break with what we termed the "Russian doll" model of management, that assumed a neatly nested hierarchy of responsibilities and a set of management roles that were miniature replicas of the job at the next level. In these and other companies studied, operating-level managers had to evolve from their traditional role as front-line implementers to become innovative entrepreneurs; senior-level managers had to redefine their primary role from administrative controllers to developmental coaches; and top-level executives were forced to see themselves less as their company's strategic architects and more as their organisational leaders. The implications of such role changes on the distribution of key tasks and responsibilities are profound.

Operating-level Entrepreneurial

Redefining their management roles and identifying the new roles and responsibilities of those running national subsidiaries, business units or other such front-line units, I studied the activities of scores of operating-level managers as they struggled to adjust to the demands of the new corporate model. The focus is on a select group of managers at ABB, 3M, and ISS, not as definitive role models, but as illustrations of the framework of management tasks.

Don Jans headed the relays business unit that was part of Westinghouse's troubled power transmission and distribution business, which it sold to ABB in 1989. Westinghouse had long regarded relays as a mature business, and Jans and his team had been encouraged to milk their slowly declining, modestly profitable operation. Yet, when exposed to ABB's decentralised entrepreneurial environment, the same management group turned their mature business into one with the performance profile of a young growth company. Within three years of the ownership change, export sales skyrocketed, new products were introduced, and operating profits doubled. Equally important, the revitalised US relays unit began developing an electronic capability to supplement its traditional electromechanical expertise, thus laying the foundation for long-term expansion into a major new growth area.

In 3M we saw a similar example of front-line entrepreneurship when, in 1989, Andy Wong became the leader of a project team that had been struggling for over a decade to commercialise a portfolio of the company's optical technologies that had never found market applications. Over the next four years, Wong redeployed the unit's resources, refocused its energy and attention, protected the operations from several threats to shut them down, and remotivated the discouraged team. By 1994, Wong's unit had become a showcase within 3M by introducing two new products, both of which proved to be highly successful in the marketplace.

And at ISS we observed Theo Buitendijk take over the company's small Dutch commercial cleaning business and double revenues within two years. He took the company into the specialised higher-margin segment of slaughterhouse cleaning, eventually becoming the company's centre of expertise in this sector and supporting its expansion throughout Europe. Like Jans, Buitendijk had previously been a traditional line manager in a classic authoritarian hierarchy (in his case, Exxon), but found that the different organisational context in ISS not only allowed, but also encouraged him, to redefine his role and change his behaviour.

In each of these companies, a similar framework of organisational structure, processes, and culture supported the entrepreneurial activities of front-line managers like Jans,

Wong, and Buitendijk, as they took the initiative to drive the performance and enhance the capabilities of their units. Among the many tasks and responsibilities they undertook, three were identified as central to the role as entrepreneurs rather than just implementers see Table 3.2 (on next page)

- They took the lead in creating and pursuing new growth opportunities.
- They worked to attract and retain the scarce resources and skills necessary to pursue growth.
- They constantly drove their business to ensure ongoing performance improvement.

The most striking set of activities and achievements common to the operating-level entrepreneurs we studied were those related to their shared successes in taking the initiative to create and pursue new business opportunities. In contrast to the role they once played as implementers of programmes and priorities pushed down from above, managers like Jans and Buitendijk found that in their new situations they were not only free to initiate new activities, but were also expected to do so. Jans rose to the challenge by expanding into export markets in Mexico, Canada, and the Far East, and committing to the development of microprocessor-based relays, despite the substantial up-front investment involved. Buitendijk's abattoir cleaning caused a sharp drop in his company's profitability before finally proving to be a much more attractive segment than the highly competitive core office cleaning business.

Beyond developing new products and markets, these front-line entrepreneurs had all expanded the assets, resources, and capabilities of their operating units. Rather than playing the more traditional passive-dependent role defined by corporate processes such as head count authorisation, capital budget allocation, and management development procedures, these individuals saw it as their responsibility to develop the limited resources they had and "to do more with less," as one of them described it. Andy Wong's actions in upgrading his unit's existing technological and manufacturing resources were

Table 3.2: Management Roles and Tasks

	Operating-level managers	*Senior-level managers*	*Top-level managers*
Changing role	From operational implementers to aggressive entrepreneurs	From administrative controllers to supportive coaches	From resource allocators to institutional leaders
Primary value added	Driving business performance by focusing on productivity, innovation, and growth within frontline units	Providing the support and coordination to bring large company advantages to the independent frontline units	Creating and embedding
Key activities and tasks	Creating and pursuing new growth opportunities for the business	Developing individuals and supporting their activities	Challenging embedded assumptions while establishing a stretching opportunity horizon and performance standards
	Attracting and developing resources and competencies	Linking dispersed knowledge, skills, and best practices across units	Institutionalizing a set of norms and values to support cooperation and trust
	Managing continuous performance improvement within the unit	Managing the tension between short-term performance and long-term ambition.	Creating an overarching corporate purpose and ambition

impressive enough, but his creation of an entirely new marketing capability in a resource-constrained operation was truly entrepreneurial. Through persistent negotiations with senior management, creative internal resource reallocations, and persuasive recruiting within the company, he was able to reinforce his small struggling unit with an experienced marketing manager and to back him with the distribution support of two other 3M divisions that agreed to help bring his unproven product to market. Don Jans's ability to develop a microprocessor-based product line, and his unit's recognition as the benchmark in cycle-time management exhibited the same commitment to build on and leverage existing capabilities. This capability led Jans to be recognised as a "giver" rather than a "receiver," as ABB terminology referred to managers who became net developers rather than consumers of the organisation's scarce resources.

The third basic responsibility of front-line managers was the one with which they were most familiar: to ensure continuous performance improvement of their operating units. In the new organisational context, however, they were given considerably more freedom, incentive, and support to find ways to do so. Thus, despite the fact that he had long been driven to maximise operating performance in Westinghouse, Don Jans was able to achieve substantial additional expense cuts, inventory and receivables reductions, and operating efficiency improvements within the ABB organisation, largely because he was given what Barnevik described as "maximum degree of freedom to execute."

Achieving current performance also became a priority for Andy Wong, who knew that by leveraging the unit's existing assets and resources, he could build the credibility and confidence he would need to obtain additional investment and support. It was for this reason that Wong initially invested a large part of his energy in focusing development attention on only two technologies and reducing manufacturing costs by 50 per cent. It was only after building organisational confidence with his operating effectiveness that he won the freedom to engage the resources necessary to implement his unit's entrepreneurial new product launch.

If these three entrepreneurial tasks do not yet describe the actual practice of most front-line managers, it only shows the untapped potential for performance improvement available to most companies. The dramatically changed behaviour of managers like Jans and Buitendijk, and Wong's rapid transition from engineer to project team leader, suggest that inside every hierarchy, even the most authoritarian, there are entrepreneurial hostages waiting to be unleashed. But the new entrepreneurial tasks can only be accomplished after the historical structures, processes, and cultural norms are replaced by a new organisational framework that not only allows front-line managers to abandon their old implementation role, but also demands they do so.

The risk of redefining the role of operating-level managers as entrepreneurs rather than implementers is that it will fragment the company's resources and capabilities and lead to the kind of undisciplined, localised expansion that conglomerates experienced in the 1960s. To prevent this, the senior-level managers—between the front-line units and the corporate-level management typically responsible for the organisation's divisions, regions, or key functions—must redefine their role from the historic preoccupation with authority-based control to a focus on support-based management and organisation development.

Traditionally, senior managers' power came from their pivotal position in large and complex hierarchies. They played a vital intermediary role, disaggregating corporate objectives into business unit targets and aggregating business unit plans for corporate review. They were the linchpins in the resource allocation process due to corporate management's reliance on their input in capital budgeting and personnel appointment decisions. And they stood at the crossroads of internal communication, interpreting and broadcasting management's priorities, then channeling and translating front-line feedback.

These classic senior management tasks have been challenged by the creation of small independent front-line units, the radical decentralisation of assets and resources to support them, and the empowerment of the operating managers in charge. They have been further undermined by the delayering of middle levels of the organisation and the impact of new information technologies on internal communication. Left to fulfil their traditional role, senior managers find themselves increasingly frustrated by the irrelevance and powerlessness of their position. Unless there is a radical realignment of their role, this group can become the silent subverters of change whose invisible, yet persistent resistance can derail even the most carefully planned transformation programme.

Some companies have succeeded in this necessary redesign of the senior-management role to the extent that this group plays a key role in supporting the front-line units by co-ordinating their activities and coaching their operating-level entrepreneurs. Ulf Gundemark, Don Jans's boss and the head of ABB's worldwide relays business area, played a central role in managing the tension inherent in the company's ambition "to be global and local, big and small, radically decentralised with central reporting and control." Similarly, Paul Guehler, vice-president of 3M's Safety and Security Systems Division to which Andy Wong's unit belonged, challenged Wong to define the focus and priorities in his business, while simultaneously helping him build the support and obtain the resources necessary to make it succeed. And at ISS, Waldemar Schmidt, head of the European region, supported Theo Buitendijk's new business initiative despite its short-term profit impact, and led the effort to leverage the expertise his unit developed into a European business capability.

In none of these cases did these managers see their roles in the traditional terms of strategic spanbreakers, administrative controllers, and information relays. Instead of dominating their front-line managers, usurping their authority, or compromising their sense of responsibility for their operations, this new generation of senior managers added value to that activity through three core tasks:

- They became a vital source of support and guidance for the front-line entrepreneurs.
- They took primary responsibility for linking and leveraging the resources and competencies developed in the front-line units.
- They played a key role in ensuring resolution of the numerous tensions and conflicts built into the management process.

When a company decides to change its dominant management model from one driven by authority to one built on empowerment, the basic orientation of the senior manager's task is turned 180 degrees from direction and control to development and support. ABB not only reflected this change in its cultural norms; it institutionalised it in the way key senior-level jobs were structured. For example, although Ulf Gundemark was the relays business area head, he had a staff of only four to help him run the $250 million worldwide business. As a result, he routinely asked managers in operating units to take on broader responsibilities, stretching their abilities and developing their contacts and support as they did so. To develop the worldwide relays strategy, he assembled a nine-person team of managers drawn from the front lines of his operating companies; and to guide the ongoing business operations, he created a business area board that included his staff members and four key company presidents, including Don Jans. As Jans put it, "I'm a much broader manager today than I was at Westinghouse. . . . We feel we are rediscovering management."

Paul Guehler described his primary job as "to help develop the people to develop the business." He worked intensively with Wong and his team, challenging them to refine their plans, forcing them to commit them to paper, and, most important, encouraging them to communicate and defend them in multiple forums in order to build their struggling unit's thin support within 3M. And at ISS, Waldemar Schmidt had a similar philosophy about his role, stating "the most important thing I can do is to show an interest, to show that I care about them and their performance." He backed his words with actions, developing a strongly supportive relationship with his front-line managers that manifested itself in frequent telephone calls to say "Well done," or "How can I help?"

The second of the common development roles we observed was focused more at the level of organisation development, as senior-level managers took on the task of linking the knowledge and expertise developed in their front-line units and embedding them as organisational capabilities to be leveraged company-wide. Gundemark's actions in forcing his front-line relays companies to rationalise and specialise in overlapping structures and responsibilities was a first step in integrating the portfolio of independent relays operations. He then appointed key specialists in each of the companies to Functional Councils, whose primary purpose was to identify best practices and capture other benefits of co-ordination in R&D, quality, purchasing, and other functional areas. Waldemar Schmidt achieved similar cross-unit linkages through his regular meetings specifically devoted to leveraging the expertise of particular country units. When Theo Buitendijk's unit in Holland was shown to have superior performance in customer retention, for example, Schmidt gave him a day at his next European Presidents Conference to discuss his approach.

Beyond these important developmental tasks, however, those in senior management positions must still accept responsibility for the performance of the front-line units they supervise. The common bottom line contribution of the three managers we described is that they all played the pivotal role in ensuring that those reporting to them kept the strategic objectives and operating priorities in balance. In ABB this task was framed by a global matrix, which was designed to legitimise rather than minimise the tensions and paradoxes inherent in most management decisions. To manage the conflict resolution vital to the organisation's smooth operation, senior-level managers like Ulf Gundemark developed and managed a portfolio of supplemental communications channels and decision forums, such as the worldwide business board and the Functional Councils we described. These and other forums, such as the steering committees that act as local boards for each of the front-line companies, not only serve a development and integration role, but they also become the place where differences are aired and resolution obtained on the conflicting perspectives and interests created by the matrix.

In 3M, this critical balancing role is so ingrained in the culture that senior-level managers like Paul Guehler have integrated it into their ongoing management approach. For example, in what he terms his "give-and-take management style," Guehler tightened the screws on Wong's operations by requiring them to make the cuts necessary to meet their financial objectives, while behind the scenes, he was defending against attempts to close the unit down and was lining up resources and support to back their proposed development initiatives.

Senior-level managers are often the forgotten and forsaken group in the organisational transformation process. Amid rounds of delayering, destaffing, and downsizing, many corporate executives have overlooked the fact that the success of small, empowered front-line units depends on a company's ability to bring the benefits of a large company to those units. Organisations that dismantle their vertical integration mechanisms without simultaneously creating horizontal co-ordination processes quickly lose potential scale economies and, even more important, the benefits that come from leveraging each unit's assets, knowledge, and capabilities company-wide. At the same time, such intense horizontal flows can also paralyse the organisation by distracting or overburdening front-line managers. It is the middle managers who can make "inverting the pyramid" operational, not only by developing and supporting the front-line entrepreneurs, but also by absorbing most of the demands of the cross-business, cross-functional, and cross-geographic integration needs. In this way, they can prevent those at the operating level from becoming overwhelmed by the ambiguity, complexity, and potential conflicts that often accompany such horizontal networked organisations, and allow them instead to focus on their vital entrepreneurial tasks.

CHAPTER 4

The Future of Emerging Markets in the Global Economy

Ever since Oswald Spengler penned *The Decline of the West* nearly one hundred years ago, many distinguished scholars and academics have made careers for themselves as harbingers of Western civilisation's demise. Recent doomsayers cite the plundering of the earth's natural resources, the growing inequality between the wealthy and poor, the decay of moral fibre and family values—among others—as the causes of this impending meltdown. The newest focus of our supposed imminent collapse is developing countries: those rogue nations who steal our jobs with cheap labour, dump inferior goods in our markets, hollow out our industrial sectors with unfair trade practices, and subject our capital to assorted financial crises.

This is unfortunate, for the truth is that there now exists such a clear, unprecedented economic opportunity for the First World (once referred to as the "West" but which must now include such Asian powers as Japan) that to wallow in our supposedly collective woes denies the future that we have laboriously created for ourselves over the last three centuries: a truly global economy and international capital market. We all can profit from embracing the economic forces that the doomsayers reject. Rather than accept the downward spiral of Western society, we should look instead to the economies of the developing countries that are being integrated into the First World's economies, and to the redistribution of economic and political power as we enter the third millennium. Instead of lamenting our purported decline, we should prepare ourselves to take advantage of the growth in Asia, Latin America, the former Soviet Union, and Africa.

During the last thirty-odd years "Western decline" literature has proliferated not only in the United States but in most of the industrialised world. The pessimism has been economic: raging inflation in the late 1970s, factory closures and the impoverishment of farmers in the early 1980s, unemployment, growing urban poverty, and rising crime rates in the 1990s—these are but a few of the problems cited by American pessimists. In Europe, it is the overburdened welfare state, compounded by low economic growth rates, worsening unemployment, and the alleged erosion of national identities through further integration into the Common Market. In Germany, matters have been aggravated by the effects of having to absorb 17 million East Germans into the economy after unification; in England, the economic crisis was underscored by the pulverisation of the pound under the fist of a single international investor; and in France, a 14 per cent unemployment rate has led to a cultural dismay over *"l'horreur economique."* The economic pessimism is not limited to the West. Even Japan, the postwar miracle nation, its stock market at this writing trading at less than half its historic high, now suffers from a socioeconomic identity crisis as it struggles to regain its financial lustre. South Korea, too, experiencing its worst financial crisis in thirty years, laments a future amid greater competition from less-developed neighbours, such as China and Vietnam.

In recent years, scores of books have espoused economic pessimism, warning us that the era of great prosperity is over; the West is losing its competitiveness; our governments operate with intolerably high deficits; we fail to save enough; economic inequality is growing; we are losing our industries to Third World nations. This list goes on. This anxiety is understandable; there is an unsettling of the First World's economies as we leap into the next century. But these facts remain clear: inflation is historically low, our collective stock markets are strong, economic growth has been fairly consistent, living standards throughout the world are at their highest at any point in history, and more people live under economic and political freedom than ever before.

But the pessimism has also become political and social. Paul Kennedy's *Rise and Fall of the Great Powers* (1987) outlined America's grim fate in a historical context of overstretched imperialism. Others have announced the twilight of democracy, the end of affluence, and increased racial strife—all of which are rooted in the notion that we are in economic decline. Our so-called deterioration has led to the rise of nationalistic movements and pundits in America, such as Pat Buchanan, David Duke, Pierre Rinfret, and the Institute for Historical Review in California, as well as abroad: Jean-Marie Le Pen and the National Front in France, the National Front in Britain, neofascists in Italy, skinheads in Germany, Georg Haider in Austria.

The pessimism has also been cultural, with many commentators expressing dismay at the effects of advanced capitalism, what Jerry Mander describes in *The Case Against the Global Economy* (1996) as the "global homogenisation of culture, lifestyle, and levels of technological immersion, with the corresponding deterioration of local traditions and economies. Soon, every place will look and feel like every place else, with the same restaurants and hotels, the same clothes, the same malls and superstores, and the same streets crowded with cars," what author Benjamin Barber has categorized as "McWorld." Similar critics in France bemoan developments such as EuroDisney as a commercial terrorist attack on the culture of Voltaire.

In general, these sentiments seem to reflect what author and social critic Thomas Byrne Edsall has called the "Era of Bad Feelings." While the observations of social dislocation seem somewhat accurate, they are only a part of the larger picture and, therefore, fail to lead to accurate future forecasting.

But the earth rotates; as the sun sets for someone, it rises for someone else. I have seen such pessimism before. In my experience on Wall Street, it has always been darkest before dawn; that is, markets are typically poised for upturns just after they have oversold. Thus, a few simple words of investment advice to the pessimists: *cover your shorts* and *go long*.

While it is fair to say that some of the pessimists' observations are correct, taken as an aggregate, they are incomplete. Arthur Herman has written in *The Idea of Decline in Western History* (1996) that "pessimism and optimism are attitudes the scholar brings to his analysis of events, not conclusions that arise from that analysis." What is certainly true is that all of us, the pessimists as well as the apparently less prolific optimists, have been experiencing change on a scale never before experienced in a single generation. Whereas population has always grown, it has never grown at the rate witnessed in the last two generations. Whereas technological change has always worked to unemploy those in backward industries, technological changes have never taken place at the rate and on the scale we are seeing today. The Agricultural Revolution that changed the nature of land use over the span of the seventeenth and eighteenth centuries could more accurately be termed as an evolution. The Industrial Revolution's impact was more concentrated, bringing rapid urbanisation and centralised production, and eliminating many cottage industries, all in a single generation. The Information Revolution, in turn, is producing innovations that profoundly affects our lives *every year*.

Today it is no longer possible for a country to insulate itself from the rest of the world. Economic developments, technological developments, and even ideological developments—both good and bad—have a *global* impact. The technology-capital-labour dynamic that changed England—first in the form of the Agricultural Revolution—and then altered all of Europe and crossed the Atlantic to stimulate technological innovations such as Eli Whitney's cotton gin (during the Industrial Revolution) today transforms the whole world by connecting the world's computer users (the Information Revolution). Change can no longer be contained. And because the effects of events ripple across the world, to confine one's observations, as the pessimists generally do, to a single country or even a single region, let alone a single segment of a society, is to depict fragments of reality and underestimate the opportunity before us.

The pessimists' inadequate picture also leaves out the dramatic improvements to human life already achieved, not only in the industrialised countries but also in those countries thought to be backward. These improvements can be measured by increased rates of literacy, daily caloric intake, and life expectancy, and decreased rates of infant mortality, for instance. Pessimists fail to recognise that what is perceived as the decline of the industrialised world is merely the narrowing of the gap between it and the erstwhile laggards, and that further integration, not inward-looking protectionism (whether economic or cultural), is what will in fact *prevent* the decline they fear.

Most multinational corporations are already capitalising on the benefits of this economic integration. While they have always had global operations, their presence abroad has increased exponentially in recent years. Their profits from global operations are at unprecedented levels and often outstrip their profits from domestic business. Cheaper labour elsewhere has shifted production and assembly away from the multinationals' home countries, and trade arrangements and organisations such as NAFTA, GATT, and WTO have only intensified this trend. McDonald's has always had restaurants abroad, but the startling rate of its expansion (with a plan to open 1,200 to 1,500 new restaurants each year, two-thirds of which will be outside the U.S.) is mindboggling to today's cautious and critical observers. Whereas these kinds of changes have been occurring, in some form, for the last three centuries, they never happened quickly, and the depth of their impact often went unnoticed and was taken for granted. The *accelerated pace of change* is what disturbs the pessimists, because *they can see it happening*. Their fear puts blinkers on their perception of the world around them and leads them to warn us of the threats to traditional ways of life, to existing global positions of power, to cultural identities to which we have all grown accustomed. Their discomfort arises from challenges to the comfort of the familiar.

Economics is no longer, if it ever was, a zero-sum game. Although the almost unqualified economic dominance of the "West" is apparently being challenged, this does not imply the West's decline. Growth in the economies of Asia, Latin America, the Middle East, Africa, and the former Soviet Union does not signal the erosion of Western living standards because jobs are being lost to cheaper labour markets. In the late nineteenth century, 90 per cent of Americans were farmers, yet as transportation improved and trade opened up, leading to increased importation of cheaper agricultural goods, the number of farmers decreased; today only 3 per cent remain. However, at no point was there mass unemployment; rather, industrialisation was the next wave, and factories quickly absorbed a newly urbanised labour force, resulting in a huge increase in living standards. Today, we are seeing a similar phenomenon, only it is industrial jobs that are being challenged, and the industrialised countries' new comparative advantage—largely rooted in technology and capital—has to be tapped. And there is evidence that advanced capitalist countries may also have an infrastructural advantage to prosper in the rapidly changing world. Just visit Silicon Valley, the centre of global innovation and the seat of America's comparative advantage. The developing world may be prospering from high growth rates, but it is the First World that still possesses "the wealth of notions"—the true essence of innovation, capital accumulation, and economic expansion.

Evolutions and Revolutions Affecting the Global Economy

As we enter the third millennium, at a time when Westerners daily see headlines proclaiming chaos, disorder, and global turmoil, we tend to ignore the news that our species is blessed by technological miracles that alter life for the better every day. Living standards—measured not only by Net Disposable Income or Gross Domestic Product per capita, but by life expectancy, daily caloric intake, infant mortality, and literacy rates—have improved to levels unprecedented in history. The West has for centuries been the leader in these statistics, and the gap between it and most of the developing world has historically been enormous. (Needham, 1994). That is because, by and large, most of the planet has not even begun to participate in the quality modernisation that has characterised the West's history over the last three hundred years, let alone become integrated with the (Western-dominated) global economy.

Table 4.1: Changes in the World from 1950-2050

Economic Indicators	*1950*	*2000 (est.)*	*2050 (est.)*
Population of developing nations	1.2 billion	4.8 billion	9.5 billion
Per cent of total world population	55	85	90
World GDP %	5	25	50
Stock market capitalisation	less than $100 million	$2.5 trillion	$250+trillion
Per cent of global stock market capitalisation	less than 1	15	40+

Sources: Economist Intelligence Unit; World Bank; United Nations; author's estimates.

But dynamic geopolitics are redrawing the global economic map. The world our children will inherit revolves most likely but will *not* revolve around North America and its Western European counterparts, but rather around the currently developing nations of Africa, Asia, Latin America, and the former Soviet Union.

Table 4.2: Quality of Life Indicators

	Developing World 1950	*Developing World 2000 (est.)*	*Developing World 2050 (est.)*	*First World 1950*	*First World 2000 (est.)*	*First World 2050 (est.)*
Life expectancy	43	63	76	65	77	82
Daily caloric intake	1215	2000	2400	2200	2800	2900
Infant mortality (Per 1,000)	140	63	12	30	8	4
Literacy rate per cent	33	64	90	95	98	99

Sources: Economist Intelligence Unit; World Bank; United Nations; author's estimates.

And for good reason there has been a huge shift in human progress over the last fifty-odd years, and the developing world's slice of the global pie grows daily. It is these countries that now have and will maintain greater economic momentum than Organisation for Economic Cooperation and Development (OECD) nations. In fact, the World Bank notes that developing economies are growing at more than 6 per cent per annum, more than double the 2.5 per cent projected growth rate for the First World. There are many reasons for this difference in economic momentum, including long-term trends in labour and technology, demographic shifts, and political reorientations. But a simpler and more intuitive perspective is this: Third World countries with average per capita Gross Domestic Product of $1,000 to $2,000 grow at 6 per cent more easily than a $30,000 GDP country grows at 2.5 per cent because of diminishing returns in the West. Diminishing returns are the result of what Lenin called "overripe capitalism," whereby rich countries saturate their own markets and become victims of their own success. To maintain living standards, rich countries seek to exploit lower production costs outside their home borders, as well as to sell goods to underserved and undersupplied consumers in less developed nations.

Historically, one dominant global economy has been the forerunner of another. The British Empire begat America in the twentieth century, as the Dutch economy begat the British two centuries earlier, and the Spanish begat the Dutch a century before that.

We have already witnessed the modern Japanese economy spring from its relationship with America, and we are beginning to see the emergence of new powers on the horizon. Now we have the second and third generations of cross-pollination: in Asia, Japan has emerged a full-fledged economic power and is now itself a progenitor. What used to be the arithmetic addition of single economic influences has now become a multiplicative process that promises to integrate the economies of most of the planet. The exploitation of free market principles first postulated by Adam Smith, based on notions of comparative advantage as defined by David Ricardo, is fuelling tremendous global economic integration and is spawning new economies. Indeed, it is estimated that world trade will grow from $308 billion in 1950 to an estimated $4 trillion by the end of the millennium. In the last ten years, annual foreign direct investment from the First to the Third World has swelled from $11.3 billion to more than $90 billion, and aggregate annual capital flows to the developing countries now total some $350 billion, compared to less than $100 billion in 1985.

New Paradigms for the New World

When analysing the late twentieth century, we see massive change: the introduction of new technologies, the rise and decline of entire industries in the First World, major infrastructural investments in developing countries, the international relocation of certain traditional industries, and other structural shifts related to labour and lifestyle. Anyone born after 1900 in the West has become accustomed to these changes, though for mankind, this scope and rate of change is a novelty. Until only some three hundred years ago, few great changes occurred in the material lives of men and women.

Keynes noted in his essay "Economic Possibilities for Our Grandchildren":

> The absence of important technical inventions between the prehistoric age and comparatively modern times is truly remarkable. Almost everything which really matters and which the world possessed at the commencement of the modern age was already known to man at the dawn of history. Language, fire, the same domestic animals which we have today, wheat, barley, the vine and the olive, the plough, the wheel, the oar, the sail, leather, linen and cloth, bricks and pots, gold and silver, copper, tin and lead—and iron was added to the list before 1000 BC—banking, statecraft, mathematics, astronomy, and religion. There is no record when we first possessed these things.

This lack of change, as Keynes observed in this chapter's opening epigraph, was due to the absence of technology and the failure to accumulate capital. Most reindustrialised societies were economically rigid, if not zero-sum games. According to most historical records, there was little economic growth anywhere on earth until the late Middle Ages. Subsistence agrarian life allowed few to accumulate wealth and prosper. In fact, crude estimates by *The Economist* suggest that for thirteen hundred years, until 1800, Western European GDP rose by only 0.1 per cent to 0.2 per cent per year. At that pace, living standards barely changed in one's lifetime, with real incomes taking some five hundred years to double.

As a result, in most of the reindustrialised civilisations sparse economic growth limited social mobility, because someone's increased wealth was generally achieved at someone else's expense. This may have been the source of the frequent wars and battles for much of recorded history; without industrialisation and the subsequent advent of a competitive, mercantilist society, theft, conquest, and inheritance were virtually the only ways to become richer. In reindustrialised societies, the notion of wealth was that it *existed*. Our more experienced view is that wealth is *created*. This notion has had a profound sociocultural impact on life.

Most reindustrialised civilisations (circa 1700 and earlier) reflected the former perspective, and it may be that many economic and social strata developed along these lines. Until approximately three hundred and fifty years ago in the West (and for billions of people still today), virtually everyone lived for per diem subsistence—working daily for food, clothes and shelter. Flatly stated, in the last 2/100ths of 1 per cent of mankind's existence, a small percentage of our species has been able to contemplate and achieve a better, longer existence within their lifetime. Undeniably, it has been the marriage of technology and capital that has led to the increase in standards of human living to their highest levels ever. In this respect, the West has been first blessed. As we stand on the cusp of the twenty-first century, it is the potent combination of technological and financial power that has accelerated our ability to enhance life faster and for more people than at any other time in history.

How All Roads Led to the Global Economy

The sudden expansion of the developing world over the last decade is staggering: Britain, for example, took some sixty years to double its output from the dawn of the Industrial Revolution in the late eighteenth century. The United States took fifty years to double its output in the mid-nineteenth century. However, at a compounded rate of 6 per cent, the developing world is doubling output every twelve years, with some regions like East Asia having doubled in ten years. China, the world's most populous country, has actually been doubling GDP in a remarkable seven years. These rates are unprecedented and are dramatically altering the distribution of power in the global economy. Many of those we consider Third World countries today will most likely attain "First World" economic status within two or three generations. This chapter answers the question, why now? In order to intelligently understand the changes and opportunities in the world today, we need to explore the evolution of the global economy from one dominated by zero-sum mercantilism into one governed by positive-sum capitalism built on the reciprocal relationships between science, technology, and the marketplace. I will touch on several reasons why the West came to dominate the world over the last few hundred years, examine the causes of the Third World's economic failures during the twentieth century, and finally identify the factors that have precipitated the developing countries) movement toward the world's economic centre stage.

How the First World Became First

The question of how and why the West took the technological and economic lead some three hundred years ago has yet to be completely answered by anyone. However, many have provided insights into what propels a global economy, how countries have historically expanded their economies, and how they can continue to increase living standards—all of which are valuable in understanding how the First World became first.

Looking at the world as it was before 1500 C.E., one would see no sign that any one civilisation would rise above the others. Many of the great scientific and practical discoveries that have allowed humanity to advance can be traced to China and the Arab world, and several indigenous groups in the Americas and Africa lived in societies as advanced as their European contemporaries.

If any civilisation looked like it would advance first technologically, China was probably the surest bet prior to the Renaissance. Chinese innovations were far ahead of Western Europe's after the fall of Rome in 476 C.E. By the first and second centuries C.E., China had already made great advances in physics, mathematics, medicine, and engineering—hundreds of years prior to the West.

By the fifteenth century, China was densely populated, with approximately 120 million people (compared to 55 million in Europe) spread over an area the size of Europe. But despite relatively advanced transportation systems making it possible to gather, harness, and apply scientific and technological advancements in a systematic way across the land, China shunned progress. In response to frontier pressures, the Ming dynasty in the mid-fifteenth century focused on recapturing the country's glorious past, looking inward and backward, discouraging trade and entrepreneurialism, discontinuing the use of paper currency, restricting printing, and neglecting municipal drainage systems and astronomical clocks. A cultural disdain for commerce and private capital, rooted in Confucian conservatism, resulted in the absence of the competitive, mercantilist spirit that was present in Europe at the time. China, enormous and steeped in a rich tradition of science, chose to bask in past glories and had little incentive to innovate.

There is ample evidence of a rich tradition of art, science, and technology in the Islamic world in medieval North Africa and the Middle East. A tolerant Islamic society left the Byzantine Empire stable and manageable until Constantinople fell to the Ottomans in 1453. Military might, particularly naval, made the Ottomans formidable adversaries in Persia, North Africa, and even southern Spain. But soon, stretched thin by imperialism and fractured by religious divisions exacerbated by a centralised despotism, the Ottomans discouraged change, fearing loss of control over the empire. Cultural and technological conservatism took hold, censoring new ideas, discouraging trade, and initiating a decline that would reach its nadir in the twentieth century.

Meso-american civilisations, such as the Aztecs and the Mayas in Mexico, and the Andean Inca civilisation similarly flourished. But while ancient Mexico had active trading relationships, commerce was carried out by barter, since neither the Aztecs nor the Mayas had invented money. Although the Incas had a vast road system that was bigger than the Roman Empire, the absence of the wheel precluded effective transport. Unfortunately, pre-Columbian civilisations were no match for the Spanish conquistadores' common diseases, such as chickenpox and tuberculosis, or for European technology, including guns and horses.

Although each of these cultures had a developed sociopolitical infrastructure and some had relatively sophisticated traditions of science and technology, it would be Western Europe, blessed with certain advantages that fostered a trajectory of uninterrupted and unencumbered growth, that would become the pacesetter of the world and ultimately dominate the global economy. As historian Paul Kennedy explains,

> however imposing and organised some of those, empires appeared by comparison with Europe, they all suffered from the consequences of having a centralised authority which insisted upon a uniformity of belief and practice, not only in official state religion but also in such areas as commercial activities and weapons development. The lack of any such supreme authority in Europe and the warlike rivalries among its various kingdoms and city-states stimulated a constant search for military improvements, which interacted fruitfully with the newer technological and commercial advances that were also being thrown up in this competitive, entrepreneurial environment. Possessing fewer obstacles to change, European societies entered into a constantly upward spiral of economic growth and enhanced military effectiveness which, over time, was to carry them ahead of all other regions of the globe

Now, at the beginning of the new millennium, after centuries of lagging behind the European innovators, much of the Third World is positioned for unprecedented growth. Technologically deprived for so long, many of these countries still live in preindustrial conditions and mass poverty, but progress is now within reach. The recent history of global economic development shows that the Western-dominated world of the last few hundred years is being dramatically transformed into a world populated by several competing economic powers.

For most of the twentieth century, the developing world could not attract hard currency; without hard currency, it could not invest in technology to expand its economies and accumulate more capital; the result was economic stagnation and contraction. Following World War II, most of the developing world locked themselves behind the doors of inward-looking economic policies. For some countries, a postcolonial sense of independence led to nationalistic economic policies and protectionist legislation. For others, the second half of the twentieth century began under the reign of authoritarian, largely military, regimes, whose economic policies included a government commitment to spending on large-scale, capital-intensive enterprises. And, many others became the pawns of the Soviet machine and were ruled by the philosophy of central planning.

The end of the twentieth century has seen a wave of change. Dictatorships have become unfashionable and are now the anomaly, as democracy—in one form or another—has become the norm and the basis for capital advancement and economic success. The Soviet experiment with communism is over, releasing a number of eager economies into the world market. Countries whose colonial heritage lasted until the middle of this century have passed beyond their neocolonial rebellion period and are now among the leaders of the emerging markets. These countries are catching up on the lead historically won by the West, following an accelerated version of essentially the West's development path, one characterised by the critical interplay of technology and capital accumulation.

Why has this happened now? One answer can be found in statistic and collectivist economic models' failure to produce the bountiful harvests, powerful arsenals, and social justice they promised, while neoliberal economies showed their ability to generate wealth and power. To best understand this ideological victory in the war of words and images, we will first look at the way in which wartime propaganda contributed to the demise of a system—how statism in the East was undermined from the outside. We will then look at the system's inherent unsustainability—how statism, in the East and elsewhere, sowed the seeds of its own destruction.

Table 4.3: Democratisation in the Modern World

Year	*Democratic States*	*Non-Democratic States*	*Total*	*Per cent of Total*
1922	29	35	64	45.3
1942	12	49	61	19.7
1962	36	75	111	32.4
1973	30	92	122	24.6
1990	59	71	130	45.4

Source: Samuel Huntington, The Third Wave (Norman, OK: University of Oklahoma Press, 1991), p. 26.

Many who analysed the fall of communism in the former Soviet Union as it was happening believed it was chiefly caused by political and human rights issues. People wanted certain social freedoms, and the government's statist economic policies could not achieve living standards anywhere close to those enjoyed in the First World. Technologies such as radio and television made the citizens under Soviet rule painfully aware of what they had been missing, and eventually they rejected the oppressive communist system, which led to a breakdown of the Soviet state.

Soviet economic ideology was further undermined when images of the success stories of East Asia, and especially postwar Japan, flooded in. Fifty years ago, Japan, Hong Kong, Taiwan, and Singapore were considered some of the poorest places on earth. Today, those countries combined hold approximately $450 billion in hard currency reserves, more than all of continental Europe. Their advances are examples for the rest of the developing world; they have found the formula to end the vicious cycle of poverty and begin the "virtuous circle" of economic success: attract capital, apply technology, grow the economy, accumulate more capital, and so on. These were not the rich, imperialist First World getting fatter by exploiting the developing world, but rather previously impoverished Asian economies that were suddenly growing by leaps and bounds. Reports rolled in, via television, radio, and underground newspapers, on the astounding growth of these nations, inspiring other developing countries whose protectionist, statist, centralised policies had been failing them. The possibility of growth, if one jettisoned compromising political agendas and followed the Asian example, was very real.

The cumulative effect of the proliferation of Genius Technologies and the abandonment of economically insular policies by the Third World is a more integrated, sophisticated, and differentiated global marketplace than ever before. Never in history have so many people on earth been bound together by capitalism, and the opportunities to produce and sell in the developing world, as well as to financially invest there, are unprecedented. In this chapter, we will analyse how strategic operators from the First World (as well as some Third Worlders) are profiting from these new economic opportunities in a mutually reinforcing manner.

MNCs: The Vanguard of Borderless Capitalism

In the last three decades, the possibility of producing and selling abroad has given rise to the multinational corporation (MNC). To understand the global impact of the MNC, First Worlders need only examine the origins of the products that fill their shopping carts: fruits grown in Chile, jeans made in Sri Lanka, and computers assembled in Taiwan—materialisations of the ideas of Smith and Ricardo. Through MNCs everyone's life is commercially touched by the developing world, and the trend should only accelerate. Meanwhile, if we look at what lines the shelves of Third World stores, we see cans of Coca Cola, bottles of Bayer aspirin, and packages of Nabisco cookies—all made by First World MNCs that are tapping into the increasing purchasing power of a growing number of emerging market consumers.

The rise of the MNC represents the same capitalist stroke of genius that Henry Ford pioneered decades ago in the United States when he decided to pay his workers a relatively high $5 per day: the creation of new and global Third World "labourer-consumers" who earn enough eventually to buy the goods they currently produce for export. MNC production-for-export ventures abroad today are ensuring future sales abroad tomorrow.

The root of First World MNCs' aggressive expansion into developing countries is cold, hard economic necessity: they are driven by profit and nothing else. MNCs look to the Third World to lower input costs, to maintain or increase margins on existing business, and to expand sales into untapped consumer markets. In theory, rich countries always become victims of their own success, as the rewards of prosperous, productive societies are high living standards and wages that drive up input costs. The wealthy economies of today's First World are populated by a growing number of older people and a shrinking number of youths. This age distribution affects spending patterns, particularly by reducing domestic demand for consumer goods. When this happens, MNCs are forced to look abroad to find new markets for sales growth. While baby boomers in the United States and Germany move toward social security, half of the population in many emerging markets is under thirty. As these young nations become more industrialised, their disposable income—and thus their consumption—increases. MNCs know this. In fact, they often work to create demand in markets that have little current purchasing power but great purchasing potential. Tea drinkers in India may not know yet that they are part of the Pepsi Generation, but they soon will. For MNCs, the developing world is the global oyster waiting to be opened.

That the MNCs of wealthy countries will inevitably expand into the developing world for profit opportunities is not a new idea. Adam Smith in 1776, Ricardo in 1817, and Malthus in 1820 emphasised capital export as necessary for the survival of capitalism. They foresaw that the costs of production would outstrip the rate of consumption and profits would decline and, even two hundred years ago, that an MNC today would have to move beyond First World borders to find ways to overcome diminishing returns in their own markets.

All of these thinkers understood diminishing returns on capital. But it was perhaps the Marxists who articulated the theory best. While Marx himself in 1894 commented on how capital needed to move around the world, it was Lenin who, in 1917, wrote about the profit motivations behind export capital in his seminal *Imperialism: The Highest Stage of Capitalism:*

> An enormous superabundance of capital has accumulated in the advanced countries. . . . As long as capitalism remains what it is, surplus capital will never be utilised for the purpose of raising the standard of living of the masses in a given country, for this would mean a decline in profits for the capitalists; it will be used for the export of capital abroad to the backward countries. In these backward countries profits are usually high, for capital is scarce, the price of land is relatively low, wages are low, raw materials are cheap. . . . The necessity for exporting capital arises from the fact that in a few countries capitalism has become "overripe" and . . . capital cannot find "profitable" investment.

In short, it is the limits of capitalism in one society that allow capitalism to be limitless around the world. Ricardo put it more kindly: "It is quite important to the happiness of mankind, that our enjoyments should be increased by the better distribution of labour, by each country producing those commodities for which by its situation, its climate, and its other natural or artificial advantages, it is adapted, and by their exchanging them for the commodities of other countries, as that they should be augmented by a rise in the rate of profits." 'Ultimately' he argued, 'consumption through comparative advantage could be increased through trade with other countries by driving costs down, allowing consumers to spend a larger portion of their income on other goods.'

First World countries find themselves exporting those things in which they have a comparative advantage and importing those in which they do not. Because of huge increases in living standards and wages, OECD countries no longer have a relative advantage in manufacturing and other labour-intensive industries. They have, however, developed comparative advantage in the high-technology and service sectors, both of which have been optimised by the applications of several Genius Technologies. At the same time, emerging market nations—now freeing themselves from market-distorting policies like Import Substitution Industrialisation—have discovered their own comparative advantages, making them viable manufacturing bases for MNCs. This allows emerging markets to generate and attract capital, and reinvest it back into their own economies. The process, in turn, builds a new class of workers who earn disposable income that can be spent on newly available consumer products, or saved and rechanneled into burgeoning emerging market economies.

The advent of new Genius Technologies at this point in history, which has propelled many First World service and high-technology sectors, has left economic voids now being filled opportunistically by the Third World's increasing capacity to manufacture and apply older technologies in the production of things such as cars and refrigerators. This process began in recent decades and has created monumental shifts in the organisation of global production of goods and services. Some developing countries, such as the Asian Tigers, are moving into their third and fourth decades of fast-paced economic growth and capital accumulation. Some, like Hong Kong and Singapore, have jumped into the First World echelon of GDP per capita. They, too, have begun to experience the limits of success, finding themselves no longer able to competitively produce low-wage manufactured goods, such as textiles—as they once did. Now these countries are moving toward more capital-intensive production—like automobiles and computer components—while moving certain manufacturing components to their less developed neighbours.

One of the first modern economists to see this "food chain" trend was Kaname Akamatsu, a scholar who studied Japan's development between the two world wars and in the postwar period. Akamatsu suggested that developing economies begin by producing simple products that are labour-intensive, and then move on to producing more sophisticated products that require more capital and more technology. This process, when graphed, resembles a "wild geese flying pattern" the name Akamatsu gave to the trend:

> The wild geese flying pattern . . . includes three subpatterns. The first basic pattern is the **sequence of import-domestic production** export. The second pattern is the **sequence from consumer goods to capital goods** and **from crude and simple articles to complex and refined articles**. The third pattern is **the alignment from advanced nations to backward nations** according to their stage of growth.

Akamatsu's theory neatly ties together three concepts: how technology is proliferated, how advanced countries continue to innovate and forge ahead, and how "backward" countries move forward along the food chain.

During the postwar period certain East Asian countries provided a good example of Akamatsu's Flying Geese pattern, first shifting exports from primary goods (raw materials) to light manufactured products (such as textiles) and then to more complex goods (electronics). According to the World Bank, the more advanced countries made way for these East Asian gains by giving up market share—the United States in virtually all manufactured products and Japan and the newly industrialised economies in lower-end manufactures.

For example, South Korea is a country in which three decades of rapid GDP expansion (averaging a remarkable 10 per cent per annum from 1962 to 1992) and accumulation of capital, in conjunction with the dramatic liberalisation of its economic policy, led to skyrocketing wage hikes. The previously low wage rates had made South Korea attractive for labour-intensive goods like sneakers and gloves. Although productivity had increased, wages had been kept low through government intervention. However, reforms in 1987 allowed real wages to reflect real productivity in a huge single leap. Since 1988 wages have increased four-fold, and certain goods from South Korea have risen in price and left the country uncompetitive in low-skill, labour-intensive production. Purchasers are now looking to other markets—like China, Vietnam, and Laos—for those goods. As a result, South Korea faces the painful challenge of shifting its production to those more capital intensive domains in which the labour advantage is not so critical, something Americans and Europeans have been dealing with for nearly two decades.

The Importance of Trade

Capitalism and globalism are natural partners because capitalism flourishes in a tariff-free, differentiated world economy. Capitalism thrives on production and consumption differences between countries. The more pronounced the differences, the greater the impetus to globalise. In their search to reduce costs and increase profits, MNCs have harnessed new technologies that have allowed trade to increase dramatically since World War II and to evolve in new ways. Much of global trade now lies in *intermediate* goods—things manufactured for use in producing other goods—often between different arms of a single MNC in order to save money and increase profits.

The modern trade in intermediate goods is made possible by the ability of producers, in Paul Krugman's words, to "slice up the value chain, breaking a production process into many geographically separate steps." Information technology facilitates instant information transfer around the globe. Innovations in transportation also make this process possible. The development of the long-distance jet airliner in 1958 and the wide-bodied jet in 1967 made air freight practical and changed the face of trade. In 1993, 29 per cent of U.S. exports departed and 21 per cent of U.S. imports arrived by air. As Krugman and Cooper remind us, many items such as cut flowers and fresh fruit are now tradable despite great distances: "Air freight also permits the international organisation of production slicing, and combines it with just-in-time [manufacturing]. Goods can leave Singapore today and arrive anywhere in the United States tomorrow." This process, according to Krugman, has led to the emergence of "supertraders" such as the Asian Tigers, and to the rise in large exports of manufactured goods from low-wage emerging economies. The net result is truly globalised manufacturing that can take advantage of the most productive mix of inputs and labour. Indeed, the automobile you drive probably is made of parts manufactured in ten different countries and partially assembled in three, all of which reduces production costs and, ultimately, lowers the purchase price you pay.

Differentiation of the world economy and the slicing up of production both stimulate and are stimulated by international trade. It is a mutually reinforcing process whereby countries can have access to cheaper goods than they are capable of producing domestically and are, thus, able to consume more. Although promoted by technology, growth in free trade has also been encouraged by mechanisms such as GATT and NAFTA, not to mention regional trade organisations.

Table 4.4: Understanding Production

Type	*Definition*	*Examples*	*Represents highest percentage of GDP for:*
Raw materials	Goods that are not processed or manufactured	Oil, rubber, minerals	Africa, Central Asia, Middle East, and several Latin American countries
Intermediate goods	Goods that are manufactured for use in production of another product	Car parts, semiconductors for computers	Parts of Asia and former Soviet Union countries
Final goods	A product that is sold to its final user	Automobiles, computers, T-shirts, electrical appliances	First World countries, parts of Asia, Central and Eastern European countries

Ninety per cent of tariffs on industrial products imported in 1947 by the industrialised nations are now gone. These reductions in trade barriers have played a crucial role in facilitating increased trade, particularly in the area of intermediate goods. The developing countries themselves have, in many cases, unilaterally reduced tariffs and created tariff-free zones in order to promote the production of intermediate goods within their borders. The MNCs have been presented with new opportunities for cutting costs and increasing profits in the First World; it enables MNCs to thrive amid increased global competition.

The wage differentials are significant between advanced and less developed countries. As of 1997, Germany boasts the highest labour costs, at more than $30 an hour, substantially higher than America or Japan, at $16 and $19 an hour respectively. By contrast, hourly labour costs are only $5.60 in South Korea, $2.40 in Mexico, and less than $1 in Indonesia. Some countries in the Western Hemisphere, like Haiti, offer labour for as low as 68 cents an hour. Based on aggregate lifetime expenses associated with employing an industrialised worker (wages, health and retirement benefits, and work environment costs), one European bank estimates that an MNC could effectively employ hundreds of Russian workers for every Japanese employee.

However, it is important to remember that low wages reflect lower productivity by individual workers. From this perspective, pay per unit produced is less divergent among countries than nominal wage scales. For instance, one U.S. worker may receive $16 per hour to sew blue jeans. In that hour he may produce eight pairs of jeans. A worker in a developing economy may receive $2 per hour and produce only one pair of jeans. In both cases the worker is paid $2 per unit produced. So labour costs per unit of output in developing countries are closer to U.S. levels than they appear. The trick for MNCs is to find the optimal mix: a worker who is paid $4 an hour who can produce three pairs of jeans—at a cost of $1.33 per unit. The overall labour/productivity mix of several OECD and emerging market nations for fabricated metal production is compared in Table 4.3.

As the table shows, low-cost labour helps in places like China and Indonesia, but note that poor productivity makes labour in the Philippines no bargain—the U.S. and Switzerland are, net, more competitive in this sector. In general, however, it becomes clear that low-skill work like metal fabrication needs to go to the developing world because of its huge comparative advantage in cost of labour. Other variables will also come into play: quality of goods produced, transportation, and storage costs—factors that may make one country more or less competitive in one kind of production versus another.

Table 4.5: Comparative Productivity, 1995 Fabricated Metal Production

Country	*Hourly Wages for Manufacturing Work (in $)*	*Hourly Labour Productivity (in $)*	*Productivity per $ of Labour*
1	2	3	4
China	0.11	0.56	5.09
Indonesia	0.25	1.08	4.32
Hungary	1.89	5.64	3.55
Mexico	2.48	8.39	3.38
Malaysia	1.55	4.06	2.62
1	2	3	4
Taiwan	4.86	12.63	2.60
Czech Republic	1.59	3.88	2.44
Chile	1.98	4.03	2.04
Japan	19.32	37.58	1.95
Switzerland	23.05	41.64	1.81
United States	16.82	28.14	1.67
South Korea	5.66	8.31	1.47
Philippines	0.79	1.15	1.46
South Africa	5.77	8.29	1.44
Germany	23.53	33.39	1.42

Source: *World Competitiveness Report 1995* (Geneva: International Institute of Management Development, 1995), p. 617.

It is important to remember that wages tend to rise over time in line with productivity increases and currency appreciation when labour markets become tight. One study of four Asian countries (South Korea, Thailand, Malaysia, and the Philippines) examined factory wages and productivity and found that 1990 factory wages and other compensation in these labour costs were 71 per cent of U.S. levels in South Korea, 86 per cent in Thailand, and actually above U.S. levels in Malaysia and the Philippines. Interestingly enough, back in 1970, unit labour costs in these four countries were less than half U.S. levels. In the intervening 20 years, a combination of currency appreciation and increases in real wages fostered by productivity gains closed the gap. The future for labour looks increasingly bright in developing economies. According to World Bank projections, the global workforce is expected to grow by approximately 600 million between now and 2010, but only 6 million of this workforce will come from high income OECD countries. While Asia will remain a key area, the Middle East and Africa are rapidly emerging as significant global labour markets. Asia is expected to contribute less than half of the growth over the next fifteen years. Sub-Saharan Africa, on the other hand, which represents less than 10 per cent of today's labour force, will account for almost 30 per cent of the growth. And though the Middle East and North Africa account for less than 4 per cent of the workforce today, these regions are expected to contribute more than 10 per cent of the growth over the next fifteen years.

Wages are only one component of total labour costs. Labour costs in the First World also include medical and dental coverage, various insurance policies (life, disability, etc.), retirement and pension schemes, and occupational safety requirements for workers. MNCs can reduce these expenses by moving production to the developing world.

The net effects of integrating the developing world seem to be beneficial for all participants. Government policies in countries that embrace global trends by aggressively engaging the international marketplace have enabled a doubling of the world's workforce over the past thirty years and a doubling of the productivity of the average worker. In an effort to stimulate economic and labour growth, as well as to attract technology and capital to accelerate modernisation, many emerging market governments are luring overseas investors with direct incentives. Tax savings are common bait: free-trade zones, tax-free holidays, attractive treatments for joint ventures, and lenient rules for the repatriation of dividends. But often governments offer other enticements, including reduced red tape regarding energy use, environmental regulations, and other potential costs to the MNC.

China has been among the most aggressive developing countries in luring foreign direct investment, as well as the most successful: in 1996 it attracted more than $40 billion in FDI, or approximately one half the world's total. A key incentive has been the establishment of twelve Special Economic Zones (SEZs), largely in the east, which have offered investors unique packages of tax breaks, including reduced land fees, reduced import and export duties, and priority treatment in obtaining basic infrastructure services. Government incentives designed to increase automobile production in China, coupled with the prospect of 1.2 billion new customers, have brought Ford and Daimler into the country. Cheap leases have also been used to attract financial firms to both Shenzen's Futian district and Pudong in Shanghai in hopes of attracting investors. A potential investor involved in China's fledgling high-tech and export-oriented industries could expect even more incentives. Going forward, it is expected that the government will use similar incentives to lure investment in China's less developed interior provinces.

Other Asian countries have followed suit. India has six specified free-trade zones (FTZs) and export-processing zones (EPZs), offering tax exemptions and other subsidies that have attracted Unilever, among others. The Indian government has targeted the garment industry for export growth and is attracting small-scale joint ventures by exempting them from selected parts of the labour legislation originally designed to prevent the exploitation of textile workers. EPZs and FTZs now can be found throughout the Asian islands, including the Philippines, Malaysia, and Indonesia.

While latecomers to the capitalist game, many Central European and former Soviet nations are quick learners. In the Czech Republic, the commercial code guarantees identical treatment for foreign and domestic investors. Companies are allowed to enter joint ventures in nearly all sectors of industry or to establish wholly foreign-owned enterprises. They have also established five free-trade zones offering a VAT tax exemption on intermediate goods. Neighbouring Poland has offered ten-year corporate tax relief and a further 50 per cent reduction in tax for the following ten years. The Polish government also offers relief on customs duties for imported plant and equipment in certain economic development zones. In Russia, Boris Yeltsin waived the oil-export tax for three years and eased the country's 23 per cent excise tax for most foreign investors.

Around the world we find more of the same. In Africa, Nigeria offers investment tax relief for a company that has incurred an expenditure on electricity, water, tarred road, or telephone for the purpose of trade when the company is located at least 20 km away.

How First World and Third World Investors are Profiting in Emerging Markets

We have seen how the developing countries are profiting from First World capital flows. However, the question remains how are investors reaping rewards from emerging markets? And, what are the risks? First, remember that a failure to accumulate capital is the chief reason developing countries have lagged economically. At this writing, the First World's financial markets are estimated at approximately $17 trillion in equity and $25 trillion in debt, versus the Third World's $2 trillion in equity and $1.5 trillion in debt. To continue the virtuous circle of reform and stoke historic growth, the Third World must rely on capital flows from industrialised countries.

The haves are now investing in the have-nots, and investors expect a higher compensation for shifting their money to developing countries, whether in debt or equity form.

Is this higher-risk premium justified? As a trader, I would hedge by answering, it depends. Often the underlying commercial risks in emerging markets are comparable to or better than those in the First World; economies are growing fast and that creates cash for dividends and debt payments. However, the political risks—reforms that may stall, new elections that might beget wayward policies, coups or civil wars that may erupt—always seem to weigh on investors' minds, and I believe this is why developing countries are forced to pay a premium for First World capital. It is this fundamental tension between great premium opportunities versus the possibility of political instability that creates both high returns and inefficiencies for skilled investors in the emerging markets. Such situations, theoretically, do not exist in First World markets because political risks—risks of nationalisation, expropriation, currency inconvertibility, civil war, radical changes in property laws—are deemed to be virtually nonexistent.

In addition to higher returns, First Worlders can achieve greater diversification from developing countries, which lowers overall portfolio risk. Furthermore, sophisticated players also have frequently chances to extract interesting returns from inefficient markets, though efficiency develops organically over time as markets grow larger with greater capitalisation. Often one hears of "arbitrage," "market neutral," or "relative value" trades that seep out from the developing world's embryonic financial markets. While none are truly risk free, many Third World investment situations do *overcompensate* investors for the market risk; these are windows of opportunity that would never remain open in the First World for more than a few moments.

For investors prepared to assume and analyse the risks inherent in the developing world, some of which are large and legitimate, others merely perceived and relatively small, enormous possibilities await, ranging from long-shot opportunities rarely seen in the OECD to low-risk arbitrage situations, and including everything in between.

The Greatest Risk?

Do emerging financial markets resemble those in the First World? Like developing economics themselves, emerging markets lie in the chrysalis between a caterpillar and a butterfly, a unique transitional period. Financial textbooks describing developed markets assert that all assets have intrinsic value and will differ only randomly.

Liquidity and Price Formation

Studying emerging market price formation means analysing the supply and demand mechanism in developing countries. If it is liquidity we're after, let's think of it in plumbing terms. For example, if a bathtub's drain is plugged, a running faucet will raise the water level. Conversely, if the faucet is closed but the drain open, the water level will fall. If the faucet is running and the drain is open, the level will depend on how fast water is flowing in and out. However, what if the bathtub itself could actually stretch and contract in size? In that case, understanding water levels becomes a bit more complicated. One needs to monitor water coming in, water going out, and the changing size of the bathtub. This is analogous to the cyclical financial patterns that are fairly common in the developing world. Price (water level) is dependent on cash inflows (water from the faucet) or outflows (water down the drain), while keeping track of the amount of stocks and bonds outstanding (the size of the bathtub). All mature markets are subject to similar patterns, but emerging market liquidity cycles tend to be more frequent and rapid. Therefore, while the fundamental analysis of politics and economics is important in developing countries, to be successful at emerging market investing one should ultimately analyse such phenomena keeping in mind:

Existing Ownership

Who currently owns stocks or bonds? What percentage is held by locals and by foreigners? What are the holders' motivations for buying and selling? Are they going to be adding or decreasing exposure in the future? Is the local savings rate increasing or decreasing? All these factors will affect liquidity.

Self-generated Inflows

What new money is coming into the market? Perhaps trade surpluses, monetary adjustments, or lower bank reserve or stock margin requirements will add liquidity to a marketplace that, ultimately, will help boost share prices.

Foreign Financial Flows

Are there changes in local laws making it more favourable for foreigners to invest? How is the economic health of the First World? Where are First World interest rates? How high are its own stock markets? All of these factors can influence whether a local market will gain or lose foreign money, ultimately affecting price.

New Issuance of Stocks or Bonds

Are companies issuing or buying back stocks and bonds? Remember, the size of the bathtub also determines price.

The bathtub theory of liquidity applies to both debt and equity. While fundamental factors affect price, always keep in mind who is buying what assets and why. Not all debt and equity markets behave the same way. In fact, the only common factor among emerging financial markets is their differences, differences that arise from the distinct histories of each country and region. As we shall see, there are two main categories of financial investing—debt and equity. Within those, however, there are very distinct categories with different risk or reward profiles. The savvy investor pinpoints those differences, assuming only the risks deemed worthwhile relative to an expected return. Let's examine those differences.

The Debt Markets: Hard Currency Versus Local Currency Obligations

Given the size and history of developing countries' indebtedness and foreign borrowings, any discussion of emerging markets should begin with debt opportunities. Note that not all debt is created equal; there are instruments denominated in local currency and others denominated in *hard currency* (largely U.S. dollars but may include some half dozen other First World currencies such as Japanese yen or German deutschemarks), with different considerations for both issuers and investors. For example, let's say Mexico is ready to borrow $100 million for one year. The country can borrow either in U.S. dollars from the market at 10 per cent per annum, or in pesos from the market at 20 per cent. At first blush, the answer seems simple: borrow in dollars, it's cheaper. But there are many things to consider. First, one should ask why interest rates are higher in Mexico. The simple answer is that inflation is higher in Mexico (approximately 10 per cent more), and the **theory of Interest Rate Parity** dictates that the Mexican peso most likely should decline against the dollar over the year at the inflation differential, in this case, 10 per cent. Theoretically, therefore, the borrowing costs for Mexico should be the same. However, this is not the whole story.

Mexico's ability to repay pesos is completely in its own hands; it has the sovereign ability to increase taxes (the primary source of government revenue) and to print pesos. Now, whether those pesos are worth anything is another matter. But repayment physically can be made by virtue of Mexico's sovereignty. However, when Mexico borrows in U.S. dollars, the only way it can meet its dollar obligations is to generate hard currency from either exports or new foreign investment (from both MNCs and financial investors) it cannot guarantee; it is completely *market-oriented*. If Mexico is having a tough time attracting FDI and exporting, and has few overseas investors interested in its financial markets, the country may not be able to generate hard currency and repay dollar-denominated debt. Therefore, investors who buy Mexican dollar-denominated bonds are assessing risk differently than Mexican peso bond investors. They are focusing not on whether they will be repaid, but rather on what the foreign exchange rate will be in one year and whether Mexico will allow free conversion from pesos to hard currency. This underscores the primary differences in risk between hard currency and local currency sovereign debt.

As the macroeconomic risks in developing countries have stabilised, the markets for both hard currency and local debt have mushroomed dramatically since the mid-1980s, a reflection of greater marketisation in the Third World.

Tradable Loans

The stock of troubled private commercial loans fuelled the rebirth of the sovereign debt markets in the late 1980s. At one point more than 90 per cent of the tradable emerging debt universe was composed of such hard-currency (largely U.S. dollar-denominated) tradable loans; today they total no more than 15 per cent. While some $300 billion has been converted to Brady Bonds, there still remain some non-performing loans from places such as Cuba and Sudan trading at steep discounts with some prospect or expectation of a Brady deal. There are loans that have been classically restructured and trade for their high yields to maturity. These loans are held for capital appreciation, and are often surrogate equity investments because they offer better liquidity than the local stock markets (if one even exists). For example, Moroccan government loans can trade in lots of $5 to $10 million, while one would be hard pressed to find a market for $2 million of a Moroccan equity locally in the Casablanca stock market.

The loan market is largely institutional investor territory dominated by banks and insurance companies, with retail investors effectively shut out. As a result, until the Brady game was played, this sector was plagued by fluctuations of liquidity, with prices being determined by who was buying and selling, much like a commodity market. Rumours on country buybacks or large international banks selling contributed to fluctuating prices. As mentioned earlier, banks often sold because of accounting problems or a realisation that they should not have extended such loans in the first place.

Interestingly, some loans trade more like equities. For example, Russian external credit—nearly $25 billion of old Soviet debt assumed by Russia in 1991—have rollercoasted in price for years. While in default in the early 1990s, these loans were priced with accrued interest at less than twenty cents on the dollar. Bids nearly doubled when Russia began restructuring talks in 1993-94, only to slide as U.S. interest rates rose, the Mexican peso plunged, and talks stalled in late 1994.

By early 1995 prices regained steam and continued up as President Boris Yeltsin was reelected in mid-1996. Over the next fifteen months, Russian debt doubled again on hopes of a finalised restructuring and the country's announced sovereign BB credit rating. However, the October 1997 Asian crisis signalled the party's end. As metal and energy prices collapsed with contracting Asian economies, Russia began bleeding in 1998. Poor tax collection created huge fiscal and monetary holes that not even a $22 billion IMF aid package could plug in July 1998. By mid-August 1998, Russia defaulted on nearly $30 billion of local treasury bills which tanked external debt prices to default levels not seen since the early 1990s. The market for new bank loans to developing countries was essentially dead for most of the 1980s and early 1990s.

Brady Bonds

Prior to Brady Bonds, traditional sovereign debt analysis was impossible; no one really knew what defaulted Polish or Peruvian government loans, for example, were worth. Few countries were paying a set interest rate, and most loans were past due with uncertain maturities. This confused investors, who simply need to know how much to invest today, when they'll be repaid, and what interest rate they'll receive. Believe it or not, that is the essence of bond investing. With old restructured loans, investors had none of this. Then came the Brady Plan. The Brady Plan provided a mechanism for replacing LDC debt with tradable bonds and, in doing so, gave birth to an entirely new asset class. It also sparked interest in developing countries that had been dormant for many years, while providing a quantitative basis for sovereign risk.

By defining when and how much investors would be repaid, and in some cases ensuring payments through cash collateral, the Brady Plan would attract more financial investors to the developing world than ever before; finally yield-to-maturities could be calculated. By 1995, nearly 75 per cent of all $400 billion in troubled commercial-bank loans to developing countries had been restructured under various Brady Plans in some fifteen countries, including Latin America (Argentina, Brazil, Costa Rica, Dominican Republic, Ecuador, Mexico, Panama, Peru, Uruguay, and Venezuela), Africa (Nigeria), the Middle East (Jordan), Central and Eastern Europe (Bulgaria and Poland), and Asia (Philippines).

The bonds, usually dollar denominated, were minted in maturities of between fifteen and thirty years. A menu of restructuring options was given to banks to provide the best tax relief possible, which created a variety of debt instruments. Most were couponbearing bonds with assortments of fixed or floating rates (or a combination), many with principal and certain interest collateralised by U.S. Treasury zero coupon bonds and other high-grade instruments.

The most common Brady Bonds outstanding today are longdated "Par" and "Discount" issues. Par bonds were converted on a 1:1 basis relative to the original face value of the loans for which they were exchanged, and carry a below-market coupon. Discount bonds carry a floating coupon, and were converted at a discount on the original face value. Approximately 75 per cent of all Bradies are either Par or Discounts, both of which have principal and some interest guarantees. In addition, other Debt Conversion Bonds (DCBs) and Floating Interest Reduction Bonds (FLIRBs) offered interest rate reductions and shorter payments, but no collateral. Past-due interest bonds have been issued to resolve interest arrears situations. Because many countries argued that falling commodity prices were the root cause of their liquidity problems, some commercial banks also required warrants that would give them more money if prices climbed back to pre-crisis levels. In Venezuela, for example, Par and Discount bond holders can increase annual coupons by 1.5 per cent if oil reaches $29 dollars per barrel for a sustained period.

As part of the Brady Plan, most of these bonds are fairly long dated to allow the countries time to repay the banks. This means that these bonds are highly susceptible to two things: **U.S. interest rates and country-specific factors**. Positive or negative developments in either could cause the bonds to rise or fall in price. Furthermore, the key to Brady Bond analysis is not a traditional yield-to-maturity calculation, but what has been dubbed "stripped yield." Given the U.S. Treasury collateral ensuring principal repayment on Par and Discount bonds, Bradies are true hybrids—a mixture of U.S. and emerging market risk. Traders are forced to dissect the cash flows to understand what the true return is on the emerging market component. In fact, because of the zero coupon and collateral, some Bradies have a "Default Return," a positive spread even if the country defaults and never makes another payment.

Investors have been interested in Bradies because of their relatively high stripped rates of return compared to U.S. high-yield (a.k.a. "junk") bonds.

New Issues

For much of the 1980s, there were few fresh dollar-denominated bond issues by developing countries. With the LDC debt overhang, most investors were petrified of sovereign defaults and, as a result, less than $1 billion a year was issued during that decade. However, ever since the first Brady Plan in 1989, the perceived fears of sovereign default have diminished dramatically. As a result, one of the favourable areas for growth on Wall Street is new bond issues for emerging market countries and companies, with an estimated $90 billion being raised in 1997. Increased issues also bring greater liquidity. As of year-end 1996, the volume of emerging market traded new issues (also known as Eurobonds because they are predominantly issued in the Euromarkets) was nearly $650 billion in a universe of debt that is estimated at more than $250 billion (larger than that of the U.S. high-yield market). This includes straight bonds, and also certificates of deposit from developing country banks and convertible bonds.

New issues carry high coupons for emerging market entities, typically 1 per cent to 5 per cent more per annum than U.S. government and corporate bonds. While this may not seem significant to laymen, returns of this magnitude are very attractive for professional bond investors who have been known to kill relatives for an extra 1/8 per cent or 1/4 per cent in yield. It is a huge premium, relative to the broader investment grade world. Moreover, as some of these entities are just beginning the ratings process, many developing country borrowers have upgrade potential, making initial issuance spreads relatively cheap.

Such capital market instruments are being utilised by sovereign, public sector, and corporate borrowers. In contrast to Bradies, new issues inject new money into countries, which helps bolster hard currency reserves. Though in certain emerging markets Eurobonds and Brady Bonds are issued by borrowers in the same country (and should, therefore, carry the same credit risk), the Euros have traded at tighter spreads. This is largely due to the market's higher expectation of default on the longer-dated Bradies: new issues are generally one to ten years, whereas Bradies are five to thirty years in maturity. Often there has been a 1 per cent to 1.5 per cent annual yield difference in some overlapping maturities, creating interesting arbitrage opportunities and relative value trades between certain sovereign issues. While it may seem counterintuitive, smaller Eurobond deals in the $100-$300 million range typically trade tighter than the Brady issues, which can be $15 billion in size. This is largely because Bradies trade in more speculative circles like hedge funds.

Local Currency

Local currency-denominated debt is one of the fastest-growing sectors in emerging market investing, mushrooming by more than $25 billion per annum. This is a healthy sign, as governments rely more on domestic savings (generated by economic growth), which helps foster the culture of money. It also reflects the creation of new currencies and monetary systems. For example, in 1990 no money market existed in the Soviet Union. When it splintered into some twenty countries, twenty new currencies and money markets were created. In the future, such markets will begin to enlarge and strengthen as pension, insurance, and banking sectors develop, sectors that never existed in most of the statist economies.

In the past, local money markets offered investors high interest rates—sometimes more than 100 per cent per annum because of high inflation. For example, according to the World Bank in 1990, the average inflation rate in the developing world was more than 50 per cent. By 1997, the same rate had declined to approximately 10 per cent. The fall was driven largely by the macroeconomic housecleaning discussed earlier. As a result, interest rates in those countries have declined dramatically.

A key feature of developing local currency debt markets is the scarcity of forward or futures contracts on the currency itself. For foreign investors, forwards is an essential risk management tool, one that is standard when dealing with the Japanese yen or Swiss franc but that is absent in the Kazakhstani tenge or Guatemalan quetzal. Therefore, in many of these markets, investors buying debt in local currency must speculate on the future foreign exchange rate and bear the market risks. This is beginning to change, and many First World exchanges are looking to offer investors currency hedge products. In Chicago and London, for example, several contracts on large currencies such as the Mexican peso and the Brazilian real are being offered. In Hong Kong and Singapore, there are contracts for several Asian currencies.

Yet most of the risk management tools are coming from the local markets themselves. In Brazil, for example, interest rate futures, currency and gold futures, stock index futures, and stock options are traded, and small but growing futures markets are emerging in South Africa, the Philippines, Hungary, China, Russia, and Slovakia. Demand for such futures and a forward product also comes from the real economy; importers and exporters need them for hedging out risks related to their underlying businesses. As global trade accelerates, one can expect to see a greater number of futures markets develop over time.

With the growth in emerging market currency instruments, there comes a need for performance benchmarks and reference assets for First World investors. To some extent, the Bradies have become a hard currency benchmark for pricing new issues in international capital markets, as well as setting reference levels of interest rates for domestic money market instruments. In June 1996 J.P. Morgan launched its Emerging Market Local Market Index (ELMI), which tracks total returns for local currency-denominated emerging market instruments. The index focuses on some of the largest and most liquid markets accessible to international investors: Mexico (22 per cent), Malaysia (17 per cent), Thailand (15 per cent), Indonesia (12 per cent), South Africa (8 per cent), Turkey (7 per cent), Poland (5 per cent), Philippines (5 per cent), and the Czech Republic (4 per cent). This is a dynamic and potentially huge growth area for global bond investors (as well as Wall Street), particularly if the European monetary union materialises and the Continent loses more than ten traded currencies.

While few formal futures markets exist for emerging market currencies, over-the-counter (OTC) products are often bought and sold to hedge rate exposure. Certain MNCs with local operations in developing countries buy and sell forward currencies, and many local banks informally offer such hedges to clients. Sometimes local central banks will offer limited coverage, often tied to a specific investment or transaction deemed to be important. Some arbitrages arise from these contracts, allowing investors to earn yields greater than comparable U.S. dollar rates, something rarely seen in First World currency markets.

Emerging Equity Markets

Beyond debt opportunities, greater economic growth in the long run should lead to greater stock market returns (See "The Mother of All Emerging Stock Markets," page 171). Emerging market stocks also offer investors great value through cheap earnings and assets. One would expect that higher emerging market growth would produce greater earnings acceleration, reflected in higher developing country price-earnings ratios (P/Es). However, on average, emerging market P/Es is considerably lower than those in the G7: 18 versus 26, according to the IFC in 1999. If emerging markets have greater economic growth, why the lower P/Es? Two simple reasons: first, low P/E illustrates the general scarcity of capital in developing countries; second, it reflects a naturally risk-averse, "show me" attitude of the market. In short, emerging stock markets need time to capitalise and prove themselves worthy of First World multiples.

Just how cheap are emerging market stocks? It certainly varies; remember, there are more than sixty emerging markets. However, in measuring enterprise value by dividing stock market capitalisation by a respective production capacity—such as in cement (price per ton of annual production) or telephony (price per telephone line)—many emerging market companies look incredibly cheap. A dramatic example is the Russian petroleum giant Lukoil. In asset size, Lukoil with 11 billion barrels of proven reserves—would rank as the world's largest publicly-traded oil company. Yet in stock market capitalisation, at $2.8 billion, Lukoil would not rate among the world's top twenty most valuable energy concerns at year-end 1998. Exxon would have been first at $178 billion, followed by Royal Dutch/Shell ($154 billion). When looking at price per barrel of proven oil reserves, investors were paying some $25 for Exxon versus only 25 cents for Lukoil. Why such a disparity?

First, let's go back to earnings. While all businesses produce different goods and services, they all should make one thing in common: profit. Companies are essentially money factories because investors are theoretically buying dividend streams. In this respect, Exxon is one of the world's great profit machines, with decades of proven profitability and netting $8+ billion after taxes in 1998. In 1998 year-end stock prices, investors were paying approximately 28 times Exxon's projected earnings—a highly confident view of the company's future. In contrast, Lukoil has only been a private enterprise for a few years; there's no real track record for investors to analyse. In terms of earnings, Lukoil netted only $300 million in 1997 and lost money in 1998. Obviously, while Lukoil professes to have huge reserves, the company cannot seem to extract, refine, and ship oil as efficiently as Exxon; thus, the difference in earnings.

There are other country-specific factors that also cap Lukoil's stock price. Its home market—Russia—has seen GDP and energy demand plummet more than 50 per cent over the 1990s. Moreover, investors fear future Russian political risks that may impair Lukoil's profitability—everything from nationalisation, dividend remittance controls, a reversion towards communism, and general economic chaos. In short, Lukoil and more importantly, Russia itself has much to prove to investors before the stock can be bid at anything close to G7 multiples.

Winners and Losers of the Future

The picture painted so far has been one of bounty, progress, and upsides. True, economic growth brings improvements in living standards and health: many Third World children today are an average of four or five inches taller than they were in the 1940s, with twenty years greater life expectancy and 50 per cent higher calorie intake. Economic growth also brings higher and more stable incomes, which means new consumer markets: today there are 200 times more TVs, telephones, and cars per household in Taiwan, for example, than in 1950. And as has been argued, faster growth in developing countries brings benefits to First World countries, by offering new and hungry markets for their exports, as well as new financial markets for higher investment returns than are available at home. In Malaysia, this dynamic is in its advanced stages. In Kuala Lumpur, the eighteen to twenty-five age range has become a target population for cellular telephone marketing, with apparently 60 per cent already signed up to cellular service. This population is one of the latest additions to the growing global consumer market that has MNCs so excited.

However exciting this future may seem, the fact is that not everyone will be a winner in this global realignment of economic power. There will be, as described, a net gain. But this is a story about comparative advantage, and it will require the First World to cede certain lower-skilled jobs to its emerging neighbours. Despite the discomfort and challenge faced by the American, European, and Japanese workers whose jobs will migrate, there are opportunities to be seized by First World workers who exploit their home country's comparative advantage, which is increasingly in the service and technology industries, including semiconductors, telecommunications, software, biotechnology, and finance. In the United States, for example, the engine of growth is increasingly to be found in Silicon Valley and its offshoots, and on Wall Street. Allowing such a dynamic to run its course will mean that, ultimately, the refrigerators that the average First World worker will buy will be cheaper, even though that worker may need to get retrained in order to remain competitive in the labour force. The average Third Worlder will now have a job, producing these refrigerators, and the value of Third World manufacturing exports will reflect production in such sectors; such goods now account for almost 60 per cent of the exports of emerging markets, up from only 5 per cent in 1955, and the Third World's share of world manufacture exports jumped from 5 per cent in 1970 to 22 per cent in 1993. Eventually, the

Third World worker will himself own a refrigerator from his factory. This same dynamic will be reproduced in other manufacturing sectors, and between other sets of economically differentiated countries. A new class of Third World consumers will have been created, with greater purchasing power and an improved standard of living. Indeed, developing countries are likely to account for approximately two-thirds of the increase in world imports over the next twenty years.

In this way international trade can raise everyone's living standards—indeed, there is an inevitability to this process, and it is only by allowing it to run freely and by adapting to the new environment that the First World can guarantee continued improvements in living standards for its citizens, in an era of skyrocketing public deficits and competitive global labour pressures.

CHAPTER 5

Global Business Alliances

Global Business Competition and Alliances

Globalisation of business has been one of the dominant characteristics of the past two decades but will develop even faster in the future. Many companies from both developed and developing countries have become multinational players seeking market opportunities across nations. Globalisation has become the cornerstone of firms' overall business strategies. Globalisation is no longer only a business option but also a part of effective corporate strategising. In other words, present business strategy is increasingly global. Today's global scope of business is markedly different from yesterday's business pattern. Presently, numerous goods and services are available across borders—even in those countries which were previously closed markets of command economies. World consumers have been exposed to a variety of products and services that had only been available to affluent consumers in industrialised countries. When customers across nations started demanding products and services for better living, companies strived to meet such demands by competing not only with local firms but also with other multinational firms.

We live in a global village today, where consumers have a chance to see and compare many products and services if not physically but virtually because of the Internet revolution.

Consequently, buyers demand quality, variety, convenience, and utility. Needless to say, Internet technology has intensified such consumer demands tremendously. Buyers today can easily search for a product or service around the world. Recent news in *The Wall Street Journal* clearly illustrates the globalisation of consumer behaviour.

These developments are not restricted to developed countries and are taking place in many emerging or developing economies. In this vein, a car buyer in Turkey looks for similar features and performance of his or her car to those made in the West. Thus, Toyota and Honda joint ventures in Turkey offer their flagship cars to Turkish customers, as well. These cases demonstrate that worldwide consumer demand for goods and services is pushing firms to engage in global productions and deliveries.

A close examination of such developments shows that a number of factors have contributed to this business globalisation. I define these factors as follows:

Liberalisation of Economies

With the demise of socialist economies, many former socialist countries such as the Soviet Union (now Russia), Poland, Czechoslovakia (now the Czech and Slovak Republics), Hungary, Romania, and Bulgaria have switched to a market economy from a command economy, which has opened their borders for foreign investment, goods, and services. The times are changing for many economic sectors in Central and Eastern Europe. The primary driver for change in this region is the eagerness of most countries to be accepted into the European Union (EU). While governments strive to meet the EU's economic requirements, the effect on the local industries has intensified because of efforts in privatisation, liberalisation, and deregulation. The markets in the region fall into three groups according to their order of EU accession. The first group of markets is Poland, Hungary, the Czech Republic, Estonia, and Slovenia. The second group includes Bulgaria, Croatia, Romania, Latvia, Lithuania, and Slovakia. The third group consists of the former Soviet states, which lag some distance behind after having suffered from the Asian contagion and a disastrous fall in foreign direct investment.

Under the terms of the Chinese WTO (World Trade Organisation) accession package, China will become a full participant in the Information Technology Agreement, eliminating tariffs on a wide range of high-tech products, including semiconductors and chip manufacturing equipment. The mandatory requirements that imported goods go through a Chinese agent or middleman will disappear, as foreign vendors will have direct contact with customers. This will permit lower marketing costs, expedient sales, better customer relations and more efficient distribution. China has traditionally imposed conflicting and arbitrary restrictions on direct investment for chipmakers. Access to China's domestic market has been contingent upon a foreign partner's willingness to transfer advanced technologies and Intellectual Property to the Chinese partner.

As in many industries, China's population represents a huge potential marketplace for prescription medicines. The Chinese market is expanding continuously, fuelled at least in part by improvements in the standard of living. Greater access to health care and changing disease patterns predicated by improving economic status drive the pharmaceutical market Many companies play an active role in creating niche markets for their products in China.

The developing economy and improvement in living standards have made Chinese consumers more aware of their health. Under those circumstances, pharmaceutical companies need to educate patients and introduce new ideas to create demand for products that did not exist previously. Smith Kline & French (SK&F) has created a new market for its painkiller Fenbid (ibuprofen). Xian Janssen has created a new market for its Motilium (domperidone) by introducing the new concept of stomach motility. Lilly has created a new market for its antidepressant Prozac by educating consumers that depression is a problem of the nervous system. Despite failing to obtain administrative protection from SDA and having lost an appeal with the Beijing High Court for protection against copies of Prozac, Lilly still plans to manufacture the drug in China at its Suzhou joint-venture site. Privatisation of state-owned enterprises in many countries has been a widespread application. Many developed and developing countries including the United Kingdom, France, Italy, Brazil, Argentina, Chile, Malaysia, and Turkey have privatised their inefficient state-owned enterprises for greater economic value. The trend towards privatisation of state-owned enterprises gives international firms and international investors an opportunity to enter potentially lucrative markets that were once closed to private enterprise. Privatisation also provides international companies an opportunity to capitalise on the comparative advantage of countries that have opened their doors to foreign companies.

Although the success in this transition to a market economy or in the liberalisation of economies varies across countries, the movement will accelerate in the next decade. Liberalisation of economies worldwide has created many opportunities for newly established domestic firms and MNCs. Many MNCs have established strategic partnerships with national firms in post-socialist countries that transformed their economies (or at least certain industries from command to market economy).

The spread of economic liberalism has been the most important driver of globalisation. "The recent and widespread change in ideology—from state socialism to market capitalism—has unleashed much internal deregulation and external liberalisation from France to the former Soviet Union." It is true that the deregulation and privatisation of industries in developed and developing countries has stimulated economic activity by opening borders for trade and foreign investment—which, in turn, stirred global competition.

Because inefficient state-owned enterprises have contributed to budget deficits in many countries, governments around the world have been privatising such enterprises at an increasing rate. By doing so, they expect the following benefits: improving enterprise efficiency and performance, developing competitive industry that serves consumers well, assessing the capital, know-how, and markets that permit growth, achieving effective corporate governance, broadening and deepening capital markets, and securing the best price possible for the sale.

A fundamental premise of most economists and management scholars is that state-owned enterprises (SOEs) are less efficient and profitable than private enterprises. Privatisation can be justified because it increases the technological efficiency of operations. Many empirical studies comparing private and public firms confirm that private enterprises are more efficient than public enterprises producing the same goods or very close substitutes, given the same or similar technology, regulatory constraints, and financial capabilities. Therefore there has been little discussion that SOEs in the former socialist countries need to be privatised. As a result of privatisation, market opportunities for domestic and international firms will continue to boom. Hoelscher, a market expert on the telecommunications industry, describes the market opportunities in Central and Eastern European countries as follows: "The Czech Republic, Poland and Hungary have undoubtedly made the most progress of all Eastern European countries in the development of their telecommunications industry during the post-1989 era. Advances include partial privatisation of and significant capital investment to the fixed-line and mobile infrastructure, market liberalisation moving towards ending monopoly in most market segments and creation of huge demand for communication services of all types among business and residential consumers."

We can extend these same arguments to SOEs in developed countries. Many developed countries around the world, including Britain, Germany, France, and Italy, have privatised numerous state-owned companies.

Privatisation in both developed and developing economies has fuelled strategic alliances. Privatised enterprises have globally engaged in strategic alliances such as licensing, joint ventures, marketing, and production partnerships to become and stay efficient and competitive. After their privatisation in the United Kingdom, British Telecom and British Airlines sought partnerships in Europe and the United States. Likewise, a number of privatised enterprises in former socialist and developing countries have sought strategic partnerships with the belief that such alliances would contribute considerably to the development of Western-like business strategies and structures. The belief exists that the links with Western firms would ensure the successful transfer of capital and technology, which are desperately needed at the time of transformation. In this vein, Russian and Azerbaijanian petroleum companies have established a number of links with U.S. and European oil companies. Similarly, telecommunications companies from Mexico to India have established collaborations with Western firms.

Strategic alliances with Western firms have injected new life into privatised firms in developing countries by revitalising commercial practices and efficient production systems. For many employees of such former state-owned enterprises, customer expectations, cost control, and building core competencies for strategic advantages were strange concepts in the past. They have quickly learned such business planning and practices through their interactions with their Western partners.

International Business Strategy and Alliances

A business strategy reflects managerial choices among different alternatives and signals organisational commitment to particular products, markets, competitive approaches, and ways of operating the enterprise. When firms formulate their business strategies, they define their objectives while considering their resources and capabilities.

Additionally, they respond to the opportunities and constraints in the marketplace. Hence, it is important to understand the driving forces of the competitive environment.

The New Competitive Dynamics

The new competitive dynamics refer to forces that shape today's business rivalries. Rapidly changing market conditions (and accordingly, emerging business philosophy) form the new competitive dynamics, which are knowledge-based and global in nature and require continuous improvements in every facet of the value chain and seeking opportunities worldwide. As technology and the globalisation of business advance with unprecedented speed and magnitude, firms in almost all industries—traditional and emerging—are engaging in unorthodox competitive modes. This new competitive mode requires product and process innovation, quick responses, and high customer service while manoeuvring between competition and cooperation. Some of the similar concepts with the new competitive dynamics are called "the new competitive landscape" and "hypercompetition" in business literature. First, we will briefly delineate these similar concepts and then illustrate the distinct characteristics of the new competitive dynamics.

The new competitive landscape is shaped by technological changes and the global economy. They noted rapid technological changes and technology diffusion, dramatic changes in information technology, and an increasing importance of knowledge. Additionally, they characterised the global economy with free movement of goods, services, and labour across geographical borders, emerging opportunities in multiple global markets, and internationalisation of markets and industries. Although the world economy has not fully reached the free movement of production factors across nations, establishment of regional economic integrations and economic liberation movements worldwide have helped substantially in changing the current global economy. In response to these global economic conditions, firms are in the midst of a revolutionary transformation from industrial-age competition to information-age competition. The rapidly changing nature of new competition "hypercompetition," which results from dynamics of strategic manoeuvring among global and innovative combatants. It is a condition of rapidly escalating competition based on price-quality positioning, competition to create new know-how and established first-mover advantage, competing to protect or invade established product or geographic markets, and competition based on deep pockets and the creation of even deeper pocketed alliances." While hypercompetition occurs among rival firms, cooperation happens between or among rival and complementary firms. This competition and cooperation coexistence is one of the dominant elements of the new competitive dynamics.

After close examination, new competitive dynamics demonstrate several essential characteristics that are interdependent. We can describe them as follows:

(a) Rapid Changes in Competitive Base

Today, a competitive edge gained in a given business will not hold long unless the firm continuously innovates it and launches new products and creates market niches. A fast slip of competitive advantage gained over the years is making firms nervous and is forcing them to initiate new alternatives.

A new business undertaking such as a merger, acquisition, or alliance in the competitive landscape can affect the competitive behaviour of other players. One move by one or two major players influences the existing competition pattern in that industry. For example, the merger of America Online (AOL) and Time Warner has major reverberations for all online companies.

This merger might lead to possible new acquisitions or partnerships; more mergers between delivery companies such as Yahoo! and content companies such as Walt Disney; more deals to extend broadband service to other platforms beyond cable, such as interactive television; and launching new portals to broadband service.

(b) Consolidations

The past decade has witnessed an increasing number of consolidations among firms in various industries. Many firms worldwide have been seeking scale advantages by combining forces. Mergers and acquisitions have become indispensable business strategies of firms. Daimler Chrysler in automobile manufacturing, Glaxo Wellcome and Smith Kline Beecham in pharmaceuticals, and Time Warner and EMI in music recording are only few examples of mergers and acquisitions seeking cost savings from consolidations while building market power and competitive advantage.

In general, the reasons for mergers and acquisitions include achieving competitive advantages through market power, overcoming barriers to entry, increasing the speed of market entry, the significant cost involved in developing new products, avoiding the risk of new product development, achieving diversification, and finally avoiding competition. Although small and medium-size firms with product and market niches continue to compete in domestic and global markets, they will have a rough time against mega companies that have plenty of resources. Under the pressure of global competition, the next decade will more likely see the continuation of mergers and acquisitions across nations in a variety of industries.

Increasing consolidations in the business world do not mean that there is no room for medium and small-size companies. But it means that giant companies will make it very hard for medium and small-size companies to compete in the global marketplace unless those companies have their product and market niches or are in alliances with others. This situation has been true for years; however, there would be more pressure on medium and small-size companies even threatening their existence. The incredible expansion of giant retailer Wal-Mart and the mergers of Exxon and Mobile, British Petroleum and Amoco, and Mercedes-Benz and DaimlerChrysler are examples of such developments.

(c) Globalisation

A number of factors including the emergence of regional economic integrations such as the European Union (EU) and North American Free Trade Agreement (NAFTA), the economic progress in newly industrialised countries such as Brazil, Taiwan, Turkey, and South Korea, the transformation of economies from a command to a market economy in Russia, Poland, Hungary, the Czech Republics, and Romania, the liberalisation of the economy in China, and the privatisation of state-owned enterprises in both developed and developing countries have led to widespread globalisation.

Globalisation is related to scale economies (discussed previously). Firms are trying to tap market opportunities in huge markets such as China, India, Indonesia, and Russia. For example, Wal-Mart—after its expansion in Latin America and Europe—is now eager to enter the Chinese market. "Others are venturing in China as well ranging from Motorola's $2 billion fabrication plant to joint venture between Enron and Singapore Power." A close look at Fortune 500 companies shows that most of these companies that have operations in numerous countries generate a substantial portion of their revenues from overseas sales. In fact, today it is futile to talk about domestic firms anymore. Even companies that are bound to only their local markets are subject to foreign competition (that is, if companies are not international but the business competition is). In fact, many firms such as McDonald's, Coca-Cola, Procter & Gamble, Nestle, ABB, Honda, Toyota, and DaimlerChrysler have commitments in so many markets around the world that they should be thought of as global players.

Global competition has improved product quality and customer service while reducing the prices of many products and services. The world consumers have been the final beneficiaries of the global competition. Without global competition, global consumers would not be enjoying Internet services, mobile phones, and broadcasting news—not to mention basic consumer goods that were only available to the consumers of industrial countries. It is interesting to see a porter or a street vendor in a developing country using a mobile phone when having a telephone had been a luxury for a long time. The competition among Ericsson, Nokia, and Motorola has enabled the spread of mobile phone services into markets where (with the wiring connections) it was impossible to provide such a service.

In a more interconnected world, firms not only from developed countries but also from third-world countries have joined international competition. Multinational firms from developing economies have emerged by making investments in even industrialised countries. For example, Petroleos de Venezuela has made major investments in North America, and similarly, Cemetex of Mexico has acquired cement plants in the United States.

(d) Operating in Hybrid Industries

Due to the advent of new technologies and emerging products and services, boundaries of a single industry have become blurred. The best example of this mix is telephone, cable, and television industries. With the addition of Internet providers, this relationship will become more intermingled. Even the most traditional industries, such as automotive and medical, have been influenced by a number of emerging industries such as computers, robots, and lasers. As a result, it is time to recognise some industries as "hybrid industries." In particular, the Internet blurs the boundaries between companies and industries. Information and entertainment industries and companies in such industries illustrate the point well. For example, Yahoo! started as a Web search engine, but now it offers so many diverse functions including a broad-paced online shopping site. Similarly, under what industry can Microsoft or AOL be classified? The giant Microsoft is rapidly diversifying itself into a number of industries, ranging from telecommunications to financial, through acquisitions and alliances.

(e) Strategic Alliances

As we explained, both academics and managers consider that cooperation is no longer incompatible with competition. In other words, competition and cooperation can coexist. Raymond Noorda, former chief executive of Novell, coined the term "co-opetition" for this emerging development. Barr J. Nalebuff and Adam M. Brandenburger used it for the title of their 1996 book. Currently, the phenomenon seems to be spreading.

In fact, today's cooperation is part of the strategic repertoire of many firms. Firms use cooperation in a variety of ways and situations to build competitive edges. A close look at the relationship between competition and cooperation reveals that cooperative ventures can take various patterns; however, the most common ones are either a firm cooperating with its competitors or with complementary firms (for example, suppliers, distributors, and firms in related industries). In addition, the form of cooperation occurs in several ways: (a) cooperate first, compete later, (b) cooperate while competing, and (c) cooperating among themselves and competing with outsiders.

Cooperate First, Then Compete

When companies feel that they need to build their competitive strengths first before full-fledged competition, they seek the cooperation of others. Partnering firms cooperate to expand the market, and then they can compete to earn their own shares.

Often, a firm finds out that developing a new technology might require acquiring resources and capabilities beyond its own or establishing an industry standard during the technology- or product-development phase.

Then, it welcomes the participation of competing firms in a strategic alliance (for example, a technology development consortium). Indeed, many R&D partnerships represent these kinds of collaborations. Resource pooling among pharmaceutical firms enables them to jointly work on formidable new drug discoveries while they reduce the risk of project failure.

Cooperate While Competing

Firms can compete and cooperate simultaneously. This simultaneous "competition-cooperation" mode has become common in the automobile manufacturing industry. General Motors and Toyota, for instance, despite their NUMMI joint venture, compete with each other worldwide. Likewise, Ford and Mazda continue to compete while they cooperate in many ways. Such collaborations capitalise on the exchange of knowhow and "tacit technology." This mode of cooperation, however, is not unique to the automobile industry.

Facing rising product-development costs, six of the world's largest semiconductor manufacturers joined forces to develop new technology for the most common type of memory chip used inside personal computers. The six companies consist of the Intel Corporation and Micron Technology of the United States, NEC of Japan, Samsung Electronics and Hyundai Electronics of South Korea, and Infenion Technologies AG, a unit of Germany's Siemens. The group—excluding Intel, which mainly makes microprocessors—accounts for about 70 per cent of the global market for dynamic random access memory (DRAM). That market reached $21 billion in 1999.

The companies thought this unusually broad alliance should be more cost effective than going alone. The accord refers to a goal of developing high-performance, advanced DRAM technology for the marketplace in 2003. This accord would provide information to facilitate the development of related PC components such as a chipset, which acts as an intermediary between DRAM and the central processing unit (CPU). Consumer interest in high-performance PCs that provide advanced multimedia and graphics is pushing companies to develop higher-speed CPUs that require more powerful yet affordable DRAM chips.

By working on technology that will be in the market in 2008, the alliance is trying to look beyond the current battle lines of industry competition. Each member of the alliance will commit a design team to the project, which will be overseen by a senior technology committee. This situation is an excellent example of how companies attempt to collaborate while they still compete. By pooling their resources, they can come up with advanced technology from which every participant can benefit.

In the same vein, there is a mutual interest of airlines for building an airport or trucking companies for building a highway. Until the facilities are built, they probably worked together to support such investments. But after the facilities are built, they might go their own ways in competing with each other. In the early stage of industry development or crises in the industry (for example, the U.S. automobile manufacturers' campaign against Japanese exports to the United States and tobacco companies acting together to fight against anti-smoking litigations), such collaboration often emerges.

Cooperate among them but Compete with Outsiders

This kind of cooperation is common among companies in Japan, where interlocking among companies is allowed. Japanese *Keiretsu,* postwar corporate networks of interlocking affiliates, plays an important role in achieving synergies within the network while building a strong competitive front against rivals. "Unlike U.S. and European conglomerates, the hundreds of companies in each keiretsu are highly decentralised. While being separate and independent, they are part of an incredible communication network that allows them to cooperate with each other when there is a mutual advantage to do so.

Mitsubishi and Sumitomo are examples of this Japanese form of conglomerates. Mitsubishi Group, for example, holds 28 core members and hundreds of other Mitsubishi-related companies. Within the Mitsubishi family of companies, because its infrastructure is already built, there is an expectation for cooperation among family members, whether drinking Kirin beer, using a Nikon camera, or buying insurance from Meiji Mutual.

Unlike the U.S. conglomerates, which accent financial management, Keiretsu is oriented to cooperate in accord with whatever contribution a family member can make to help the other family members. Business units may be cooperating as suppliers of parts, lenders of capital, contributors of production know-how, or providers of access to markets. All these happen quietly. It takes a lot of digging to find out who is supplying what to whom. Even then, many of the arrangements cannot be uncovered. Most of the agreements will never be known. Keiretsu behaviour epitomises cooperation based on mutual advantage. Keiretsus actively seek out joint ventures with a broad range of partners, all over the world.

Similar to Japanese Keiretsu, South Korean firms have their own conglomerates called Chaebols, which function in the same fashion. Although many conglomerates also exist in the United States and Europe, their structure and operations are different from the Keiretsus in terms of building intense cooperation among family members. Antitrust laws in the United States do not allow such close knitting within the same corporation when it hinders the competition in the marketplace.

We can see another form of building a network of cooperation in the Internet industry. Some of the leading Internet firms are creating Internet "ecosystems." They evolve together, sometimes linked by cross holding, and continually pull more companies into their orbits. For example, Softbank of Japan holds more than 120 Internet investments. Softbank brings a new company, such as Webhire, into the fold and blends it with a more established asset, such as Yahoo!, in which Softbank holds a stake of 23 per cent. Softbanks can be deemed today's Internet *zaibatsu*, referring to several powerful companies in prewar Japan that had strong intragroup ties.

This kind of Internet cooperation is sometimes called "Netbatsu" because it combines the words Internet and

Zaibatsu. Internet moguls in action today remind us of this powerful model. The American version of Netbatsu is Safeguard Scientific, which operates in Internet-related areas such as software, communications, and services by compromising partner companies and incubating companies.

The second form of interfirm collaboration embraces cooperation between a focal firm and its complementary players. In recent years, the most common ones include agreements between manufacturer-supplier and pharmaceutical and biotechnology companies. To avoid the high inventory cost and to benefit from quality improvements and speedy deliveries of components and raw materials, manufacturers have developed long-range relationships with their suppliers. For example, automotive and PC manufacturers have benefitted greatly from close ties with suppliers. Today, in developing new drugs, more and more pharmaceutical companies rely on biotechnology companies.

Automobile Manufacturing Industry and Global Alliances

The principal objective of this section is to enhance our understanding of patterns of strategic partnerships in the automobile manufacturing industry from economic, organisational, and strategic management perspectives. To fully understand interfirm partnerships in automobile manufacturing, we must first grasp the industry's dynamics and then describe the alliance patterns and processes.

Industry Dynamics

Market Size

The global market represents about 44 million vehicles per year in sales. This number is expected to grow to about 64 million by 2008. The biggest growth is expected in China, India, the Pacific Rim, South Africa, and South America. The global market in the automotive industry is well more than $1 trillion and involves more than 10 million employees, meaning that it is the world's largest manufacturing business. The major producing countries are the United States with 23 per cent, Japan with 20 per cent and Germany with 10 per cent. The largest single market is the United States with annual sales of about 15 million units.

Demand is projected to reach 69 million units by 2008, and capacity is expected to be 80 million units for the same period. The slow growth can be attributed to recent price increases, outpaced income growth, and the increase in the age of registered automobiles (the average car is eight years old). Presently, it takes 24.5 weeks of family earnings to purchase an automobile compared to 17.5 weeks of income in 2008.

Scope of Competitive Rivalry

The automotive industry has become globally competitive and has undergone significant restructuring and consolidation. All of the major industry participants are continuing to increase their focus on efficiency and cost improvements while announced capacity increases for the North American market and excess capacity in the European market have led to continuing price pressures.

General Motors (GM), Ford, and Chrysler (now DaimlerChrysler), known as the Big Three, accounted for 69.4 per cent of the U.S. market in 1999, down from 1998's 71.0 per cent and 1997's 71.7 per cent. Their 1999 market shares (cars and trucks combined) are as follows: GM with 29.5 per cent, Ford with 24.1 per cent, and Chrysler with 16.8 per cent. Japan accounts for 31 per cent of the market with Honda at 10 per cent, Toyota at 9.9 per cent, Nissan at 5.7 per cent, Mazda at 2 per cent, and Subaru at 1.4 per cent, other foreign manufacturers sustain a 10.2 per cent market share. In the mature European market, Volkswagen stands as the market leader with GM in second position. In Japan, foreign automakers are experiencing sluggish sales growth, with U.S. manufacturers only gaining 3.1 per cent. In the Asian market, Japanese automakers are dominating while the U.S. manufacturers are pursuing strategies such as local production and distribution. By 2005, some are projecting that total industry sales in the South American and Asian regions will double more than 35 per cent of the worldwide market. There are three global developments that put U.S. automakers in a shifting competitive position: The fastest-growing auto markets are in countries that are struggling to develop their own industries; new technologies must address environmental and safety concerns; and manufacturers depend increasingly on the important players in a long and complex supply chain.

There are basically four categories in the motor vehicle market. The U.S. manufacturers dominate the truck and sport utility vehicle (SUV) market; the Japanese dominate in family sedans (such as Toyota Camry and Honda Accord); the Europeans lead in luxury sedans (Mercedes and BMW); and the economy market is highly fragmented. The major manufacturers have ranges of products that play to all the major market segments. Only a few manufacturers have chosen to focus on niches, such as Isuzu (trucks) and Subaru (all-wheel drive passenger cars). The primary battle is now in light trucks, which include minivans and SUVs. These vehicles yield the greatest unit profits. In addition to the big three, virtually all of the major importers have SUVs.

For GM, competing on a global basis is a priority that is driving the largest international production capacity expansion in the company's history. GM has five new manufacturing facilities either under development or up and running in Argentina, China, Brazil, Poland, and Thailand. These facilities are the cornerstone of GM's expansion into new markets. GM derives 20 per cent to 25 per cent of its revenues from international vehicle sales and only six per cent from the Asia/ Pacific region. Ford, which garners about 20 per cent of its profits from outside North America, has been losing money in Latin America. But profits have been increasing in the bigger European market.

Market Growth and Product Life Cycle

While the market in the United States and Europe is mature, in developing countries there is room for growth. A worldwide growth is expected to be significant, with approximately 10 million units added in the next 10 years.

Over the past few years, American automakers have seen a steady 2 per cent to 3 per cent growth. This growth has been fuelled by increases in light truck sales. Passenger car sales have remained at or below 9 million units since 1992. The peak was reached in 1986 at 11.5 million units. Growth will have to come from developing countries as the developed nations represent mature auto markets. Barriers to growth in these markets, however, are that they are developing their own automotive industries and/or preventing access to foreign automakers. On the other hand, auto parts manufacturers' long-term prospects are promising, despite the fierce competition. Growth arises from several sources: the rush to add more high-tech features to vehicles, the United States-Japan trade accord, global expansion, and the standardisation of parts. In addition, growth in the United States has also been observed in the sales of light trucks and SUVs over the past several years.

Although the automobile industry is mature, cyclical, and saturated, manufacturers can still rev up the demand for vehicles by making them more affordable.

Number of Rivals and their Relative Sizes

The automobile industry worldwide is concentrated. The big three are now the big six, as Toyota, Nissan, and Honda continue to expand their assembly and powertrain (engines and transmission) operations in North America. Over the past several years, many foreign manufacturers, such as Honda and BMW, have seen great opportunities for growth in the U.S. market. Building plants in the United States and producing vehicles that are sold in the United States and Canada have produced this growth. Not only can they promote their vehicles by claiming "Built in the USA," but they can also nearly eliminate tariffs, take advantage of currency fluctuations, reduce logistic costs, and operate close to the customer. Many non-U.S. automakers are targeting for more growth, because part of the corporate strategy is focusing on future products for the light truck market.

The automobile industry is global, given the fact that all players are competing in each other's markets. The principal players in the vehicle manufacturing industry include GM, Ford, and DaimlerChrysler (an American-German company) in the United States, and other major players include Toyota, Nissan, and Honda from Japan; Volkswagen and BMW from Germany; Renault and Peugeot-Citroen from France; Fiat from Italy; Saab (owned by GM now) and Volvo (owned by Ford) from Sweden; and Hyundai and Kia from South Korea. The U.S. auto market is the only truly open market. All other markets are protected to some extent. The bulk of the import nameplate vehicles are actually assembled in North America. Although GM, the number one manufacturer, is continually losing market share to foreign competitors, it is aggressively trying to regain market share with rebates and discount financing.

Number of Buyers and their Relative Sizes

The majority of buyers are consumers at large. According to the U.S. Industry Survey, the average family owns 1.5 cars, and in fact this average number might rise by two or three. Other major buyers are industrial and business organisations. Government and car-rental companies (some are vertically integrated with automobile makers) are also important customers. Overcapacity ensures competition for sales, and this situation has taken pricing power away from the automobile makers.

The Degree of Vertical Integration

The automobile industry has been very competitive. Although, in the U.S. market, which is the largest market, the big three have been dominant in controlling a large portion of market share, foreign competition has eroded their strong position.

Increasing competition and weaknesses in some world markets are causing some horizontal integration among manufacturers and increasing consolidations. The most recent merger was Chrysler and Daimler-Benz. Automobile manufacturers with cost containment and safety reasons assert a high degree of influence over supply and distribution channels. Most manufacturers have full control over their dealers. It is common to observe strategic alliances between automobile manufacturers and their suppliers. The suppliers are rewarded with long-term contracts as they incur most of the programme costs. GM is the most vertically integrated manufacturer, buying only 30 per cent of its components. The parts industry consists of more than 10,000 U.S. suppliers, 2,300 European suppliers, and 2,100 Japanese suppliers and does more than $50 million in business. More than 2,500 worldwide original equipment manufacturers (OEMs) exist that help produce the 15,000 components that automakers need to build a new vehicle. Companies such as Johnson Controls, Goodyear, Dana, and Tenneco are among the largest independent OEMs. Some suppliers are OEM subsidiaries within large, diversified companies such as GE, 3M, Allied Signal, and Eaton. Generally speaking, vehicle manufacturers are mainly concerned with assembly but are not extremely vertically integrated, meaning that they outsource a good share of their components. For example, Ford and Chrysler purchase more than 55 per cent and 70 per cent, respectively, from OEMs. Furthermore, Japanese manufacturers are not highly integrated either, often purchasing around 65 per cent of their components from American or Japanese OEMs.

Besides manufacturing, all firms are highly integrated. Most have rental car subsidiaries to ensure sales, some have their own part manufacturing subsidiaries, and most have their own financial arms to provide consumer loans. In addition, the big three are running their own dealerships (and service departments) to further integrate. Currently, 22,000 car dealerships exist in the United States, many of which have common ownership (in other words, an individual or corporation has multiple ownership).

Scale Economies

Automobile production requires a very large investment in plant and equipment. While improvements in technology and production methods have reduced some of the traditional economies of scale, the initial and ongoing investment in the plant and equipment presents a formidable barrier to any new entrant into the industry. To realise innovation, which is essential for becoming and staying competitive, a large amount of R&D spending is required.

The Ford 2000 programme and copycat programmes at other multinational automobile manufacturers will enable firms to realise tremendous cost savings from scale economies. With the homogenisation of products, costs associated with line retooling and other product-diversification costs will also decrease. In the past several years, there has been a great degree of consolidation as companies seek to create alliances to share infrastructure costs.

The need for economies of scale is driving the urge to merge in the automobile industry. Specific operational strategies include reducing the labour costs and overcapacity through closing plants, consolidating operations, merging, and forming joint ventures. A large production volume is needed for a new model. Batch engineering enables GM and DaimlerChrysler to market multiple vehicles that share basic platforms and components.

Experience Curve

The automobile industry has a history of major production innovation breakthroughs based on a firm's experience. Henry Ford's ability to produce consistent interchangeable parts and simple assembly production provided the basis for automobile mass production and produced a significant competitive advantage. Similarly, today's lean production techniques, resulting from years of continuous improvement experience, have provided a sustainable competitive advantage for the Japanese. The automobile industry's high experience curve poses a significant barrier to new entrants.

The experience curve battle in the automotive industry is primarily concerned with the time it takes to bring a vehicle to the market. The Japanese are the best at new model development, with model changeovers occurring at roughly four-year intervals. Model runs for U.S. automakers are typically in the five to seven-year ranges. Honda is the champion at model launches with model-year changes. On the other hand, GM has had problematic launches of all its new vehicles over the past few years.

Dove suggested that manufacturing knowledge is one of the core competencies in the automotive industry and that management of knowledge provides a competitive advantage. The other area where experience plays a significant role is in new product design, or the period from conception to production.

Overall, experience curves play a vital role in helping to lower costs, improve efficiencies, and improve quality. The more experienced the company in the automobile industry, the more familiar and knowledgeable its employees are with design, process, manufacturing, sales, and marketing of the vehicle. Reaching efficient and profitable levels does not occur overnight, however. This goal requires many years to reach sustainable, productive, and profitable levels. Companies that have sustained themselves in this industry have a big advantage over newcomers. These advantages are observed in the areas of capital, manufacturing efficiencies, skilled labour, and capacities.

Capacity Utilisation

The world automobile industry has an excessive capacity of uncompetitive mass-production and an under-capacity of lean production manufacturing plants as automobile manufacturing capacity is increasing in developing countries. The automobile industry in Korea, Brazil, China, and India is going through impressive growth. Governments have played a key role in the evolution of the industry in all these developing countries. The Korean industry, despite its recent setback, has made the most significant progress and is now exporting cars to developed markets. It is the only country that invested in R&D for product development, retained management control in joint ventures with multinational companies, and had ambitious export targets. The industry in Brazil is controlled entirely by multinational corporations (MNCs). Although this situation has led to growth and the adoption of lean production, indigenous product development is lacking. Tariff barriers have come down, forcing domestic production to become more market responsive. Fluctuating tariffs and taxes and cyclical demand have characterised the industry. The Indian automotive industry is experiencing a revolution with rapid growth and the entry of nine MNCs, and another three planning to enter in the next two years. The Chinese industry is also growing very rapidly, although it is still highly fragmented. Passenger cars are only 15 per cent of total vehicle production in China. Demand in Brazil, India, and China is highly price sensitive, and growth is led by the demand for a small car. Higher taxes on mid- and large-size cars give the small car a big price advantage. Import duties for components imply that the supplier base in these countries needs to develop fast. The supplier industry in the emerging economies could become a bottleneck for growth.

A major implication is that the future in China and India, the two biggest potential markets with the highest growth rates, is uncertain (although bright). Governments seem to appreciate the necessity for stable policies and progressive deregulation and regard the automotive industry as one of the pillars of economic growth. Uncertainty exists about the extent of growth, the degree to which suppliers can meet demand, and the number of players that will be able to survive in the long run, however. The automotive MNCs have kept introducing their models that succeeded in the West to emerging markets. It remains to be seen whether this strategy will succeed. The Brazilian industry, which is much older than that of China or India, will probably continue to experience significant growth. Capacity is expected to increase in the next couple of years. Korean carmakers are also entering India and could enter other emerging markets, as well. Korea is a lucrative market for the automotive MNCs but is emerging as a trade partner rather than as a major net importer of cars. Daewoo, one of the Korean manufacturers, is a takeover subject by a Western multinational. With stagnation in developed markets and huge additions of capacity in emerging markets, market power of MNCs over car production could erode, although they will continue to dominate product development.

Nevertheless, with companies rushing to capture new markets in Asia and Latin America, analysts predict that the industry will have the capacity to produce about 22 million more vehicles than the world wants.

Table 5.1: Production Profile in the Global Automobile Industry—1999

Companies	*Annual Production (in Thousands)*
General Motors (GM, Opel, Vauxhaul, Saab)	7.497
Ford (Ford, Jaguar, Volvo)	7.100
Toyota (Toyota, Lexus, Duihatsu, Hino)	5.314
Renault-Nissan (Renault, Nissan, Mack)	4.820
Volkswagen (VW, Audi, Seat, Skoda, Lamborghini, Rolls-Royce)	4.818
DaimlerChrysler (combined for 2000)	4.749
Fiat (Fiat, Iveco, Alfa Romeo, Lancia, Ferrari, Maserati)	2.663
Honda	2.593
PSA Peugeot Citroen	2.270
Mitsubishi	1.542
Suzuki	1.253

R&D Partnership

Cooperation with a Non-Competitor: Genset (United States) and Algene Biotechnologies Corporation (Canada) entered into a strategic alliance for research on Alzheimer's disease. As a result of internal research activities over the past several years, Algene has compiled an extensive and comprehensively phenotyped collection of clinical samples from Alzheimer's patients within the Quebec population. A large number of patient phenotypes were confirmed by the presence of senile plaques and high concentrations of protein bundles (neurofibrillary tangles) in post-mortem diagnosis. By applying its gene mapping and statistical analysis platforms to these samples, Algene has identified several chromosomal regions that are susceptible to contain genes associated with Alzheimer's disease.

Under the strategic alliance, Algene will license its proprietary gene mapping results and provide access to its existing Alzheimer's disease DNA collections exclusively to Genset. In return, Genset will fund a one-year research programme at Algene to pursue further sample collection and analysis to provide DNA samples to Genset, which satisfies optimal genetic, epidemiological, and biostatistical criteria for a large case control association study.

Genset will use its integrated genomics technologies to rapidly generate proprietary biallelic markers in the chromosomal regions identified by Algene, perform high-throughput genotyping of the complete sample collection, and apply its advanced biostatistics and bioinformatics tools to analyse the resulting association data. Under the terms of the agreement, all intellectual property rights to the results of the programme will belong to Genset. Algene will receive licence fees and one-year programme funding with possible milestone payments based on the results of Genset's continued research and future revenues from the commercialisation of the programme's discoveries.

By combining its unique genomics approach using association studies with Algene's clinical expertise and exceptional clinical collection with well-characterised phenotypes, Genset hopes to rapidly discover and patent novel genes that will put it on the path towards better therapeutic options to deal with Alzheimer's disease. On the other hand, this agreement with Genset represents a major milestone for

Algene. Its Alzheimer's programme had reached a point where rapid progress towards the identification of associated genes required the scientific expertise, proprietary technology base, and critical mass of a major genomics partner. Genset is clearly the ideal ally for Algene to pursue the next phase of research in this programme and to eventually commercialise the results. This alliance also reflects the new business strategy at Algene, which aims for early strategic partnering of its gene discovery programmes to accelerate research and to generate revenue for the company.

Genset intends to establish targeted collaborative projects in the field of Alzheimer's research with pharmaceutical companies and to license its related gene discoveries for the discovery and development of novel drugs. Although both companies are collaborating on this Alzheimer's research, there was no indication that they would collaborate on the commercialisation of the results. Each company would more likely pursue their own paths after the research is completed.

Airline Industry and Global Alliances

In the past two decades, rising concentrations through mergers, acquisitions, and bankruptcies has marked the airline industry. "The top airlines have gained greater control over markets since the mid-1990s through code-sharing agreements with regional carriers, and more recently, through global marketing alliances." The U.S. deregulation of the airline industry in 1978 has dramatically modified the market, which required the carriers to adopt the use of a hub-and-spoke system of airport networks. Control over hub airports has intensified the competition and contributed to big losses, mergers, and several major bankruptcies in the United States.

Airlines derive most of their revenue from passenger fares; however, they also earn ancillary revenues from transporting mail, shipping freight, selling in-flight services, and from serving alcoholic beverages. The commercial airline industry concentrates its efforts on attracting the business traveller segment because it is the primary revenue for airline companies. Business travellers yield higher margins because they typically book flights that are paid for by their companies. Therefore, business travellers have a tendency to be price inelastic with regard to airfares. Consequently, airlines offer special deals to attract business travellers. These special services can include priority check-in, expedited baggage handling, luxury lounges, and in-flight amenities such as cellular phones, faxes, and outlets for laptop computer usage.

In contrast, leisure travellers are highly price conscious. They usually try to save money by using the Internet for comparisons, looking for discounted airfare, and accepting unusual flight schedules.

Airlines are classified according to their size of operation. There are primarily three kinds of airlines: major airlines, national airlines, and regional airlines. Major airlines encompass the most common types that travellers use because they have the greatest geographical reach. To be considered a major airline, an airline must have at least $1 billion in revenue. They usually operate with 130 to 450 seats per aircraft. Some even have aircraft that can travel 5,000 miles before refuelling. In this book, the focus will be on major airlines and their international partnerships.

National airlines are more limited to regional markets. A national airline can have between $100 million and $1 billion in revenue. National airlines usually operate aircraft with 100 to 150 seats. They operate short-haul trips because of their limited geographical reach. They specialise in point-to-point services. Regional airlines (called commuter airlines) serve low-density and short-haul markets. They primarily have point-to-point service up to 400 miles with fewer than 100 seats. Charter airlines usually transport passengers on an "on-call" basis. These are unscheduled services to various destinations.

Competitive Dynamics

Airlines compete for price and service to attract the consumer and vacationer market. But business travellers require flight frequency and reliability when choosing an airline. Airlines usually differentiate themselves from the competition through frequent-flyer programmes. These programmes enable travellers to accumulate bonus miles to receive discounts on future travel. They are often redeemed for free air tickets or service upgrades. These programmes are designed to promote repeat business and to solidify a customer's choice to use one airline carrier.

Airline fares fluctuate frequently. Airlines often reduce fares to attract leisure travellers; however, they rarely discount business fares because the demand for these seats is highly price inelastic. Passengers flying coach might get a variety of quoted fares. Walk-up fares (paid by passengers at departure) are the highest because consumers have less of a chance to compare competitors' fares. Airline seats are perishable inventory. To reduce the revenue loss, the airline industry develops sophisticated computer programmes to determine the demand by the hour, day, week, or month. Airlines also attempt to calculate how much a flight should be booked by a given point in time through a practice known as "yield management." Yield management alerts airlines to abnormal booking patterns, an estimated number of passengers, overbooking, the number of seats that can be overbooked, and how many customers will cancel.

Airline Operating Costs

Labour represents 35 per cent of an airline's costs. This amount includes costs for flight crews, flight attendants, ground service personnel, despatchers, maintenance crews, and customer service (booking and boarding). Most airline personnel belong to a union in the United States. Most union negotiations last a year before a settlement is reached. Then, a settlement lasts for about three years. Fuel costs are the second-largest operating cost category, representing approximately 10 per cent of costs. Some airlines hedge fuel prices by buying and selling futures on the commodity market. Weather can also affect airline costs and operations. Wind speed and air temperatures influence how much fuel an aircraft needs.

Weather is the second-largest cause of airline fatalities. The airline industry must obtain a detailed weather forecast that includes cloud height, horizontal visibility, wind speed, and direction. Aircraft itself represents about 10 per cent of total costs. Airlines either buy or lease their fleet of aircraft. Most airlines perform routine maintenance, but many outsource heavier repairs to firms that specialise in such business. Airlines are strictly regulated by government agencies (for example, the Federal Aviation Administration, or FAA, in the United States) for safety, labour, and operating procedures.

As major airlines face the competition of group alliances in the global market, they are subject to competition in domestic markets by other major players and regional players. Regional airlines have gained new ground with the development of newer, smaller jets that are faster than turbo-prop planes and that have greater ranges. The new regional jets have also made operating in previously underserved markets more cost-efficient. Recognising their potential, major U.S. carriers such as Delta Airlines, which owns regional carriers Delta Express, Atlantic Southeast, and COMAIR, and American Airlines, with its American Eagle, have sought to control all or part of the upstart regional airlines. There is a similar trend in Europe, where regional airlines are seeking partnerships with major airlines to more effectively gain access to certain hubs.

Major carriers merging with each other have not found an easy solution as they consolidate operations and fend off competitors. They have encountered strict scrutiny by regulatory agencies in the United States and Europe, as has been the case with United Airlines' bid for US Airways (still held up in review). Similar efforts have been stymied in Europe, as was the failed merger between KLM and Alitalia. Given this background information on the airline industry, we will turn to strategic alliances between airline companies and examine the salient characteristics of interfirm collaborations in the global airline industry.

Strategic Alliances Between Airlines

Airlines worldwide have been trying to strike a balance between cooperation and competition. They have been seeking alternatives to their conventional merger and acquisition strategies, such as strategic alliances, to expand services rapidly and to buttress market share without undertaking the difficult task of acquiring a rival. Nonetheless, collaboration in the airline industry presents a different picture from other industries we have examined so far. While airlines continue to establish links in the forms of equity participation and contractual alliances with the leadership of major airlines, others engage in networks of constellations of players. As we will explain, STAR and OneWorld as networks of airlines include a number of individual airlines. On the other hand, there are also a number of dyadic relationships reflecting cooperation between two airlines. For example, British Airways and Aer Lingus signed a cooperative agreement while American Airlines and Swiss/Sabena agreed on a code-sharing. A number of European and U.S. airlines have also developed trans-Atlantic alliances.

Table 5.2: Trans-Atlantic Airline Alliances

Airline Pairs	*Flights per Week*	*No. of U.S. Cities*	*No. of European Cities*
American Airlines—Sabena (Belgium)	49	5	1
Delta Airlines—Air France	147	9	3
Northwest Airlines—KLM (Netherlands)	126	13	1
United Airlines—Lufthansa (Germany)	268	11	3
United Airlines—SAS (Denmark, Sweden, and Norway)	82	4	3

Source: The airlines' annual reports.

Many airlines are still partially owned by their respective nations, and treaties between them determine which airlines can land in which locations. To get around national laws and regulatory problems and to compete effectively, airlines have formed global networks and individual alliances.

Basically, major airlines from the United States, Europe, and Asia-Pacific have forged their own alliance groups to offer better services internationally. It is estimated that international travel will grow faster than domestic U.S. travel. Consequently, U.S. domestic carriers find it advantageous to create collaborative ventures with international carriers as an entry point into new markets. Thus, airline alliances can be studied in three primary forms as referred to in the general Strategic Alliance Model. First, *equity participation* refers to one airline buying equity into another to build an organic tie and to control a target airline. Second, *bilateral cooperative alliances* mean an agreement between two airlines involving non-equity in dyadic relationships. Third, *network alliances* are a group of airlines collaborating on a number of marketing activities.

Equity Participation

A number of airlines have bought equity stakes in other airlines to build a formal link and to mould their collaboration into a formal structure. Principal equity participations by major airlines into others are given in Table 5.1. Through such equity holdings, the investing airline company can influence strategic directions of the target airline and develop complementary activities to its own operations. Of course, building such a formal link between two airlines brings them closer to each other and entices cooperation between them.

Bilateral Cooperative Agreements

Commonly, we see two airlines cooperating on code-sharing, frequent-flyer mileage programmes, and other expanded passenger services. A major component of many airline alliances, however, is code-sharing, which refers to replicating seamless travel that would be provided by a single airline. This system is called "interline service" in the industry. Interline service offers airline passengers the convenience of single ticketing and check-in. With code-sharing, a passenger carrier can advertise its alliance partner's flights as its own, and without adding new aircraft it can increase the number of destinations and frequency flights it offers.

Table 5.3: Equity Holdings between Airlines

Investor Airline	*Nationality*	*Target Airline*	*Nationality*	*Equity Stake*
British Airways	U.K.	Qantas	Australia	25%
British Airways	U.K.	Iberia Airlines	Spain	9%
SAir Group	Switzerland	Sabena	Belgium	49.5%
SAir Group	Switzerland	LTU	France	49.9%
SAir Group	Switzerland	LOT Polish	Poland	37.5%
Singapore Airlines	Singapore	Virgin Atlantic	U.K.	49%
Singapore Airlines	Singapore	Air New Zealand	New Zealand	25%
SAS Scandinavian	Sweden	British Midway	U.K.	20%
SAS Scandinavian	Sweden	Widoroe	Norway	63%
SAS Scandinavian	Sweden	Cimber Air	Denmark	26%
KLM Royal Dutch	Netherlands	Kenyan Airlines	Kenya	25%
KLM Royal Dutch	Netherlands	Air Littoral	France	35%
KLM Royal Dutch	Netherlands	ALM Antillean	U.S.	40%

Bilateral Cooperative Agreements

British Airways	Aer Lingus
American Airlines	Swissair/Sabena
United Airlines	Singapore Airlines
SAS	Singapore Airlines
Air Canada	Singapore Airlines
Lufthansa	Singapore Airlines
Northwest Airlines	KLM Royal Dutch Airlines
Air France	Delta Airlines
Air France	Aeromexico
Air France	Korean Airlines

Alliance Networks

Recently, many airlines around the world have joined in alliance networks to compete effectively by providing superior customer services. Principal airline networks include STAR, OneWorld, SkyTeam, and Qualiflyer.

STAR: The first alliance group was STAR, which was established on May 14, 1997. The Star Alliance group consists of United Airlines, Lufthansa, SAS, Air Canada, Mexicana, Air New Zealand, British Midland Airways, Austrian Airlines (former Qualiflyer member), Lauda Air Luftfahrt AG (former Qualiflyer member), Tyrolean, Singapore Airlines, Thai Airways, All Nippon Airways, Varig, and Ansett Transport Industries. The STAR group seems to be the most established and the largest alliance network, consisting of 15 airlines. It offers a wide range of flights in many countries.

OneWorld: It consists of eight full members including American Airlines, British Airways, Cathay Pacific, Finnair, Aer Lingus, Qantas Airways, Iberia, LanChile, and 23 affiliates. Between them, they offer services to 550 destinations in 133 countries, with their 270,000 employees operating fleets of more than 1,850 aircraft, carrying some 210 million passengers in 2000. The alliance is largely restricted to sharing frequent flyer schemes, airport lounges, and some marketing. Because all the members of OneWorld have their own frequent-flyer programmes, OneWorld has created a set of symbols: OneWorld Emerald, Sapphire, and Ruby. Regulators refuse to let them make the next steps of selling seats on each other's flights and coordinating schedules and prices.

SkyTeam: It consists of Delta Airlines, Air France, Aero Mexico, and Korean Air. The SkyTeam airlines carry a combined 174.3 million passengers per year, trailing the Star Alliance (which is led primarily by United Airlines and Lufthansa). The group sees the Star Alliance as its only real competition, but the alliance still has a long way to go.

In addition, we will discuss two airline network attempts that resulted in failure.

Qualiflyer: The network, which was initiated by SAir Group (Swissair and Sabena), consists of Swissair, Sabena, Crossair, OAM, Air Liberte, Ait Littoral, TAP Air Portugal, PGA Portugalia Airlines, Air Europe, Volare, and LOT Polish Airlines. Swissair, a leader in the group, introduced a symbolic gesture by painting its aircraft with a blue belly as a sign of the Qualiflyer membership. The group focused on only the European market, which limited its geographic scope. Swissair admitted failure in its attempt to build the Qualiflyer alliance around a group of carriers in which it was taking substantial minority stakes, although some frequent-flyer programmes still continue among the member airlines.

WINGS: The Wings Group used to include Northwest Airlines, Continental Airlines, KLM, and Alitalia, but after KLM's disengagement with Alitalia, the group dissolved. The original cooperation between KLM and Northwest goes back to 1993. It appears that the two leading partners were KLM, with its affiliate Alitalia, and Northwest, with its affiliate Continental Airlines. Obviously, the group had limited partners, most notably none from the Asia-Pacific region.

Through such networks, airlines seek to exploit each other's resources, which include additional routes and marketing strategies as well as code-sharing agreements, without incurring the high costs of expansion. For customers, airline alliances offer broader frequent-flyer programmes, stream-lined travel, and simplified systems for purchasing tickets. A review of those airline networks indicates that most airlines feel that to compete effectively with less regulatory hassles and minimum risky investments, they must have connecting flights in three continents: North America, Europe, and Asia-Pacific. All strategic groups have flight connections to North America, Europe, and Asia-Pacific. Thus, the present strategic networks seem to ignore Latin America, but all major U.S. airlines cover Latin America sufficiently. Also, Iberia Airlines in OneWorld and Aeromexico in SkyTeam have numerous flights to South America. Additionally, some airlines have, if not network alliances, dyadic relationships with major Latin American airlines to complement their North American flights.

Telecommunications Industry and Global Alliances

Like other industries, one of the dominant characteristics of the telecommunications industry is the augmenting number of consolidations (mergers and acquisitions) and alliances. Competitive advantage in this industry depends considerably upon economies of scale. Consequently, many firms in the telecommunications industry worldwide have sought economies of scale through numerous mergers, acquisitions, and alliances. Bell Atlantic first merged with Nynex and then merged with GTE and formed Verizon Communications, while SBC Communications and Bell South formed a joint venture called Cingular Wireless. Qwest Communications acquired U.S. West, and SBC Communications acquired the Ameritech Corporation.

Major Telephone Mergers in 2000

As the industry continues to consolidate, it seems that the remaining players are shifting their focus away from slow-growth core markets, such as local and long-distance service, to emphasise greater growth areas such as broadband data, wireless, and international markets. These top-tier global players include WorldCom, AT&T, SBC Communications, and Verizon Communications (formerly Bell Atlantic and GTE). The second tier of global competitors includes Global Crossing, Sprint Phone Group, Qwest Communications (with merger partner U.S. West and investor Bell South), British Telecommunications PLC, and Deutsche Telekom AG.

Table 5.4: Top Telephone Company Mergers as of August 2000

Companies	*Amount (billion $)*
Vodafone-Mannesman	180.0
SBS-Ameritech	109.1
Bell Atlantic-GTE	95.0
Vodafone-AirTouch	66.0
AT&T-Media One	55.0

Source: Companies' annual reports.

British Vodafone (now a partner in Verizon), Deutsche Telekom, and France Telecom appear to be aggressive suitors with an appetite for U.S. exposure and the necessary cash to back it up. Deutsche Telekom has already agreed to acquire wireless provider VoiceStream Wireless, which will give a valuable extension of its Global System for Mobile (GSM) communications network.

On the European side, France Telecom acquired Orange plc of Britain from Vodafone AirTouch plc for 25.1 billion pounds ($37.66 billion U.S. dollars) in cash and stock. While the transaction creates the second-largest mobile-phone group in Europe, it also intensifies the battle for wireless customers in Europe. France Telecom will combine its own mobile operations with those of Orange and sell 10 per cent to 15 per cent of the combined wireless concern in an initial public offering in 2001. In actuality, Vodafone was forced to dispose of Orange to win regulatory approval for its acquisition of Mannesmann AG of Germany. France Telecom already owns the Itineris wireless network in France and controls operators in Belgium, the Netherlands, Denmark, and parts of Eastern Europe. The combined wireless operation has 21 million subscribers now and expects to raise that number to 30 million by adding Orange, which is the third-largest mobile-phone operator in Britain. France Telecom's more immediate plan is to bid for more third-generation wireless licences in Europe that would enable the company to offer Internet and data services on cellular phones. Nevertheless, several ambitious cross-border mergers recently in Europe have collapsed over disagreements about issues ranging from government ownership to management positions to a fight about the location of a company's headquarters. Previous unsuccessful merger attempts include Deutsche Telekom-Telecom Italia, Telia-Telenor, British Telecom-Telefonica, and Telefonika-KPN. The most recent resistance to WorldCom's attempt to buy Sprint PCS originated in Europe and resulted in a refusal by the U.S. government.

Principal characteristics of and trends in the telecommunications industry can be outlined as follows:
(a) Falling telecommunications costs: Technological advancements such as fibre optics, digital transmissions, and

satellite communications have reduced prices and will continue to do so. In the future, quality or bandwidth will determine telecommunications prices rather than distance between users or the duration of a call; (b) Privatisation of state-owned telecom monopolies: A number of nations around the world have allowed new entrants into their markets with newer and cheaper services especially in wireless market. Quite a number of nations have either privatised or been in the process of privatising their telecommunications monopolies to attract advanced technologies or raise capital. They have relatively opened their markets to foreign competition in long-distance and wireless markets, although most are reluctant to open their local voice markets; (c) The Internet and related technologies: As the Internet connections augment tremendously every year through a variety of devices (computers, wireless phones, televisions, and automobiles), traditional telecommunications services such as telephony, facsimile, e-mail, and audio and video files are sent over the Internet at a lower cost. Although many of these services do not provide the same quality and reliability yet as standard telecommunications do, the high demand for these services will enhance the current quality by greater R&D and applications. As a result of Internet advancements, there is a transition from voice telecommunications to data telecommunications. It is estimated that there will be a reversal of voice and data transmission in global traffic in the future. Data networks, private networks, network intelligence, and network applications are the high-growth markets of the future.

Telecommunications in information markets represent three major segments: **content** (creating information), **communication** (moving information), and **application** (using information). The communication segment will consist of only one-third of the total market. It was recommended that companies in the telecommunications industry use effective segmentation to exploit the opportunities in the information market. However these segments have become blurred in recent years. As we will describe, forging alliances between companies is one way to deal with these different or converging segments and services.

Another emerging characteristic of the telecommunications industry is the rapid advancement of wireless communications by adding text and pictures to voice transmissions. Because of wireless communication's significant impact on the industry, we will look at it closely.

Wireless Communications

Wireless communications present the fastest growing segment of the industry. There has been a growing demand for wireless services for both voice and data transmissions. Although voice communication has dominated the telecommunications market from the beginning, as wireless carriers scramble to integrate data applications into their wireless services, this trend has been changing rapidly. "The catalyst driving this trend is the third-generation (3G) of wireless communications, which is making inroads into Japan and Korea and should spread throughout Europe in a few years. This information wave should hit U.S. shores around 2004, giving consumers the opportunity to use one mobile device for all of their communication needs." The potential market of cellular phones is huge. It is estimated that one billion people, or one of every six people on Earth, will own cell phones in three years. Many of the newer digital models will carry software that enables the user to access basic information—sports scores, stock prices, airline schedules, and the weather—from the Web. The most sophisticated "smart" phones will include an operating system, which means that users can retrieve files, manage address books and calendars, and even compose documents with a mini keyboard. But the bulk of the market is likely to be in "feature" phones that lack full operating systems.

Primary competitors in the U.S. wireless industry are broadband personal communication services (PCS) providers and cellular wireless companies, both of which operate networks based on a system of geographic cells. Other players include enhanced specialised mobile radio (ESMR) operators, which concentrate their signals on despatch channels. Industry wireless revenues topped $40 billion in 1999, up 21 per cent from 1998. As of year-end 1999, roamer revenues represented about 10 per cent of the revenue base. The industry's cumulative capital investment in wireless rose 18 per cent year to year to $71.3 billion in 1999. Based on 1999 wireless revenues, the largest domestic operators were Verizon (a joint venture between Bell Atlantic/GTE and Vodafone AirTouch, with $16 billion, which we will discuss next), SB Communications and Bell South ($10 billion), AT&T Wireless Services ($7.6 billion), Nextel Communications ($3.3), and Sprint PCS ($3.2 billion). In 1999, British wireless provider Vodafone Group acquired AirTouch, forming Vodafone AirTouch. Subsequently, the company formed a strategic U.S. national wireless alliance with Bell Atlantic (and its merger partner, GTE) called Verizon. In April 2000, SBC and Bell South formed a national wireless joint venture called Cingular.

In terms of the population of the U.S. markets (called U.S. POPs) that a firm is licensed to serve, the leading wireless companies as of year-end 1999 were AT&T Wireless Services (314.6 million POPs), Sprint PCS (234 million), Verizon (179.3 million), Nextel (165.3 million), NextWave Personal Communications (152.9 million), and Omnipoint (126.6 million). This listing by POPs differs markedly from market share rankings by revenues or number of subscribers. POPs rank the major wireless players as far as prospective customers are concerned. The list suggests potential market position as the industry enters a phase of accelerated development, expansion, and in all probability, consolidation.

British-based Vodafone is the biggest mobile phone company in the world, with more than 65 million customers in 25 countries on five continents. Vodafone took over Mannesman of Germany and Omnitel of Italy in 2000. These takeovers made continental Vodafone the fastest growing division, with 4.38 million new customers. The company added more than 1.46 million new customers in the Americas and

Asia-Pacific region, taking its total to 16.25 million. Its newly formed United Kingdom, Middle East, and Africa division (grouping four countries) added 770,000 customers. The company, however, uses strategic alliances in numerous countries. Another big player is NTT DoCoMo, which holds the highest market share in Japan. Both companies have been pursuing strategies to enter and expand in the U.S. wireless market, as we will describe next.

The mobile-phone sector presents a dynamic, competitive landscape with interesting developments. While major players are competing fiercely, they are cooperating to develop new technologies and services because they want to combine the convenience of cellular phones with the use of the Internet. To accomplish this task, a variety of collaborations are underway.

While alliances are common in the industry, the latest agreements did not preclude further alliances with others in the future. It seems that this situation is really the future of modern telecommunications, because no company can excel in every area.

Telecommunications Alliances

Although it is futile to try to describe the state of affairs in telecommunications alliances because they change on a regular basis, examining some of the major attempts and events provides insight into this industry's dynamics and future. There had been three primary global alliances—Concert, Global One, and World Partners—of which the first two are already over. These alliances illustrate different approaches to globalisation. Concert and Global One were primarily equity relationships. First, in Concert, British Telecom purchased a 20 per cent stake in MCI, which was acquired by WorldCom later and became MCI WorldCom. Second, Deutsche-Telekom, France Telecom, and Sprint (United States) formed Global One. According to the agreement, each European partner purchased 10 per cent of Sprint. But there was disappointment with Global One, and at the end French Telecom took over the venture. The third global telecommunications business, World

Partners, is a combination of equity stakes and agreements on billing, marketing, interconnection, and so on. Operated largely by AT&T and Unisource, a European alliance that has included Telecom Italia (Italy), Telia (Sweden), Swiss Telecom, and KPN (Netherlands), World Partners also includes KDD (the incumbent international carrier for Japan), Telstra (Australia), and Unitel, a Canadian long-distance carrier. World Partners largely relies upon contractual agreements. Because of the large number of companies involved in this partnership, it seems to be the only practical model. It might also be that many of the relationships have grown out of the pre-liberalisation contract and settlement arrangements. It is not yet clear whether World Partners' business model will succeed. Two major companies, Telefonica and Telecom Italia, have had inconsistent relationships with the alliance. Telefonica left the alliance while Telecom Italia has made moves to leave World Partners to join Cable & Wireless in multinational ventures.

A close examination of strategic alliances in the telecommunications industry reveals that most of such alliances are "pure play" alliances; that is, ventures in which partners offered unlike (but closely related) products, technologies, and markets. These markets are usually in the same market segments, such as content, communications, and applications. Verizon Wireless is an example of such a pure play alliance between Bell Atlantic/GTE and Vodafone Air Touch, a joint venture established to compete head-on with AT&T in the U.S. wireless market. Another type of alliance is "converging alliances," which means two companies from different industries collaborating because of converging technologies, enabling innovative services.

Microsoft, for example, invested $1 billion for an 11.5 per cent share in an alliance with Comcast, the fourth largest U.S. cable operator, to support cable modem entry into telephony and data access to homes. Microsoft also invested $10 million in Teledesic, a low-Earth orbit satellite communications network of which McCaw and Boeing are also partners. Converging alliances are formed when participating technologies or markets are on a converging path. In studying telecommunications alliances, we will again use the typology introduced in Chapter 3 as equity (joint ventures and equity participation) and non-equity alliances.

We will analyse joint ventures in the telecommunications industry, the Ericsson-Microsoft mobile venture, and the Vodafone joint venture in New Zealand. Each case presents different dimensions of the model, but they all are attempts to achieve the objective of market penetration.

Verizon Wireless Joint Ventures

In 2000, the Bell Atlantic Corporation/GTE and Vodafone AirTouch formed a joint venture called Verizon Wireless with $16 billion, creating a major player in the industry. Verizon Wireless is the largest wireless communications provider in the United States, with 27.5 million wireless voice and data customers. The new company includes the assets of Bell Atlantic Mobile, AirTouch Cellular, GTE Wireless, PrimeCo Personal Communications, and AirTouch Paging. The company has a footprint covering nearly 90 per cent of the U.S. population, 49 of the top 50 and 96 of the top 100 U.S. markets. Verizon Wireless, with its 38,000 employees, is a strong contender in the U.S. wireless phone market. Verizon Wireless will have the national scale and scope to realise revenue enhancements, cost savings, and capital efficiencies. The company will achieve expense savings through reduced roaming costs and increased economies of scale in transport, billing volumes, handset purchases, and advertising. Combining common Code Division Multiple Access (CDMA) technology platforms will also yield capital efficiencies, simplified integration, and superior network quality.

At the initial stage, both partners concluded that they needed each other or that they were not self-sufficient, so they preferred a joint venture to internalisation or market transactions. At the formulation stage, Bell Atlantic/GTE—despite its experience and capability in traditional telecommunications areas—wanted to deploy asymmetrical competencies of Vodafone, which has been the largest wireless company in the world. Also, it needed a cash infusion for its infrastructure investments. From the standpoint of Vodafone, Bell Atlantic/GTE looked at suitable partners with established market shares and experience in the traditional telecommunications business but with little experience in wireless communications. Vodafone's perception was that by deploying the organisational capabilities of its partners, it could easily expand in the U.S. wireless market rather than struggling for a green-field investment or searching for another qualified partner.

At the operational stage, both partners hold sufficient equity of the joint venture to control operations. After the close of the Bell Atlantic-GTE merger, Bell Atlantic-GTE will own 55 per cent and Vodafone AirTouch will own 45 per cent of the wireless joint venture. The board has seven members with four designated by Bell Atlantic and three chosen by Vodafone AirTouch. It is too early to draw any conclusions concerning Verizon's financial performance, however. It is apparent, though, that Verizon presently holds the highest market share in the U.S. wireless market. The assessment at the outcome stage is not appropriate at this point because the venture is so recent. Time will decide the satisfaction level of the partners—whether they will continue with this business or exit from the current joint venture.

Ericsson Microsoft Mobile Venture

The software giant Microsoft has been struggling to expand its software, Windows CE, for use in the cellular phone sector. It has not shown the same success as its Windows operating system in personal computers (PCs), however, as in the cellular phone market. As a result, Microsoft has developed Mobile Explorer, which enables browsing the Internet through mobile phones.

Microsoft got its foot in the door in what could be a hot market for cell phones that surf the Internet—a field where big phone makers had shunned the software giant. Sweden's

Telefon AB LM, Ericsson agreed to form a joint venture with Microsoft. Ericsson would use a scaled-down Web browser from Microsoft in some of its phones. We must also note, however, that Ericsson had also been engaged in Epoc, a competing operating system developed by Sambian (which we will discuss later). Ericsson owns 70 percent of the joint venture and also supplies most of the initial staff of 100 engineers. The venture company is based in Stockholm with regional offices around the world. The venture's first product—e-mail for cell phones—has already been launched.

The two companies with different backgrounds combined their resources to establish a viable product/service. This joint venture is a typical example of converging alliances, as we defined previously. The joint venture breathes new life into Microsoft's desire to become a major supplier of software for Internet-based cell phones. Microsoft's attempts to market its Windows CE operating system to cellular handset manufacturers have been a disappointment. Cell-phone makers and service providers have complained that Windows CE requires too much processor power to use in compact phones. As a result, the large mobile-phone manufacturers had ignored Microsoft's efforts.

Microsoft, nevertheless, still hopes that Windows CE will displace Epoc. But in the meantime, it has made an important move in penetrating the mobile-phone market with its new Mobile Explorer, a "microbrowser" that runs on multiple operating systems in addition to Windows CE (including the Epoc system). This concept is a kind of defence on the part of Microsoft, instead of fighting with four major cellular phone manufacturers. Microsoft expects the following benefits from this partnership. Once Microsoft's Mobile Explorer is up and running on Epoc-based phones, Microsoft is likely to persuade Ericsson and others to take the next step—installing Microsoft's Windows CE on newer models that pack more computing power. Microsoft also hopes to gain an advantage by attracting more traffic to its online service, MSN, and it intends to sell software that powers large computers that run the new wireless services. Its whole strategy is to tie the client's handsets to its server. On the other hand, Ericsson expects to benefit from this venture because it could sell more of its handsets to users, especially those who use some form of Windows applications on their personal computers (such as Outlook, an e-mail service). The new venture also plans to develop tools to synchronise software from PCs and mobile phones, which will enable users to carry updated electronic calendars on their mobile phones.

At the initial stage, both companies—Microsoft and Ericsson—expected some synergistic benefits from combining their resources and capabilities (such as Microsoft's Windows CE and Ericsson's widespread market) as an established wireless handset manufacturer and seller. The partners wanted to exploit their core competencies for a competitive advantage.

At the formation stage, Ericsson has chosen Microsoft, which happens to have the Windows CE operating system for wireless units at a risk of damaging its earlier alliance in Symbian, where its major competitors are also partners. The company probably wanted to go alone or to not lose time in incorporating an effective operating system into its wireless handsets. On the other hand, Microsoft needed a lift from a major mobile-phone operator such as Ericsson that would adopt its Windows CE operating system.

Therefore, Microsoft perceived Ericsson as a suitable partner. The joint venture partnership represents the deployment of asymmetrical competencies of both partners.

Ericsson's decision to link with Microsoft threw the old alignment with other manufacturers into confusion. Its Symbian partners might have considered that Ericsson had defected to Microsoft. Ericsson, however, announced that it had no intentions of abandoning Epoc. By this action, Ericsson has developed strategic alliances in both areas to ensure its competitive positions in the future.

As far as the operations and outcome stages are concerned, it is inappropriate to comment on them at this point because it is too soon to say whether the Windows CE operating system will find a wide acceptance as a result of this alliance.

Vodafone's Joint Venture in New Zealand

We can examine Vodafone's joint venture in New Zealand in the context of the joint venture model, as well. At the initial stage, while Vodafone wanted to expand into the New Zealand market, Telstra Saturn, cable TV, landline, and Internet companies in New Zealand decided to diversify themselves with the help of a major mobile-phone player such as Vodafone so that the synergies of two companies would lead to a considerable competitive advantage in the New Zealand market. Consequently, Vodafone of the United Kingdom and Telstra Saturn of New Zealand formed a strategic alliance, creating the biggest "cross network" competition to Telecom, an existing mobile phone operator in New Zealand. In other words, the telecommunications players Vodafone and Telstra Saturn are increasing the pressure on the local company Telecom by teaming up to offer combined services at sharp discounts. The joint venture will mean new services for customers in 2001, such as using the same number for both landline and cell phones, both at home and for business, and a single electronic voice mailbox for both phone services. Also, the companies will offer bundled services, including Telstra Saturn's fixed phone line, TV, and Internet and Vodafone mobile phone services.

Bundling services invariably meant cheaper deals on the standalone costs. It also meant "huge opportunities" to bundle other services for the thousands who presently bought pre-pay phones. The discounts for bundled services would be significant, although they would not be drawn on likely price cuts. Both companies would have the capability to bundle the combined products and send one bill by the company that made the sale. The alliance would not mean any shareholding arrangements between the two companies. In other words, cross-shareholdings had not been subject.

Vodafone has 638,000 mobile phone customers, about 38 per cent of the total market, and 50,000 mobile Internet users. Vodafone has spent $300 million since arriving in New Zealand at the end of 1998. Vodafone already has an alliance with Clear in New Zealand, but the new link with Telstra Saturn would not affect that relationship. Interestingly, Vodafone is a competitor with Telstra in Australia.

Telstra Saturn put a fixed-line backbone network through New Zealand and had a range of services. Telstra Saturn has about 33,000 landline phone customers in Wellington and 20,000 pay TV customers, about 5 per cent less than Sky TV's market share in Wellington. It is expanding in Christchurch and Auckland.

The joint venture would develop integrated products and services across the combined fixed and mobile networks. It would also strengthen the existing supply agreement where Telstra Saturn and Vodafone use each other's networks. The alliance would not affect either company's individual developments, including the purchase of second and third-generation spectra. Again, although it is early to judge the operations and outcomes of the joint venture, it has been stable so far.

Equity Participation

The following examples illustrate a different form of alliances: equity participation—one telecommunications company buying some equity stakes into another telecommunications company to establish organic ties so that mutual interests of both companies can be pursued in collaboration. Through equity stakes, telecommunications companies have built an important link to work towards their mutual objectives.

The AT&T-NTT DoCoMo Alliance

NTT DoCoMo, the Japanese telecommunications giant, after achieving a spectacular growth in cellular phones in Japan, used equity participation to expand its mobile Internet services worldwide. The company's objective is to use its stakes in cellular phone carriers to promote 3G services worldwide and to build economies of scale that would motivate Websites to build interesting applications for 3G phones and to give phone makers a larger market for their wares. To that end, it invested around $17 billion in minority stakes in cellular operations in Asia, Europe, and most recently in the United States. For example, it invested $9.8 billion for a 16 per cent stake in AT&T's Wireless unit—one of the largest investments ever by a Japanese company in a foreign company. NTT DoCoMo has an ambitious plan for the U.S. market, such as repeating its Japanese success in the United States. In Japan, "it has signed up 15 million subscribers to its wireless Web service in under two years and has added as many as 50,000 new customers a day. DoCoMo's mobile Internet service, called i-mode, allows people to do such things as download news and cartoons, and check their bank balances on cell phones." After its first launch in early 1999, I-mode has become popular among young Japanese. DoCoMo combined standard Internet technology and flashy marketing to quickly expand the service beyond its initial projections. The key to its success was getting others—newspapers, restaurants, and video game makers—to format miniature versions of their Internet sites to fit on I-mode's tiny screens. Now, Japanese can order sushi, book plane tickets, or play a video game on their mobile phones. The company already offers a small number of English-language I-mode services in Japan, such as ones from CNN and Bloomberg News, and is helping Japanese content providers set up services for the U.S. market. DoCoMo eventually could increase its stake in AT&T Wireless to 17.2 per cent and will acquire five-year warrants to purchase up to an additional 41.7 million shares of AT&T Wireless at $35 each, the deal represents an important step towards closing the gap between mobile phone technology in the United States and Japan. Japan has more advanced mobile phone technology, such as 3G telecommunications and I-mode technology.

CHAPTER 6

Global Banking

The Continuous Restructuring of Global Financial Services

Financial people know in their bones that their profession goes back a long way. Its frequent association with "the oldest profession" may occur simply because it is almost as old. After all, the technology of finance is very basic, requiring little more than simple arithmetic and minimal literacy, and the environment in which it applies is universal—that is, any situation that involves money, property, or credit, all of which are commodities that have been in demand since humankind's earliest days.

These financial commodities have been put to use to facilitate trade, commerce, and business investment and to accommodate the accumulation, preservation, and distribution of wealth by states, corporations, and individuals. Financial transactions can occur in an almost infinite variety, yet they always require the services of banks, whether acting as principal or as agent, and financial markets in which they may operate.

Banks, too, therefore have a long history—a history rich in product diversity, international scope, and, above all, continuous change and adaptation. Generally, the latter have been required to adjust to changed economic and regulatory conditions, which have on many occasions been drastic. On such occasions banks have collapsed, only to be replaced by others eager to enter this traditionally dangerous but profitable business. New competitors have continually appeared on the scene, especially during periods of rapid economic growth, opportunity, and comparatively light governmental interference. Competitive changes have forced adaptations too, and in general have improved the level and efficiency of services banks offer to clients, thereby increasing transactional volume. The one constant in the long history of banking is, perhaps, the sight of new stars rising and old ones setting. Some of the older ones have been able to transform themselves into players capable of competing with the newly powerful houses, but many have not. Thus the banking industry has much natural familiarity with economic restructuring.

It is doubtful, however, that there has ever been a time in the long history of banking that the pace of restructuring has been greater than the present. Banking and securities markets during the 1980s and 1990s in particular have been affected by a convergence of several exceptionally powerful forces—deregulation and re-regulation, rapidly increasing competition and disintermediation, product innovation and technology—all of which have occurred in a spiralling expansion of demand for financial services across the globe. Bankers today live in interesting, if exhausting and hazardous, times.

The Legacies of Global Banking

The legacies of global banking history reveal that both bankers and credit were plentiful and active in the ancient world. The recorded legal history of several great civilisations started with elaborate regulation of credit, such as the Code of Hammurabi, about 1800 B.C.E., where the famous Babylonian set forth, among other laws, the maximum rate of interest for loans of grain ($33^{1}/_{3}$ per cent) and of silver (20 per cent).

In the Ancient World

Maritime trade abounded in the Mediterranean, and was already highly developed by the Greeks and the Phoenicians in 1000 B.C.E. Such trade involved long-distance shipment of commodities that were not locally available. Wherever trade occurred there had to be a means of payment acceptable to both sides, often obtained only through the good offices of a bank represented in both countries acting as a foreign exchange or bill broker.

Banks also helped the merchants, shipowners, and, later, public officials manage their money—sometimes by accepting it on deposit, sometimes by investing it for them in precious metals, stones, or the financial assets of the day. One could make money on money long before Alexander the Great.

By the second century C.E., the Romans, then at their peak, had reorganised everything. Their power in the Mediterranean was absolute, peace reigned along its shores, piracy had been eliminated, trade flourished, and coinage was available throughout the Empire. Bankers and financiers prospered. Will Durant described them as follows:

> One of the streets adjoining the forum became a banker's row, crowded with the shops of the moneylenders and money-changers. Money could be borrowed on land, crops, securities, or government contracts, and for financing commercial enterprises or voyages. Cooperative lending took the place of [commercial] insurance; instead of one banker completely underwriting a venture, several joined in providing the funds. Joint-stock companies existed chiefly for the performance of government contracts . . . they raised their capital by selling their stocks or bonds to the public in the form of *partes or particulae,* i.e., "little parts," or "shares."

Under other circumstances this financial and commercial infrastructure might have grown to produce large international banking and trading companies of the kind that exist today. However, this didn't happen in the Roman period, largely, it seems, because the state, focused as it was on conquest and strict control of its empire through efficient administration, reserved for itself the principal financial powers in the society. As the state was the principal holder of capital, it became the principal dispenser of it too, lending large sums to the public, no doubt accompanied by some degree of corruption. Perhaps to preserve this convenient arrangement the Roman senate did not permit limited liability companies to be formed, thus keeping the private wealth of the Empire where it could best be controlled, among individuals.

In any case, large banks and commercial houses never emerged in the Roman days, though banking transactions themselves were plentiful on a small scale. This may have proved to be a contributing cause in the decline of the Empire, which along with political deterioration suffered acute economic decay. In the third century much economic difficulty was experienced, including the "great crash" of 259—after the Emperor Valerian had been taken captive—when markets collapsed and there were runs on banks in various parts of the empire.

During the following century Roman economic decline was irreversible. Money and gold bullion were leaving the Empire in a great payments drain (they ended up in the Near East and in India). The population was declining and barbarians had to be brought in to replenish the dwindling supply of workers. Wealth had become highly concentrated at the top, and the nouveau riche had been suppressed. Society's savings were dissipated in consumption, military conquests were no longer being undertaken to resupply the state with plunder and slaves, and the Empire itself was breaking into two parts, with most of the action taking place in the eastern capital, Constantinople.

After the Romans

The rest, sadly, we know, though one historian of the period, Harold Mattingly, a distinguished Cambridge University scholar and expert on Roman finance, makes a curious observation:

> The possibilities at the disposal of an all-powerful state are enormous, if it can [utilise] its resources in money, natural wealth and man-power. If the Roman State could have been administered by a syndicate of men of modern capacity in banking and industry, there might have been rationalisation on a magnificent scale. The State might have been able to meet all demands upon it and still have left its subjects to enjoy a very fair measure of prosperity. If it failed to realise all these possibilities, that will have been due to lack of knowledge as well as lack of interest.

This thought brings to mind the Communist "empire" of our century, the collapse of which in the late 1980s might equally have been avoided if its rulers (like the Chinese) had understood free-market capitalism just a little bit better.

The Roman Empire collapsed in the fifth century. It was succeeded by the Byzantine Empire, which ruled in the eastern Mediterranean until the Arab conquests in the seventh century, which in turn diminished its scope and power.

In the western Mediterranean, in the absence of Romans, trade between the great ports and up the rivers leading into them was sporadic, again interrupted by pirates, but totally lacking in finance. After the Arab conquests, trade flourished but European trade did not. For all practical purposes it was in limbo for several hundred years. From the point of view of European bankers and financiers, these truly were the Dark Ages.

Where there was no trade, economic life collapsed back upon villages or counties. People consumed what they grew or raised or made, and no more. There were no surpluses beyond local needs, as there were neither markets to send them to nor any way to send them. No trade, no money, no finance—there was nothing to buy with money anyway. From this stagnant, landlocked condition the feudal system emerged, digging its roots deeply into European life.

Upward Mobility in the Middle Ages

With the rekindling of trade, of course, came opportunity for those seeking it—often, no doubt, those on the bottom rungs of society as it was then inflexibly cast.

A French historian of the Middle Ages, Henri Pirenne, repeats the story of one St. Godric of Finchale as an example of the way the nouveau riche were formed in the latter part of the eleventh century. Godric was born of poor peasant stock in Lincolnshire, and was forced, no doubt, to leave his parents' meagre holdings to make his own way. He became a beachcomber, looking for wrecks, which were numerous at the time. Finding one, he put together a peddler's pack and set out on the road, where in due course he fell in with a band of "merchants" (possibly bandits). In time he amassed enough money to form a partnership with others, owning a ship engaged in coastal trade, which subsequently branched out into long-distance trade, merchanting, and banking. He became very rich, subsequently made his peace with God, and became a saint, no doubt leaving much of his fortune to the Church. Pirenne is emphatic that there were many Godrics operating at the time in Europe, though few among them were saints. They emerged as the bourgeoisie, and the commercial rebirth of Europe was soon an accomplished fact.

By the late twelfth century, business schools were in operation for those seeking a career in commerce to learn basic reading, bookkeeping, and arithmetic. By the thirteenth century, banking and finance had become quite sophisticated. Great textile factories were established in Flanders, furnished with wool from Britain and flax from Egypt, and the cloth was sold all over Europe with financing provided by expatriate Italian bankers speaking French. By the fourteenth century long-term credits were available, offered by merchants seeking to place their excess cash, or by bankers acting on their behalf.

Public authorities and noblemen were also borrowers as, for example, when they needed to buy grain during a famine or to outfit a regiment to be sent off to the Crusades. It became easier to borrow from moneylenders than to send one's plate to the mint.

The Italian Era

By the fifteenth century the mighty house of Medici reigned supreme in Italy, with its various branches throughout Europe acting as bankers, merchants in wool and cloth, dealers in spices and silks, goldsmiths, shipowners, deposit takers, and foreign exchange brokers. The influence of the Medicis and other houses like them reached into the papacy and the Church, and to princes and noble families all over the continent.

By this time the modus operandi of relations between merchants and the Church was reasonably well fixed, if complicated. To redeem his soul, the merchant would make contributions to the Church and its charitable works and alms houses, perhaps leaving a substantial part of his fortune to the Church upon his death. He would also suffer, as an ordinary cost of doing business, numerous fines and other charges for violating religious laws restricting commerce. He could purchase benefices or indulgences from the Church to expunge his guilt; before long literally hundreds of such benefices were offered for sale by the Church. He might also, as a lowly member of the bourgeoisie, have to renounce high social position in his community, though it is unlikely that Lorenzo de Medici ever did so.

On the other hand, having done these things to the extent required, he would be left alone to grow as rich as he was able, to likewise ascend in society and to leave most of his fortune to his heirs. It was a delicate balance perhaps, but one that was efficient for both the Church and the emerging middle classes. Each became mutually supportive of the other, despite the unbridgeable chasm of their intellectual and spiritual positions, and each prospered.

The more developed Italian banking became during the Renaissance, the more it was exposed to the great risks of the times, mainly shifts in political and religious power and influence. These were in constant turmoil during the sixteenth century, and even the Medicis couldn't last. They were succeeded in the world of merchants, after the Reformation, by German and Swiss protestant bankers, many of whom developed ties in Britain, Holland, and France. The modern era developed in which commercialism and finance were substantially freed of the stern admonitions of the Church.

Financial Markets Appear

The Dutch moved especially quickly, and had set up organised markets for trading in financial instruments by 1602. The Amsterdam Stock Exchange followed in 1611, on which trading and speculation in securities of all types developed rapidly. The "tulip mania," in which the prices of bulbs temporarily reached extraordinary levels (one traded as high as £20,000), came in 1636. The Amsterdam market permitted various forms of short selling, puts and calls, and futures transactions in many different commodities (tulip bulbs being one) and securities, including shares of the dominant and prosperous Dutch East India Company. Insider trading was first made an illegal practice in Amsterdam in the seventeenth century. The shrewd and profit-minded Dutch traders knew that insider trading was not in fact a victimless crime.

By the beginning of the eighteenth century trading in bills of exchange and other financial instruments, including shares of a limited number of corporations, took place daily in the City of London in an area called Exchange Alley. This was the scene in 1720 of the *"Great South Sea Bubble,"* in which thousands of British investors developed a mania for shares of a new company that would have monopoly rights to trade off the east coast of South America, the prospects for which were never much better than dim. Many people bought their shares on margin, an early example of financial leverage at work. The bubble burst, of course.

British Capitalism

During the latter part of the eighteenth century the American and the French Revolutions had occurred, changing forever the way ordinary people would think about their lives, and how much they would come to value the freedom to take one's own chances and venture one's own capital on a better, more prosperous future. Also at this time Adam Smith's influential work, *The Wealth of Nations,* appeared and helped to ensure nearly a hundred years of prosperous laissez-faire economic policy in Great Britain.

Britain's defeat of Napoleon at the battle of Waterloo in 1814 set the stage for nearly a century of economic dominance. It also was the occasion for the House of Rothschild to rise from obscurity to supreme prominence from the great killing it made in the market by getting the jump on the outcome of the battle and the defeat of Napoleon, and then wrong-footing everybody else on the Exchange by at first selling, then buying large amounts of British paper. The Rothschilds had earlier amassed a smaller fortune in buying and selling commercial bills from both sides during the war. Neither of their activities was illegal or considered improper at the time, though both would be condemned today.

With the end of the Napoleonic era came a great era of capitalism, nourished by the industrial revolution and the ascendancy of "the people" in Europe and America. The result has been that since 1800, the general growth in the economic well-being of those people affected has been several times that which had been experienced over the entire four thousand years that preceded it. Indeed, in those areas of the world still ruled by conquerors or by religious groups, not much general improvement has been experienced. And in those areas where old regimes have been toppled by peoples' (i.e., communist) revolutions and capitalism was stamped out, some, but far less, growth has occurred, a fact that has become painfully obvious in recent years.

The Roots of Modern Banking

Our modern economic and financial heritage, then, begins with the coming of democratic capitalism, around the time of Adam Smith. Under this system the state does not prevent or discourage anyone willing to work hard enough, and who also has access to capital, from becoming a capitalist himself.

A hundred years after Adam Smith, England was at the peak of its power. Politically, it ruled 25 per cent of the Earth's surface and people. The British economy was by far the strongest and most developed in the world. Its competitors were still partly asleep. France was still sorting itself out after a century of political chaos and a war with Prussia that had gone wrong. Germany was just starting to come together politically, but still had quite a way to go to catch up with the British in industrial terms. The rest of Europe was not all that important. There was a potentially serious problem, however, from reckless, often irresponsible, competition from America, which fancied itself a rising economic power, but otherwise the horizon was comparatively free of competitors. British industry and British finance were very secure in their respective positions of world leadership.

English financial markets had made it all possible, according to Walter Bagehot, the editor at the time of *The Economist,* who published a small book in 1873 called *Lombard Street* that described these markets and what made them tick. England's economic glory, he suggested, was based on the supply and accessibility of capital. After all, he pointed out, what would have been the good of inventing a railroad back in Elizabethan times if there was no way to raise the capital to build it? In poor countries there were no financial resources anyway, and in most European countries money stuck to the aristocrats and the landowners and was unavailable to the market. But in England, Bagehot boasted, there was a place in the City of London—called Lombard Street—where "in all but the rarest of times, money can be always obtained upon good security, or upon decent prospects of probable gain." Such a market, Bagehot continued, is a "luxury which no country has ever enjoyed with even comparable equality before."

However, the real power in the market, Bagehot went on to suggest, is its ability to offer the benefits of leverage to those working their way up in the system, whose goal is to displace those at the top. "In every district," Bagehot explained, "small traders have arisen who discount their bills largely, and with the capital so borrowed, harass and press upon, if they do not eradicate, the old capitalist." The new trader has "obviously an immense advantage in the struggle of trade."

> If a merchant has £50,000 all his own, to gain 10 per cent on it he must make £5,000 a year, and must charge for his goods accordingly; but if another has only £10,000 and borrows £40,000 by discounts (no extreme instance in our modern trade), he has the same capital of £50,000 to use, and can sell much cheaper. If the rate at which he borrows be 5 per cent, he will have to pay £2,000 a year [in interest]; and if, like the old trader he makes £5,000 a year, he will still, after paying his interest, obtain £3,000 a year, or 30 per cent on his own £10,000. As most merchants are content with much less than 30 per cent, he will be able, if he wishes, to for go some of that profit, lower the price of the commodity, and drive the old-fashioned trader—the man who trades on his own capital—out of the market.

Thus, the ambitious "new man," with little to lose and access to credit through the market, can earn a greater return on his money than a risk-averse capitalist who borrows little or nothing. The higher return enables the new man to undercut the other man's prices and take business from him. True, the new man may lose on the venture and be taken out of the game, but there is always another new man on his way up who is eager to replace him. As the richer man has a lot to lose, he risks it less, and thus is always in the game, continually defending himself against one newcomer or another until finally he packs it in, retires to the country, and invests in government securities instead.

"This increasingly democratic structure of English commerce," Bagehot continued, "is very unpopular in many quarters." On one hand, he says, "it prevents the long duration of great families of merchant princes . . . who are pushed out by the dirty crowd of little men."

On the other hand, these unattractive democratic defects are compensated for by one great excellence: no other country was ever so little "sleepy", no other was ever so prompt to seize new advantages. A country dependent mainly on great "merchant princes" will never be so prompt; there commerce perpetually slips more and more into a commerce of routine. A man of large wealth, however intelligent, always thinks, "I have a great income, and I want to keep it. If things go on as they are, I shall keep it, but if they change I *may* not keep it." Consequently he considers every change of circumstance a bore, and thinks of such changes as little as he can. But a new man, who has his way to make in the world, knows that such changes are his opportunities; he is always on the lookout for them, and always heeds them when he finds them. The rough and vulgar structure of English commerce is the secret of its life.

In 1902, a young American new man named Bernard Baruch took Bagehot's essay to heart and made himself the first of many millions in a Wall Street investment pool, buying control of a railroad on borrowed money. The United States had come of age financially around the turn of the century, and Wall Street would soon displace Lombard Street as the world's centre of finance.

The Rise of the Americans

Early in the century, J.P. Morgan organised United States Steel Corporation, having acquired Carnegie Steel and other companies in a transaction which valued at $1.5 billion, an amount worth perhaps $20 billion today. This was the largest financial deal ever done (until the RJR-Nabisco transaction in 1989) and it occurred in 1902 during the first of four merger booms to take place in the United States. Each of these booms was powered by different factors, but in each, rising stock markets and easy access to credit were major contributors.

By the early 1900s New York was beginning to emerge as the world's leading financial centre. True, many American companies still raised capital by selling their securities to investors in Europe, but they also sold them to American investors. These investors, looking for places to put their newly acquired wealth, also bought European securities, perhaps thinking they were safer and more reliable investments than those of American companies. By the early years of the twentieth century European issues in the New York market were commonplace. This activity proved especially beneficial when World War I came—both sides in the conflict sought funds from the United States, although the Allied Powers raised by far the larger amounts.

After the war, American prosperity continued while Europe's did not. Banks had a busy time, raising money for corporations, foreign governments, and investment companies and making large loans to investors buying securities. Banks were by then "universal," that is, they were free to participate in commercial banking (lending) and investment banking, which at the time meant the underwriting, distribution, and trading of securities in financial markets. Many of the larger banks were also involved in a substantial amount of international business. There was trade to finance all over the world, especially in such mineral-rich areas as Latin America and Australia. There were securities new issues (underwritings) to perform for foreign clients, which in the years before the 1929 crash aggregated around 25 per cent of all business done. There were correspondent banking and custodial (safekeeping) relationships with overseas counterparts, and a variety of financial services to perform for individuals, with respect to both foreigners doing business in the United States and the activities of Americans abroad.

The stock market crash in 1929 was a global event—markets crashed everywhere all at the same time, and the volume of foreign selling orders was high. The Great Depression followed, and the banks were blamed for it, although the evidence has never been strong to connect the speculative activities of the banks during the 1920s with either the crash or the subsequent depression of the 1930s. Nonetheless there were three prominent results from these events that had a great effect on American banking. The first was the passage of the *Banking Act of 1933* that provided for the Federal Deposit Insurance system and the Glass-Steagall provisions of the *Banking Act,* which completely separated commercial banking and securities activities. Second was the depression itself, which led in the end to World War II and a 30-year period of banking being confined to basic, slow-growing deposit taking and loan making within a limited local market. And third was the **importance of the government** in deciding financial matters, especially during the postwar recovery period. There was little for banks or securities firms to do until the late 1950s and early 1960s.

By then, international business had resumed its rigorous expansion and U.S. banks, following the lead of the First National City Bank (now Citicorp), resumed their activities abroad. The successful recovery of the economies of Western Europe and Japan led to pressures on the fixed-rate foreign exchange system set up after the war. The Eurodollar market followed, then the Eurobond market and the reattraction of banks and investment banks to international capital market transactions.

Global Banking Emerges

Next comes the 1971 collapse of the fixed exchange rate system in which the dollar was tied to gold. Floating exchange rates set by the market replaced this system, obviating the need for government capital controls. In turn this led to widespread removal of restrictions on capital flows between countries, and the beginnings of the global financial system that we have today.

This system, which is based on markets setting prices and determining the flow of capital around the world, has drawn in many new players, both users and providers of banking, and capital market services. Competition among these players for funds, and the business of providing them, has greatly increased the stakes of individual institutions and indeed the risks of the banking and securities businesses.

The effects of competitive capitalism have been seen and appreciated during the past decade as they have not been since 1929. The 1980s witnessed further rounds of deregulation and privatisation of government owned enterprises, indicating that governments of the industrial countries around the world have found private sector solutions to problems of economic growth and development preferable to state-operated socialist programmes. Thus there have been radical changes in Europe, where massive deregulation of financial markets in the United Kingdom and several other countries has occurred, and where the Single-Market and Economic and Monetary Union initiatives of the European Union (EU) promise similar effects on European business and finance. Deregulation in Japan has freed vast sums of capital to seek investment overseas and to create an active global securities market in Tokyo.

Most financial businesses are now effectively global. Banking and capital market services have proliferated, and numerous new competitors have emerged on the scene—many of which are not banks at all. Indeed some, like General Electric Capital Services (GECS), are customers of banks. New regulations are constantly being introduced and old ones changed. Telecommunications provides an ease of access to information that separated banks from their clients, pushing much of today's business into trading markets in which advice and service are less valuable than the latest quotation posted by securities and foreign exchange traders. It is a time of great and widespread change, affecting everyone. It is a time of massive restructuring for all financial service firms.

The purpose is to gain a better understanding of the evolution of international banking and finance, the services represented in today's market, the competitive processes involved, and the impact these have on prominent public policy issues. By treating the services of commercial banks and investment banks separately we are not acknowledging that these are or should be separated—we are simply using a traditional distinction for examining what these services are and how competition works in each.

Evolving Competitive Strategies

Our main emphasis is on the issues of formulation, implementation, and evaluation of competitive strategies (that is, strategies that succeed because they are ultimately shown to be competitive) of banks and capital market institutions. Each financial services business will have to reformulate its own global competitive strategy over the coming years. There is no single strategy that will work for all. Indeed, there are so many different types of firms, from different countries and possessing different strengths and weaknesses that an enormous variety of different strategies is likely to result.

International Commercial Banking

International Commercial Lending

International lending has changed drastically over the years. Major, highly rated corporations, public-sector enterprises, and governments have largely migrated to the capital markets, where their own securities command terms that are competitive (and often superior) to those banks which can provide. This has largely supplanted straight bank-to-client lending, and even smaller and less highly rated borrowers have found it possible to tap the capital markets using various kinds of credit and liquidity backstops and asset-backed structures. And as a result of the less-developed country (LDC) debt crisis of the 1980s, a major class of sovereign borrowers disappeared—borrowers for whom the capital markets have traditionally been closed—with the exception of forced loan rescheduling and new-money packages in the 1980s as the debt crisis wore on, and some renewed interest in banking lending to LDCs (emerging market borrowers) more recently.

Nevertheless, international bank lending continues as an important part of global financial markets. In times of financial instability, the capital markets tend to shrink and in some cases even disappear as viable sources of finance, and borrowers flock back to the banks. Many creditworthy corporate borrowers, for example, maintain sizable bank lines even in the best of times, partly to make sure the banks are there when and if they are needed. And for certain kinds of financings, such as short-term lending to finance merger, acquisition, and leveraged buyout transactions, as well as longer-term lending on project financings, there are no good substitutes for traditional bank loans. This may be because the borrower cannot be sure precisely when the funds will be required or when they can be repaid out of the proceeds of stock or bond issues or asset sales, or because the transaction is likely to encounter significant and unanticipated developments over its life that requires a form of financing where the added flexibility is worth more than the added cost. Bank lending provides one of the few alternatives for close borrower-lender contact and monitoring, and therefore maintains significant advantages in contracting and information costs.

Commercial Lending Facilities

There are various ways to classify international bank lending to corporate, government, and other types of borrowers.

First, a bank may *lend to local clients out of branches or affiliates* in foreign countries in which it operates, funded by local-currency deposits or by local money-market borrowings. This is purely local business, competing mainly with local banks. Foreign-based banks normally have to compete purely on price or by focusing on a specific market niche—special industry expertise, for example. Foreign banks lending in local markets may also focus on affiliates of multinational companies based in their own home countries, or on financing international trade transactions. It nevertheless remains essentially "domestic lending abroad," and the only thing international about it is the transfer of product or credit know-how, or client relationships, from the parent organisation or from affiliates in third countries.

Second, a bank may undertake *direct cross-border lending to clients located in another country*. Such loans appear to be relatively minor in importance. They focus on special kinds of transactions as part of close bank relationships to particular clients, including foreign affiliates of multinationals; as part of workouts of earlier troubled loans; or as part of international private banking relationships. In many cases such loans take the form of syndicated Eurocurrency facilities.

Lending facilities, whether direct or syndicated, can take a number of forms. There are "revolving credit agreements" (called "revolvers"), which permit clients to borrow, on demand, up to a certain maximum amount over an agreed period under an agreed interest formula. In return the bank earns a commitment fee for standing ready to lend, whether or not such lending actually occurs. These are usually "committed facilities," and the commitment is legally enforceable and covered by appropriate legal documentation. Committed facilities require the same kind of careful credit analysis as actual loans, especially since, for some clients, committed facilities will be taken down only when capital market financing is unavailable or more expensive. Such facilities often take the form of "backstop lines," which rating agencies like Moody's and Standard & Poor's require issuers of commercial paper to have in place in order to assure investors that the liquidity will be there when the paper matures. Borrowers may also arrange for "uncommitted facilities," which are not legally enforceable and hence involve lower fees. Clients may find these attractive because of the lower cost if they believe there is little likelihood of difficulty in accessing financial markets in the foreseeable future.

In the course of ordinary credit relationships with clients, banks will have in place limits on the amount of lending exposure they are willing to incur, sometimes called "undisclosed, unadvised guidance lines," which may be increased or decreased at the bank's own discretion on the basis of changing circumstances. Whether committed or uncommitted, international commercial lending facilities may be associated with a range of other banking products, especially those involving interest-rate or exchange-rate protection. Examples include "forward-rate agreements" (FRAs), which permit a client to lock in an interest rate today for a loan to be taken at some future date; interest-rate caps or collars; and currency swaps. The bank, in turn, will hedge these transactions in the market and keep whatever spreads or fees it is able to earn on these collateral services.

Bank Financing of Foreign Governments and Government Entities

Lending to units of foreign governments gained major importance in the 1970s. The reasons include:

- The rapid growth of balance-of-payments financing needs on the part of national governments, particularly after 1973.
- The use of government agencies as intermediaries to secure external financing for a wide variety of borrowers domestically.
- Major borrowing needs on the part of governmental and quasi-governmental entities like power authorities, sewage systems, trading companies, airlines, and shipping companies and the like, both at the national and state-local level.
- Active participation of governments as owners of manufacturing and trading companies, as well as financial houses and banks.
- The growing use of government guarantees to facilitate foreign borrowing on behalf of private ventures.

Sovereign lending collapsed after the debt crisis in the early 1980s and the migration of Organisation for Economic Cooperation and Development (OECD) government entities to the global bond markets, but has revived gradually in the 1990s.

Government borrowing abroad may be undertaken by a national entity charged with managing the country's external finance, for example, its central bank, monetary authority, ministry of finance, or similar institutions. It may also be undertaken by other government-owned authorities or corporations, often called *parastatals,* although such external borrowing usually must have the approval of a coordinating agency such as the central bank.

Balance-of-payments borrowing is undertaken by countries with current-account payments deficits that are not offset by private capital inflows, resulting in a balance-of-payments deficit. The proceeds of external borrowing by the country's monetary agency are often used to intervene in foreign exchange markets to support the external value of the national currency, the exchange rate. Balance-of-payments borrowings may be *seasonal* or *cyclical,* in response to periodic underlying variations in export receipts and import disbursements or capital flows, or they may be *structural* due to an essentially permanent shock (e.g., a major drop in export prices) to which it will take time to adjust. Such borrowings may also be *chronic* as a result of a more or less permanent excess of domestic absorption over production, capital flight due to lack of confidence in the country's future, and similar factors.

Seasonal and cyclical balance-of-payments borrowing is essentially self-correcting and finds its everyday parallels in corporate working-capital borrowing and personal finance. To the extent that such needs cannot be handled from a country's own reserves, short-term borrowings under bank credit lines, reviewed periodically, may be an alternative method of handling. Structural balance-of-payments borrowing is designed to ease the problem of adjustment to new economic realities and can also be fully justified provided the necessary adjustment actually comes about within an acceptable time frame. This is not the case with a country essentially living beyond its means and engaging in chronic external borrowing, its government unable or unwilling to take the steps needed to restore balance via domestic macroeconomic or exchange rate policies, ultimately heading for a rough landing for debtors and creditors alike.

Fiscal borrowing concerns external financing to cover budgetary deficits, and is linked directly to the balance of payments and its financing. In many cases fiscal borrowing involves short-term loans made in anticipation of government receipts, and therefore it tends to be self-liquidating.

Development borrowing involves the financing of infrastructure projects—schools, hospitals, roads, railways, airports, port facilities, communication networks, power grids, sewer systems, public housing, and a variety of others. Some projects are direct producers of foreign exchange (generating exports or saving on imports), while others are not. As distinct from development *project* lending, *programme* lending may involve literacy training or vocational education, for example, with potentially far-reaching domestic and international consequences that are usually extremely difficult to forecast.

Loan Syndication

As noted, most of the major international lending facilities are *syndicated*. In simple form, a syndicated credit facility involves the combined activities of a number of banks in the assembly of a relatively large loan to a single borrower under the direction of one or several banks serving as lead managers.

The borrower has the advantage, under such an arrangement, of being able to raise a larger sum than any single bank would be willing to lend, at substantially lower cost and more efficiently than the same amount of borrowing from multiple sources on its own. Moreover, the borrower enters the market fewer times and thus may improve its future access to financing in less jeopardy. Borrower "visibility" is enhanced by major syndications involving a large group of banks, possibly making future financings easier. The lenders have the advantage of:

- Better diversification of their asset portfolios
- Participation in lending they might not otherwise have access to
- Cooperation with multiple banks (often home based in a number of different countries) having greater collective expertise and information than any single bank

- Reduced risk of borrower default due to the enhanced penalties of such action in terms of limited future access of the borrower to financial markets
- Certain legal protection inherent in syndicated loan agreements

Banks also find participation in a variety of syndicated loans an efficient way to obtain necessary expertise, market exposure, and visibility without incurring unacceptable financial exposure.

Essentially, international syndicated loan facilities represent a cross between debt underwriting and traditional commercial bank lending. They open medium-term financing opportunities to many borrowers who might not otherwise be able to obtain credit on comparable terms through the international or domestic securities markets, private placements, and other financial vehicles.

Historically, international syndications of medium-term credit facilities began in the late 1960s, when changes in interest-rate levels and volatility increased the attractiveness of major financings on floating-rate terms, as opposed to fixed-rate bond issues, and borrowers' needs outstripped the lending capabilities of individual banks. Their antecedents include the longstanding practice of multibank term lending to corporate customers in the United States, priced at or above the domestic prime lending rate. During the 1970s and 1980s, somewhat over half of all medium- and long-term borrowings in international capital markets, well over 80 per cent of such borrowings by developing countries, and almost all such borrowings by centrally planned economies were in the form of syndicated loans. While LDC lending and project financing took up the bulk of syndications in the 1970s, mergers and acquisitions (M&A) and leveraged buyout (LBO) syndications took their place in the latter part of the 1980s. Both continue at far lower levels in the 1990s.

The geographic centre for syndicated lending has always been the City of London. Much smaller centres have developed to serve the Asian markets in Hong Kong and Singapore. New

York has played a relatively minor role. The actual booking of syndicated loan participation is done as well in the various offshore banking centres like Luxembourg.

The Syndication Process

Borrower contact—with a national government agency, an electric power authority seeking to finance a significant capacity expansion, a corporation seeking a standby facility for a major acquisition, perhaps a national development bank intending to take up a large sum internationally which it will then on-tend in smaller amounts to domestic enterprises, or anyone else—is maintained routinely by lending officers of major international banks. The better the "relationship" between the bank and the potential borrower, the better the bank's information about the client's evolving financing needs and the greater its chances of playing a significant role in meeting those needs. In seeking syndication business, banks rely on:

- Their own branches, representative offices, or other affiliates maintaining contact with the prospective borrower.
- Referrals from other units of the bank, or referrals through established corporate and other client relationships.
- Referrals from other banks anxious to render a service to their own clients, yet not in a position to take leadership position themselves, with whom good relations have been maintained.
- Direct solicitations from potential borrowers or, in the event of joint lead-managed syndications, other banks.
- Approaches by investment banks acting as advisers to borrowers, one of whose functions is to facilitate capital-market access through introductions to a competent bank active in loan syndication

Knowing the borrower and conditions in international lending markets, a prospective *lead bank* will carefully draw up a proposal to arrange the loan, thereby seeking a *syndication mandate.* The proposal will specify pricing, terms, fees, and other pertinent aspects of the loan and will indicate whether the syndication will be *fully committed.* If so, the bank will undertake to provide the full amount of the loan to the borrower according to the terms of the mandate, whether or not it is successful in its efforts to interest other banks in participating in the loan. If the syndication is *partially committed,* the bank will guarantee to deliver part of the loan, with the remainder contingent on market reaction to the loan. In a *best-efforts syndication* the borrower will obtain the funds needed only if sufficient interest and participation can be generated among potential participating lenders by the good-faith efforts of the bank seeking the mandate.

By this time, or shortly thereafter, the bank may have brought in one or more co-lead managers to help with the syndication and share in the underwriting commitment, especially if the amount to be raised is very large or the deal is rather complex. Generally, the larger the loan, the larger tends to be the management group involved, including several *lead managers, managers,* and *co-managers,* each group accepting a different share of the underwriting responsibility, and several "brackets" of *participants,* whose role is usually confined to supplying funds.

The terms of the formal letter seeking the mandate will follow extensive discussions with the borrower and will be carefully tailored to its needs as well as market conditions. It will have to be fully competitive with other banks going after the same mandate. The mandate letter will also specify *exclusivity* of the mandate, and repeatedly note the leading roles the mandated bank is to perform in the syndication.

There are a variety of negotiable trade-offs, as between the tenor and size of the loan, drawdown schedule, grace period, amortisation schedule, spread, fees, tax issues, borrower information, and legal covenants. In seeking a mandate, the prospective lead bank must strike a balance between what the borrower wants and what the market can live with, that is, what will result in a successful syndication—always keeping a watchful eye on what competitors may propose. Sophisticated borrowers will often accept "second best" proposals from highly responsible and prestigious lead banks over more "imaginative" or lower-cost proposals from aggressive competitors if they feel that this will better serve their long-term standing in the market. Still, the tolerance for less than fully competitive bids is generally very low.

If the borrower decides to go ahead with the syndication, the mandate will be awarded to one of the competing banks or to joint bidders, who then become lead manager(s) of the syndicate. Suppose a single bank has won a mandate on a $100 million fully committed syndication, and the lead bank wishes to keep $15 million of this in its own portfolio—its *target take.* It will then have to find a way to *sell down* the remaining $85 million to other banks. To do so it will have to develop a *syndication strategy* that will successfully raise the required sum yet call for minimum sharing of the management fee that will be paid or of the visibility the bank attracts for putting the loan together. Several other banks may have to be asked to manage or co-manage the loan jointly, however, and thus be allocated a portion of the total funds to be raised. Part of these funds they will take into their own portfolios in turn and the rest they will sell down to other syndicate participants, in return for a share of the management fee.

The lead bank is generally expected to take a share in the loan that is at least as large as that of any other lender. The management group (lead manager(s), managers, and co-managers) may retain as much as 50 to 70 percent of the total loan for their own portfolios.

The syndicate will be put together by the lead manager and the management group who will send offering faxes to banks around the world followed up quickly with elaborate writ Deciding which banks to invite into the syndicate is a major part of a lead bank's task and will help determine its strategy. It must be able to judge the invitees' country and industry exposures, past client relationships, degree of sophistication in syndicated lending (especially in complex deals), its own relationships with invitees, and similar factors that will determine individual banks' receptivity to the deal. In some cases the borrower will express a preference as to which banks should (and should not) be invited to participate. Contacting 200 or 300 banks to obtain twenty or thirty ultimate participants is not unusual. Banks invited to participate will usually decline, accept, or request further information on the basis of the offering fax, and careful track will be kept of the responses by the lead manager or management group.

If there are several lead managers, one of them is assigned to keep track of responses from each of the banks that have been approached. This can be rather complex when several hundred banks in a variety of countries are involved, with responsibility for contacting them divided among members of the management team.

Meanwhile, the lead manager will work on preparation of an *information memorandum,* in which the borrower will disclose financial and economic—and sometimes historical and political—facts pertinent to current and projected creditworthiness. This, together with a *term sheet* restating the conditions of the loan, will be sent to interested banks and carefully prefaced by an emphatic disclaimer of all responsibility for its content on the part of the lead manager. A disclaimer is necessary to avoid possible legal liability in case of default or other problems with the loan that may arise later. The information memorandum, although prepared by the borrower, will be carefully checked for accuracy and completeness by the lead bank(s).

If things go well, the loan will be fully subscribed. If it is oversubscribed, participations will either be *prorated* among the interested banks, or occasionally the total amount of the loan will be increased at the option of the borrower. In the latter case, however, prospective syndicate members may wish to consider whether they are comfortable with a larger loan to the borrower concerned. An oversubscribed syndication may well result in an unhappy borrower (who thinks the interest rate or fees are too high) or unhappy banks (who are unable to get as much of the loan as they were initially offered). The competence of the lead manager is called into question by both sides.

If insufficient funds are raised, the borrower will have to make do with less if the syndication is on a best-efforts basis, or the banks in the management group will have to book the balance themselves and thereby exceed their target take if the syndication is fully committed. In such a case the syndication is considered "unsuccessful," with potentially serious adverse consequences for the future prospects of the borrower as well as the lead manager(s) in the market. Again, the competence of the lead manager will be called into question.

Both under-subscribed and oversubscribed deals must be avoided, and this is why tailoring the terms of the loan to perceived market receptivity—accuracy in pricing—is such an important determinant of competence in loan syndication leadership. Particularly desirable participations are those that present a favourable risk/return profile, both in comparison with other loans available in the market and with those offered in the months immediately ahead. Lead banks with a track record of completing such deals are rewarded by further leadership roles and, obviously, adding attractive paper to their own portfolios.

The Principal Players

Investors in the Euronote/ECP market include:

(1) Banks and other financial institutions looking for spreads over LIBOR or their own cost of funds, and

(2) Nonbank investors whose short-term assets include bank deposits, CDs, short-term government securities, and commercial paper.

Borrowers in the market include sovereign and corporate issuers. The latter can be subdivided between companies viewed as high-quality credits, which tend to use uncommitted CP programmes, and those of lesser credit standing, which require committed, underwritten facilities.

Commercial paper and Euronote facilities are extremely flexible. Borrowers are not locked into any one interest-fixing date as they are, for example, in syndicated Euroloans or floating-rate notes in the Eurobond market. So they have more opportunities to take advantage of interest-rate windows as they occur—clearly of great interest in volatile market conditions. This speed of response may be especially valuable in multioption facilities, which allow the borrower access to a range of currencies and credit forms. They can play the yield curve and respond to particular openings of investor interest. One large programme can serve both to retire outstanding, more expensive debt and to rationalise debt management requirements. For a competitive commitment fee, the borrower using Euronotes can access cheap funds as and when needed, expanding or contracting the level of debt at will, safe in the knowledge that if market conditions are not receptive to the notes, funds are nevertheless assured. The broken or odd-dated maturities, which are a common feature of many CP programmes, also provide a great deal of flexibility, allowing issuers to tailor the period of their financing precisely to their specific funding requirements.

Although the ECP market still is nowhere near the depth of its U.S. counterpart, it nevertheless has certain distinct advantages that have contributed to its growth. It offers longer maturities at competitive rates and caters to a global investor base, whereas demand in the U.S. market is almost wholly domestic. Investors from Australia, continental Europe, the Far East, and the Middle East (corporate treasurers as well as central and commercial banks and other institutions) constitute an investor base that allows a broad range of maturities, while the speed with which the leading ECP houses are able to arrange and distribute deals is greatly helped by limited regulation.

Asset-Related and Project Financing

There are, several specialised forms of lending that have limited recourse to ultimate borrowers and their balance sheets, or sometimes none at all. These can provide attractive lending opportunities but also can expose banks to significant risks. Some such transactions, in which the asset is a major basis for the financing, also lend themselves to securitisation, selling to other financial institutions, and repackaging. This section discusses the various types of lending that are based on the value of assets underlying trade financing, ship financing, commodities financing, international leasing, and project financing. Each has its own unique characteristics and poses unique challenges to banks hoping to compete effectively.

Financing International Trade

Banks have been involved in the financing of international trade and effecting payments for international trade transactions since at least medieval times. The basic *transactions* services involve circumventing information and transactions costs for importers and exporters, making payment for international transactions as expeditiously and cheaply as possible, and providing associated foreign exchange and risk-shifting services. The basic *credit* services involve the direct extension of credit from the time merchandise leaves the factory door (and sometimes before that) to the time the buyer completes payment or, alternatively, making possible credit extension for this purpose by the financial market in terms of providing backstops for the risk involved, again in the most cost-effective available form.

Forms of International Payment

Probably the easiest and cheapest forms of payments for international trade transactions of sales from an exporter to an importer are made on an open-account or consignment basis, or against payment in advance. Both are possible only if the two parties know each other well and trust each other.

If a transaction is done on a consignment basis, the exporter ships the merchandise and sends the shipping documents to the importer, who is then able to claim the goods when they arrive. When the importer sells the merchandise, it sends the proceeds minus its markup to the exporter. The same thing happens when the transaction is done on an open-account basis, except that the importer remits payment to the exporter on arrival of the goods or within an agreed period thereafter. Selling on consignment loads the entire risk (that the merchandise will actually be sold and that the importer will actually pay), as well as the financing of the goods while in shipment and in the importer's inventory, on the exporter. Selling on open account loads the credit risk on the exporter as well, and also part or all of the financing. Nevertheless, the exporter may be willing to accept the risks involved in selling on consignment depending on its underlying competitive position. Selling on open account is normally done when there is a close connection between importer and exporter, as when the importer is an affiliate of the exporting company. Serious collection problems arise in the event of default, in part because all claims must be filed under the laws of the importer's country.

Payment in advance may be specified in certain cases where the exporter is able to load onto the importer all of the credit costs and the risk that the goods will actually be shipped and will arrive as specified and the cost of credit during the time the goods are in transit, and sometimes even as the goods go through the production process. This form of payment is sometimes specified for custom-made products that cannot be sold to anyone else, or when the exporter has very substantial bargaining leverage.

In all three cases (payment in advance, consignment, and open account), banks get involved only in the payment function itself, and receive customary fees for this service as well as for the spot or forward exchange transactions involved.

International Collections

Perhaps the most straightforward, direct involvement of banks in international trade is collection of amounts due on arm's-length transactions between importers and exporters. Suppose the two parties do not know each other well. The exporter would not want to ship merchandise on a straightforward basis, because he could not be sure of getting paid. The importer could take care of this problem by simply paying in advance, but then could not be sure the merchandise actually got shipped. This calls for an intermediary who takes care of the risk exposure on both sides.

The exporter prepares a "trade bill," or draft, which the importer is supposed to pay either when it takes possession of the merchandise *(documents against payment,* or D/P draft) or when it accepts the draft (D/A draft) for payment at some specified future date, such as 30 or 90 days down the road. The exporter prepares the merchandise for shipment and obtains a *bill of lading* (B/L) from a common carrier such as an airline or shipping company attesting to the fact that the goods are as specified and that they were shipped on a given date and along a specified route. The B/L and the D/P or D/A draft is sent to the exporter's bank, which in turn sends the draft and documents to its correspondent bank in the importer's country with instructions to hand over the documents (permitting the importer to claim the merchandise) against payment or against acceptance of the draft, as the case may be.

If it is a D/P draft, sometimes called a *sight draft,* the payment is collected by the bank in the importer's country, transferred to the bank in the exporter's country, and credited to his account. No credit is extended, and the collection process is compensated by fees—plus a spread and fees on a foreign exchange transaction in the middle. The same thing happens if it is a D/A draft, a *time draft,* except that the payment is collected for the account of the exporter on the specified date 30, 60, or more days in the future, after shipment has been accepted by the importer. In the meantime, the time draft may be held to maturity by the exporter, or it may be accepted by the importer's bank and either held to maturity or sold in the local banker's acceptance market, with the discounted proceeds collected for the exporter immediately. In this case, credit is extended by the holder of the time draft, who collects interest in the form of the discount.

Letters of Credit

Documentary time drafts for collection provide one vehicle for access to credit to finance international trade transactions, other than straightforward bank loans to the exporter or the importer. An alternative is the *letter of credit* (L/C), which efficiently takes care of properly allocating the credit risks to those best able to carry them and at the same time greatly facilitates access to financing at the best available terms.

Assume the exporter and importer do not wish to extend credit to each other or to take payment risk. The exporter asks the importer to request his bank (the *opening bank)* to issue an irrevocable letter of credit for the transaction amount in the exporter's favour. By doing so, the bank commits itself to paying the specified amount if the importer is unwilling or unable to pay—assuming the merchandise has been shipped precisely as specified in the terms of the L/C. The opening bank will then send the L/C to its correspondent bank in the exporter's country (the *advising bank)* which will forward it to the exporter. The transaction will subsequently take place using a sight or time draft, as discussed earlier, with the credit risk covered by the opening bank. An L/C of this type will cover only a single transaction, with tight specification of what will be shipped and how it will be shipped.

It may also be, of course, that the exporter is unfamiliar or uncomfortable with the importer's bank. In that case it may request that the opening bank's L/C be confirmed by the advising bank in its own country—a "confirmed, irrevocable letter of credit." Should the importer default, the importer's bank will pay. Should both be unwilling or unable to pay, the exporter's advising bank will pay. Of course, the advising bank must be comfortable with the credit standing of the opening bank and with the country-risk involved (e.g., the risk that exchange controls may be imposed that prevent the necessary currency from being made available to the importer or his bank). Again, the transaction will take place as specified earlier, and in the case of a time draft the acceptance can take place in the exporter's country and be discounted in the local banker's acceptance market at money-market rates. This shows how the process works.

In addition to unconfirmed and confirmed irrevocable letters of credit, there are other variants. Revocable letters of credit may be amended or cancelled by the opening bank at any point, and will therefore offer the exporter less protection and a lower price. Revolving letters of credit will cover multiple or continuous shipments of merchandise. If a revolving L/C is cumulative, any amounts used become reavailable once the transaction has been consummated, which is not the case in a noncumulative revolving L/C unless specifically amended. A "transferable L/C" permits the exporter to assign the proceeds to one or more secondary beneficiaries (e.g., subcontractors), while in a back-to-back L/C the exporter uses the first L/C (opened by the importer in his favour) as the basis for requesting his bank to open a second L/C in favour of his own supplier(s). This would tend to be used by exporters who are middlemen between domestic manufacturers and foreign buyers and do not have acceptable credit standing of their own.

In the case of international trade transactions covered by L/Cs, banks have a number of opportunities to earn fee and interest income. Fees go to banks for issuing (opening) L/Cs and for advising and confirming them, for collections, for foreign exchange transactions, for accepting time drafts, and (when the draft is held on the bank's own books) for extending credit—with the rate of interest reflected in the associated discount. Obviously, this is a highly competitive, transactions-intensive business. Banks that are best at it have strong client bases involved in international trade; procedures that are convenient to use, efficient, and error free; and substantial networks of correspondent banks. Another form of international trade financing, particularly common in Europe, is *forfait financing*. Under this structure, a bank (forfaiting house) will buy from the exporter the obligations due it on the part of importers in various countries without recourse to the exporter itself. The exporter will receive the discounted proceeds immediately, against evidence covering the quality, quantity, and shipment of the merchandise. The discount reflects both the interest charge and the credit risk (commercial as well as country) the forfaiter is assuming. The promissory notes involved are usually endorsed by the importer's bank. The notes, now endorsed by both the importer's bank and the forfaiting house, can be held to maturity or resold in the market.

To some extent, a forfait transaction is similar to *factoring*, which is familiar in the United States and certain other domestic markets. Factoring involves a bank that believes it is sufficiently familiar with the customers of a particular client to buy the client's accounts receivable on a nonrecourse basis at a discount. The goods have already been shipped and the bills sent out, and it is up to the bank to collect. Factoring is common in the garment industry. It is a specialised business in which risk must be carefully managed through intimate knowledge of the industry and creditworthiness of customers as well as diversification. It can be highly profitable for banks that know how to manage the risks involved. Internationally, factoring is more difficult because risk management is a problematic, a domestic bank having the basis to understand the risks associated with a client's foreign customers is difficult to imagine, unless two or more banks (or branches of a single bank) work together, swapping factored receivables involving customers in each bank's home country.

Government Export Financing, Backstops, and Counter Trade

Governments in most industrial and many developing countries provide export assistance of various kinds to stimulate foreign sales of domestic companies. These involve guarantees covering commercial risks as well as political and economic risks associated with the importing country, as well as concessionary financing of various types. For example, in the United States the Export-Import Bank (Eximbank) provides direct loans to exporters and importers, export credit insurance and guarantees, and backstops for banks involved in international trade financing. Short-term credit support, up to 180 days, is run through the Foreign Credit Insurance Association (FICA) run by Eximbank and private insurance companies. Export financing of commodity transactions is handled by the Commodity Credit Corporation (CCC). There are similar agencies in other countries, such as Hermes in Germany and COFACE in France. All permit the lodging of certain risks with the government at concessionary prices, thereby taking them out of the commercial market. Often these can result in very attractive profits for the banks involved, in light of the limited foreign risks they have to assume.

Banks in several countries have become very active in arranging and facilitating "countertrade," "barter," "buybacks," "switchtrade," "offset," and other transactions with countries experiencing foreign exchange problems. For example, a company may ship a piece of capital equipment to a particular country in return for which it is obligated to take back (or buy for cash) certain other commodities or arrange their sale to third parties. Or it may build a plant on a turnkey basis, for which it gets paid in a stream of production from that plant. This business is highly specialised and risky. Normally the companies involved are in the best position to price countertrade services and to manage the risks. Banks in some countries get involved in facilitating such transactions, and in a few cases in taking on the role of principal as well, but in general they are in a poor position to carry the risks.

Ship Financing

One of the most risky sectors of international lending involves ship financing. Shipping is a cyclical business, shipowners often put up very little equity, and the value of used ships that are attached in cases of default may be little more than scrap value.

Ships are generally financed with a first mortgage, covering perhaps 70 or 80 per cent of the construction cost. The remainder may be financed by the shipyard or the export finance agency of the exporting country, with the shipowner often putting up only a small amount of equity. Since the secondary ship market is so uncertain and becomes critical at precisely the time conditions in the industry are likely to be at their worst, other sources of comfort must be sought by lenders. Shipowners usually "charter," or lease, the ships they own to operating companies, which range from major oil companies, grain transporters, and container ship operators to cruise lines, under one of two basic types of charters. The first is a "bare boat charter," in which the operator is responsible for all operating charges and risks of the vessel and the costs of labour, fuel, insurance, maintenance, and repairs. The second is a "time charter," in which the operator rents the ship from the owner for a specified time but the owner bears the costs and risks. Charters may range from a comparatively short-term leasing arrangement to 10 years or more. If a vessel is to be operated under a succession of short-term charters, but seeks financing of a longer term, then the banks carry the risk that successive "charter hire payments" will be sufficient to cover the required amounts of debt service on their ship loans. In such cases the credit standing of the shipowner is of principal importance. On the other hand, in cases where a shipowner has arranged an adequate long-term bare boat charter with a major oil company, the shipowner's own creditworthiness is of lesser importance.

History is full of cases of bank-owned ships sold at great losses or scrapped. To be in this business a bank has to develop not only a firm understanding of the shipping business and the reputation of shipowners and their ability to comply with the terms of charters as well as their ability to operate ships profitably), but a sixth sense as well. To the extent that financial projections are reliable, they will cover the ship operator's cash flows, cost structures, competition, demand conditions, and related with the high risks can come high returns, and the spreads on shipping loans are commensurately high. This has from time to time attracted inexperienced banks into shipping loans, often to their great distress. The risks also prevent shipping loans from being easily syndicated, sold, or participated-out. Nor do ships lend themselves to financing via securities issues, for risk-related reasons and because of the need for flexibility in the case of restructuring.

Commodities Financing

A further aspect of international asset-based bank financing involves commodities like grains, timber, oil, pulp, natural fibres, with traders heavily financed with short-term bank debt. The traders' profit margins are small and turnover is rapid, with the liquidation of assets expected to provide fully for debt service. There is generally little sense in looking for recourse to the commodity trading company, which frequently takes speculative positions that could wipe it out, so financing has to be structured fully along asset-based lines. Commodity traders, as opposed to dealers, often match buy and sell orders so that the commodities are presold and therefore the final customer's ability to pay becomes critical.

Banks in the business of financing commodities must assure themselves of the credit quality of the ultimate buyers, the diversification of the commodity firm's exposure to buyers, and the volume of business. Critical are the firm's own financial controls, its credit standing, and its ability to hedge its exposure. Like much of asset-based financing, this is a specialised activity that requires banks to have equally specialised knowledge. At times it can be quite lucrative, especially when the bank gets paid handsome spreads for effectively taking risks associated with top-quality customers such as the multinational oil or grain companies.

International Lease Financing

Another important form of asset-based financing involves leasing of mobile capital goods. These can include aircraft, barges, containers, drilling rigs, pallets, power generation equipment, computers, production machinery, medical equipment, materials handling equipment, and the like.

In leasing, the lessor owns the equipment and leases it to an operator, receiving the lease payments and the residual value, which cover the equipment's acquisition cost plus profit. Lessors may or may not have the option to acquire the equipment during or at the end of its useful life. Such *financial leasing* is distinguished from *operating leasing*, where the lessor is responsible for maintaining and insuring the equipment and covering any applicable taxes. Financial leases are noncancellable, whereas operating leases are often used by customers to cover their short-term equipment needs and can be cancelled at any time. Operating leases tend to be the province of specialised leasing firms that finance themselves with bank loans or in the capital markets, with full recourse to the lessor, on the basis of their own credit standing

Project Financing

The financing of large-scale projects such as pipelines, oil and gas production, tunnels and bridges, energy plants, major office buildings, and similar long-gestation, highly capital-intensive ventures has evolved into a major competitive arena for international financial services firms. The sheer size of the financing needs that are frequently encountered, and the complex financial-structuring and specialised risk-evaluation requirements have concentrated leadership in this business in the relatively few banks that developed the financial resources and technical skills needed.

Driven by increased competition and growing pressure on the profitability of conventional international lending, a number of commercial and investment banks have succeeded in developing capabilities in a broad range of banking functions, enabling them to offer comprehensive financial support and advice through the life of a major project.

Background

Modern project financing appears to be largely an American invention. It can be traced to bank financing of independent oil companies during the 1930s, particularly in Oklahoma and Texas. Few of the "wildcatters" who dominated the oil business at the time had the financial resources to bring new discoveries into production, or strong enough balance sheets for ordinary unsecured bank borrowing on anything but a very limited scale. Secured borrowing was likewise precluded, since the principal "assets" to be financed were usually a hole in the ground and some associated equipment and supplies with questionable resale value. Yet it was clear that the resources in the ground themselves represented a prospective value as a future revenue stream that could become the basis for attractive lending opportunities. Bank loans could be serviced from the proceeds of the future sale of the resource without necessarily looking exclusively to either the operating company's balance sheet or to production assets for credit support.

Called *production payment financing*, this early approach in effect mortgaged the resource in the ground, with financial institutions betting that it was actually present in sufficient quantity, that it could be lifted economically, and that it could be sold at a price that lived up to a set of initial expectations, all within reasonable margins for error. Given the nature of large-scale energy projects such as offshore oil and natural gas ventures as well as terminals, pipelines, and other facilities relying for cash flows on throughput charges, "project financing" eventually grew in volume and international scale. The concepts underlying project financing were later extended from energy to other ventures such as power plants and cogeneration facilities, tunnels, bridges, pipelines, office buildings, and telecommunications facilities. Here, the loan is based on the future receipts of the project.

Global Retail Banking

The foregoing discussion raises the question whether most retail banking services really lend themselves to globalisation, as do many wholesale banking and securities services discussed in other chapters of this book. We have pointed out that most retail services are really local and even regional in nature, and it is unclear what foreign-based institutions bring to the table. Whatever it is, it must be sufficiently superior in quality or lower in cost to convince mass-market customers to defect from their local institutions. Given the absence of patents, copyrights, and other statutory entry barriers in the financial services industry, sustaining such a basis for competitive advantage—assuming it can be achieved in the first place—is not easy in local markets around the world. Foreign-based institutions, in short, must win a local franchise against entrenched local competition, which may be quick to react to encroachments on what it regards as its turf. Either that, or foreign banks may simply buy good local franchises and run them essentially as portfolio investments. Failures in international retail banking are perhaps more common than successes.

The high-net-worth private banking client is likely to remain an important factor in international banking for the foreseeable future, although the pattern of wealth ownership will probably shift steadily from inherited wealth to that created by the current generation. The passing of property rights from one generation to another is constantly subject to fiscal and political challenge. At the same time, newly created wealth appears ever more acceptable alongside market-oriented economic policies. Economic structures are becoming increasingly competitive, which simultaneously diminishes the chances of successive generations successfully retaining the wealth earned by their forebears and increases the chances that the newly wealthy will be sharper thinking and more international in outlook. Private banking players will have to adapt to these changes, remembering that their fate ultimately will be sealed by the quality of the human resources they are able to attract to what essentially remains a "people business."

Retail banking is one part of the financial services industry that does not lend itself particularly well to globalisation. Some retail activities such as travellers checks and "plastic" are important exceptions. Others are highly idiosyncratic and local—Herr Mueller behaves differently from Monsieur Meunier, who behaves differently from Mr. Miller in terms of what he expects his bank to do for him—and this requires a great deal of adaptation of competitive advantages in products and processes. Indeed, the key success factors in retail banking may in the end be more related to a keen awareness of the market than to technology and systems.

Nonetheless, it is clear that international and even global niches exist in specific retail financial services, ranging from mortgage and consumer lending, stockbrokerage and mutual funds, to family financial planning. The jury remains out on whether there is a role for truly global retail financial services players in the future. And it is clear that "global branding," such as Coca-Cola or McDonalds, is possible in the financial services sector as well. So far, only American Express and perhaps Citicorp have succeeded in developing a global consumer franchise. Banking and finance comprise a highly sensitive sector of the economy. There is an inherent element of price and liquidity risk in maturity-mismatching in asset and liability management, trading, and merchant banking activities. Despite careful diversification in asset deployment, exposures incurred in lending activities always involve solvency risk. The very role of financial intermediation entails the assumption of risks. Moreover, fraud, misrepresentation, financial collapse, predatory behaviour, selfdealing, bubbles, busts, and shocks have afflicted financial systems over the centuries, in the United States, Europe, and elsewhere in the world. Problems that afflict an individual institution may spill over to damage the entire fabric of the national financial and economic system. To cope with this problem, countries have tried to establish safeguards that are robust enough to contain external damage triggered by crises in the financial sector, yet that do not materially impair financial efficiency or the creative forces of private enterprise. Deposit insurance limits erosion of confidence by banking customers. The central bank as official lender of last resort exists to inject liquidity into individual institutions in trouble (e.g., via its discount facilities) and into the financial system as a whole (via open market operations and changes in reserve requirements).

Along with institutional safeguards comes regulation to further support the safety and soundness of the financial system. The apparatus is familiar—reserve requirements, bank examination and supervision, maximum lending limits, securities regulation, activity limitations on commercial and investment banks, mutual savings banks and savings and loan institutions, and interest-rate ceilings, among the traditional techniques. Countries use different kinds of safeguard structures, but the need for them is universally recognised. Indeed, some use bank nationalisation to "socialise" both the risks and the returns, and not coincidentally to achieve a direct government role in credit allocation.

The problem with financial regulation and control is that it invariably erodes the *efficiency* of the system. All regulatory and supervisory measures have the potential of displacing financial resource allocation from that which is most efficiently driven by the free interplay of market forces. This is as true of reserve requirements as it is of interest-rate ceilings on deposits. Further costs are associated with eroded innovativeness and competitive vitality of the industry. So the combination of financial safeguards and regulation results in a lessening of financial efficiency and dynamism. Greater security is never free—there is always a price to be paid. Here we are buying increased safety with respect to the national financial system and paying for it in the form of reduced financial market efficiency. This is a logical trade-off. Yet there is always the question whether we are paying too high a price for the increased financial stability we are purchasing through regulation and control. Many countries would surely regard bank nationalisation as an extortionate price to pay for any prospective increase in financial safety that would create.

These issues become especially difficult in the international environment, although much progress has been made to create a more coherent regulatory apparatus and at the same time a more level playing field. This has focused on more careful assignment of regulatory responsibility to branches and affiliates, coordination of national prudential policies, and perhaps most important, alignment of capital adequacy standards.

Structural Change in Global Financial Flows

The previous sections have focused in some detail on the structure of *intermediated* global financial flows, that is, flows that run through the balance sheets of financial intermediaries such as commercial banks. This differential comprises the operating costs, losses, and profits incurred in the intermediation process. The lower this differential, the more efficient is the intermediation process. Banks (and banking systems) compete with each other to a significant degree on the basis of intermediation efficiency, which in turn is driven by their respective comparative advantages and regulatory burdens. They also compete with alternative forms of financial intermediation, notably securities transactions, both within national financial systems and globally. In this section we shall outline the dynamics of alternative financial intermediation flows, their dramatically shifting patterns in recent decades, and their prospective future development. These dynamics, in turn, have a pivotal effect on the strategic positioning and performance of banks and other financial firms, their wholesale and retail clients, and the competitiveness of entire financial systems.

Financial Intermediation Process

The central component of any model of a modern financial system is the nature of the conduits through which the financial assets of the ultimate savers flow through to the liabilities of the ultimate users of finance, both within and between national economies. This involves alternative and competing modes of financial intermediation, or "contracting," between counterparties in financial transactions. Here we shall discuss the intermediation framework in terms of a model that can be useful in explaining and forecasting structural shifts in national and global banking and financial markets through ultimate sources of surplus funds raised in the household sector (deferred consumption or savings), the corporate sector (retained earnings or business savings), and the government sector (budgetary surpluses).

Ultimate *users* of funds comprise the same three segments of the economy—the household or consumer sector, the business sector, and the government sector. Consumers may finance purchases by means of personal loans from banks or by loans secured by purchased assets (hire-purchase or installment loans). These may appear on the asset side of the balance sheets of credit institutions on a revolving basis, for the duration of the respective loan contracts, or they may be sold off into the financial market in the form of securities backed by consumer credit receivables. Corporations may borrow from banks in the form of unsecured or asset backed straight or revolving-credit facilities and/or may sell debt obligations (e.g., commercial paper, receivables financing, fixed-income securities of various types), or equities directly into the financial market. Governments may likewise borrow from credit institutions (sovereign borrowing) or may issue securities directly.

Under the third alternative, savings surpluses may be allocated directly to borrowers through various forms of private placement and other direct-sale mechanisms. Under the second model of funds flows, savings may be allocated directly to the purchase of securities publicly issued and sold by various governmental and private sector organisations in the domestic and international financial markets. Under the first or "classic" model of financial intermediation, savings (or funds sources) are held in the form of deposits or alternative types of claims issued by commercial banks, savings organisations, insurance companies, or other forms of financial institutions entitled to finance themselves by placing their liabilities directly with the general public. Financial institutions then use these funds flows (liabilities) to purchase domestic and international assets issued by nonfinancial institution agents such as firms and governments. With the exception of consumers, other borrowers such as corporations and governments also have the possibility of privately issuing and placing their obligations with institutional investors, thereby circumventing both credit institutions and the public debt and equity markets. But even consumer debt can be repackaged as asset-backed securities and sold to private investors.

International Capital Market Services

International Money and Foreign Exchange Markets

As long ago as the fifteenth century, organised international money and foreign exchange markets existed. Merchants in Italy, for example, wanting to import tapestries made in Belgium from wool gathered in England, had to find ways to finance these transactions that occurred outside their own country. Italian banks, such as the Medici, set up foreign branches to effect payments and arrange for the delivery of the goods on behalf of their clients. The banks had to deal in currency exchange and in deposit collecting and loan-making in countries outside Italy. These activities have continued throughout the nearly 500 years of modern banking history, though during the past 20 years or so they have been especially subject to new developments, growth, and change.

Just as international banking refers to activities of banks outside their domestic national markets, international money-market and foreign exchange transactions deal with the issuance and trading of money-market instruments in various currencies in markets other than their domestic national markets. In the domestic U.S. market, money-market instruments include U.S. government and government agency paper of approximately one year or less maturity, as well as commercial paper, bankers' acceptances, and bank certificates of deposit. These instruments conform precisely to U.S.

regulatory requirements and market practices; if foreigners wish to buy them, they must take them as they are—in registered form, in which the identity of the purchaser is disclosed, and subject to withholding taxes on interest and bank reserve requirements. If these conditions are not satisfactory, alternative instruments will be sought; if these don't exist, they will be invented through the creative processes inherent in a freemarket system that allows capital to cross borders without impediment.

Origins of Eurocurrencies

The history of the international money market, since its modern (postwar) rebirth in the 1960s, is a confluence of three parallel and mutually influential events: major changes in the international monetary system, the evolution of an international investor base, and continuing deregulation of domestic capital markets in major countries to conform to overpowering international alternatives.

In 1944, at Bretton Woods, New Hampshire, the Allied Powers agreed to a postwar international monetary system in which the dollar would be the principal reserve currency (i.e., used as reserves by other countries). The dollar was to be pegged to gold, at the rate of $35 per ounce, and all other currencies were to be fixed to the dollar. When balance-of-payments difficulties arose, it was understood to be the obligation of both the deficit and the surplus countries to modify their domestic fiscal and monetary policies so as to reduce the problem. Governments periodically intervened in foreign exchange markets to help the process along, but usually they relied on broad economic policy changes to effect adjustment. If the imbalance could not be redressed after suitable effort, then the currency could be refixed to the dollar, after which it would have to be defended at the new rate. For the system to work, the world's principal economies would have to grow at about the same rate and the world's military and other burdens would have to be shouldered equally, which was not the case. Further, at the national level, strict economic discipline and controls would be needed, and voting publics would refrain from blaming others for problems and would understand that it was necessary from time to time to take bitter medicine in the interest of their country's long-run well-being. These conditions were not commonly found in the 1950s and 1960s any more than they are now.

In 1971, after several years of large U.S. balance-of-payments deficits, the Bretton Woods system collapsed. It was replaced by a floating-rate mechanism, in which all currencies were to be priced continually by the market and economic imbalances would generate corrective pressures on the foreign exchange rate. The mechanism obviated the need for capital market controls that restricted cross-border transfers, as harsh policies were no longer necessary—the market would administer the medicine that countries were unable to administer to themselves. In time, all the major industrial nations removed their controls on international capital movements. This meant that users and providers of capital could look overseas for capital market opportunities that were superior to what was available at home. It also meant, however, that interest-rate and foreign exchange market volatility would be much greater in the new floating exchange rate environment than in the old fixed-rate regime. Increased volatility led to a great expansion of trading activities and hedging strategies, by banks and other market-makers.

The postwar investor population was affected by these events and by the rapid institutionalisation of markets in the United States, the United Kingdom, and some other European countries. There was also a large increase in the population of otherwise law-abiding Europeans who wanted to transfer funds into foreign bank accounts that were beyond the scrutiny of tax authorities in their countries, as well as an increase in irregular or illegal accumulation of funds in tax-haven countries by corrupt government officials, flight capitalists, and criminals. These individuals, mostly investing through banks in Switzerland, Luxembourg, and other European centres, were highly focused on preserving their anonymity. The institutions, though not subject to tax concerns, were sophisticated investors looking for underpriced investments. Together, these investors were looking for opportunities that were not available in the United States.

Such opportunities were soon discovered in the Eurocurrency markets—an informal, unregulated, over-the-counter market made up of banks and other professional dealers from around the world transacting in instruments that were not available in national markets. Occasionally the Eurocurrency market would devise a financial instrument that was not available in the home market, and it would attract a large volume of activity on the part of home market nationals. Soon the pressure to deregulate the domestic market to make the same type of financing available became too great to contain. Often involuntarily, most countries have had to give in to the process of imported innovation. The result has been a large increase in the number and type of financial instruments available in international and foreign markets.

Eurodollars

Though there was some activity in Eurodollars before World War II, it did not become significant until the early 1960s. At this time, dollars were accumulating in Europe as a result of increased economic growth and investment, the U.S. balance of payments deficits, and investor preference to hold dollars but not in the United States. A dollar-denominated bank deposit outside the United States, for example, in London (or Frankfurt or Zurich), was called a Eurodollar. If you wanted a Eurodollar investment, you had to have it in the form of a bank deposit—in the beginning that was all there was. Eurodollars (and all Eurocurrencies) are priced in terms of the London Interbank Offered Rate (LIBOR), which is the rough equivalent of the Federal Funds rate in the Euromarket: the rate a bank will offer for a loan to another major bank for a specified maturity, such as 30 or 60 days. Major banks post their own rates daily. The rate to be paid on a deposit from another bank is expressed in terms of the London Interbank Bid rate (LIBID).

A nonbank borrower can expect to pay a premium over LIBOR (e.g., LIBOR + 1/4 per cent), and a nonbank depositor would receive a rate reflecting a discount (LIBID – 1/4 per cent). The spread between LIBOR and LIBID has generally been about 1/4 per cent, much less than the difference between U.S. prime rate and bank deposit rates

Other Eurocurrencies

Banks also quote rates for loans and deposits in other currencies, which in a way they manufacture synthetically. They do this by adding the cost or benefit of a forward foreign exchange contract for the prescribed maturity in the desired currency to the U.S. dollar LIBOR rate. If a customer wants a loan based on 60-day sterling LIBOR, the bank first acquires the required amount of sterling in the spot market, then sells sterling forward against dollars in 60 days, and the cost or benefit of this transaction (in percentage) is added to the dollar LIBOR cost.

Euro Certificates of Deposit

Banks, especially U.S. banks, were eager to build up their Eurodollar deposits as a source of funding for their growing international activities. The deposits could be used to fund Eurodollar bank loans or loan syndicate participations. They could be loaned to branches in the United States to support lending activity there, if and when the rates were right. And they could serve as a means of diversifying the banks' wholesale source of funding for their overall deposit base. Investors were other banks (there were more than 400 foreign bank branches in London in 1980, all looking to "buy" assets in the interbank market), multinational institutions, and corporations with temporary funds to invest.

In 1961 Citibank devised the first transferable Euro certificate of deposit (ECD). This was a major innovation that soon led to secondary market trading in dollar instruments and to the creation of the Eurosecurities market. The first Eurobond was offered in 1963, and was sold to investors willing to extend their investment for 15 years, at somewhat higher rates. Both ECDs and Eurobonds were in bearer form (identity of purchaser not disclosed) and were free of withholding taxes on interest.

During the next 30 years the Euromarket was a constant source of innovation, with new instruments being introduced as soon as changing regulatory or investor preferences dictated. Inevitably, ECDs and Eurobonds were introduced in currencies besides the dollar. The Eurobond market soon took off on a continuous expansion that has made it into one of the world's principal sources of finance

A Euro Money Market

The money market, however, developed much more slowly than the Eurobond market. It was because in the Euromarket well-known international banks had a lock on the market for short-term investments. The banks were also prepared to offer ECDs of whatever maturity an investor might wish. Mostly there was little demand for trading the instruments; the investors were happy to hold them until maturity unless a special requirement to sell them arose.

Investors were extremely quality conscious at a time when limited international investment-grade rating information was available. Unlike domestic markets, the U.S. and European governments did not offer short-term securities internationally, so investors had to make do with banks and other corporate issuers.

If they were prepared to go out a bit in maturity, investors could buy outstanding or newly issued Eurobonds of high-grade, well-known issuers, including some major European governments. The issuers began to shorten the maturities of their bonds (e.g., to two or three years in some cases) to attract these investors as well as to avoid the extremely high interest rates of the late 1970s. As trading volume increased in the secondary markets, investors began to accept that they could rely on the liquidity in the market to facilitate a sale of Eurobonds before maturity.

Money-Market Instruments

The following is a description of the different international money-market instruments traded in the Euro securities market.

Euro Certificates of Deposit

ECDs are issued by banks directly or through dealers or brokers. Banks prefer to sell their own ECDs to their clients and correspondent relationships, but often, to extend the market and increase the volume of ECDs outstanding, they resort to dealers to sell the paper for them, for a modest commission. The banks post their own rates for a spectrum of maturities. These rates are closely tied to LIBOR, which is quoted in most major currencies. Newspapers such as the *Financial Times* of London publish averages of these posted rates daily.

Banks will often negotiate with large customers for special rates for ECDs with custom-made maturities or other terms. The bank's posted rates may be slightly higher or lower than rates posted by similar banks, reflecting the bank's greater or lesser desire to take in funds at particular maturities. Such decisions are made by the bank's treasury department, which has to balance the entire bank's requirement for funds and currencies at particular maturities. For most banks, the treasury function in the London branch will conduct most of these Euro funding operations, generally in close contact with the Head Office.

The secondary market in ECDs is very active. Banks maintain markets in their own ECDs, and encourage their customers to trade with them. As rates change, banks will either increase their issuance of ECDs or attempt to buy in outstanding paper. Brokers may work with the banks as agents, on a nonexclusive basis, to place or buy in ECDs for a commission of a few basis points. Such brokers do not take positions in the bank's ECDs for their own account. Often the brokers represent individual investors seeking the best rates for deposits. Dealers, on the other hand, purchase and sell bank ECDs for their own account. They hope to create opportunities

Table 6.1: Volume of Euro Money Market Instruments Outstanding (amounts outstanding at year-end, $ billions)

	Market Opening	*1986*	*1987*	*1988*	*1989*	*1990*	*1991*	*1992*	*1993*	*1994*	*Compounded Growth Rate*
Euro Commercial paper and other short-term notes (NIFs and RUFs)	Early 1980s	29	50.2	66.7	69.6	89.4	106.4	115.7	110.3	114.1	18.7%
Euro-medium-term notes	Mid-1980s	0.4	2.6	5.6	9.6	21.9	38.5	61.1	146.6	292.01	28.0%
Total		29.4	52.8	72.3	79.2	111.3	144.9	176.8	256.9	406.1	38.8%

Source: Bank for International Settlements.

Table 6.2: Euro Currency Interest Rates

Apr 13	*Short Term*	*7Days Notice*	*One Month*	*Three Months*	*Six Months*
Belgian Franc	51/16-5	$6^{1}/_{2}$-$6^{3}/_{8}$	5-$4^{7}/_{8}$	$5^{1}/_{4}$-$5^{1}/_{8}$	$5^{1}/_{2}$-$5^{3}/_{8}$
Danish Krone	7-$6^{3}/_{4}$	7-$6^{3}/_{4}$	7-$6^{3}/_{4}$	7-$6^{3}/_{4}$	$7^{1}/_{8}$-$6^{7}/_{8}$
D-Mark	$4^{5}/_{8}$-$4^{1}/_{2}$	49/16-47/16	49/16-47/16	411/16-49/16	$4^{3}/_{4}$-$4^{5}/_{8}$
Dutch Guilder	47/16-45/16	$4^{5}/_{8}$-$4^{3}/_{8}$	$4^{5}/_{8}$-$4^{1}/_{2}$	$4^{3}/_{4}$-$4^{5}/_{8}$	$4^{7}/_{8}$-$4^{3}/_{4}$
French Franc	$7^{3}/_{4}$-$7^{1}/_{2}$	713/16-79/16	$7^{3}/_{4}$-$7^{1}/_{2}$	$7^{5}/_{8}$-$7^{3}/_{8}$	$7^{1}/_{8}$-$6^{7}/_{8}$
Portuguese Esc.	$9^{3}/_{8}$-$8^{7}/_{8}$	$9^{5}/_{8}$-$9^{1}/_{4}$	1011/32-105/32	1013/16-$10^{1}/_{8}$	$11^{1}/_{4}$-$10^{1}/_{2}$
Spanish Peseta	823/32-819/32	$8^{3}/_{4}$-$8^{5}/_{8}$	9-$8^{7}/_{8}$	915/32-911/32	$9^{3}/_{4}$-$9^{5}/_{8}$
Sterling	$6^{3}/_{8}$-$6^{1}/_{4}$	63/16-6[illegible]16	$6^{1}/_{4}$-63/16	611/16-69/16	7-615/16
Swiss Franc	$3^{1}/_{2}$-$3^{3}/_{8}$	$3^{1}/_{2}$-$3^{3}/_{8}$	$3^{1}/_{2}$-$3^{3}/_{8}$	$3^{1}/_{2}$-$3^{3}/_{8}$	$3^{5}/_{8}$-$3^{1}/_{2}$
Can. Dollar	8[illegible]16-$7^{7}/_{8}$	8-713/16	8-$7^{7}/_{8}$	8-$7^{7}/_{8}$	715/16-713/16
U.S. Dollar	6-$5^{7}/_{8}$	6[illegible]16-515/16	$6^{1}/_{8}$-6	$6^{1}/_{4}$-$6^{1}/_{8}$	67/16-65/16
Italian Lira	$10^{1}/_{4}$-$9^{3}/_{4}$	105/16-103/16	$10^{3}/_{8}$-$10^{1}/_{4}$	$10^{5}/_{8}$-10[illegible]	11-$10^{7}/_{8}$
Yen	$1^{7}/_{8}$-$1^{3}/_{4}$	113/16-$1^{3}/_{4}$	$1^{3}/_{4}$-111/16	111/16-$1^{5}/_{8}$	$1^{5}/_{8}$-19/16
Asian $Sing	$3^{7}/_{8}$-$3^{3}/_{4}$	$3^{1}/_{4}$-$3^{1}/_{8}$	213/16-211/16	215/16-213/16	3-$2^{7}/_{8}$

Source: Financial Times, April 18, 1995.
Short-term rates are call for the US Dollar and Yen, others: two days' notice.

for capital gains from trading in the ECDS, as they would in all money-market instruments. Dealers will call the bank in the morning and offer to buy or sell ECDs at particular rates. Then they lay off their positions to customers, or hold them for a few days to wait for an expected market change to occur. Large dealers offer ECDs along with a complete menu of other Euro money-market instruments to customers on a continuous basis.

As an example, a dealer such as Salomon Brothers might be aware that Mitsui Life Insurance Company is seeking to place $100 million in high-grade short-term investments tomorrow morning, Tokyo time. Mitsui actually wants the investments to have a maturity of 75 days.

The posted rate for 60-day ECDs might be 4 per cent, and for 90 days 4.3 per cent. Salomon will call a dozen or more high-grade banks the evening before the opening in Tokyo to offer to buy 75-day ECDs at a rate of 4.25 per cent, in order to offer them at, say, 4.20 per cent, to Mitsui Life. Many banks will turn Salomon down, but one or two may have a need of their own for a large placement of 75-day ECDS and be willing to pay the somewhat higher rate. Such intense market coverage together with the willingness of dealers to position paper of all types has greatly improved the efficiency of the Euro money market in recent years. The improving efficiency of the market largely explains its rapid growth since the early 1980s.

Floating-Rate Notes

In the early 1980s, many banks began to offer floating-rate notes (FRNS) as a supplement to their funding activities. These notes were not deposits, and therefore were subordinate to them. The FRNs might have a maturity of 10 years, but interest would be reset every 90 days at three-month LIBOR (say, 4.5 per cent) plus a small spread (say, 1/8 per cent). Because of the continuous resetting, the price of the notes was expected to return to par (100 per cent) every 90 days, assuming that the reissue rate continued to be LIBOR + 1/8 per cent. An investor was now given a choice between 90-day ECDs (say, at 4.3 per cent) and purchasing and reselling 90 days later a

FRN at a rate of 4.625 per cent, a difference of 32.5 basic points. The investor would have to realise that there was a risk that the FRNs could not be sold at 100 per cent 90 days later, so part of the 32.5 basic points was a reserve to protect against selling it at a price below par, plus commissions. The investor might ask a dealer to quote a repurchase rate at which the firm would agree to buy the FRNs back 90 days hence, and if a positive spread still existed (and the investor was willing to take the credit risk of the dealer meeting this obligation 90 days later) the investor might prefer the FRN trade to the ECD. On the other hand, the investor may prefer to remain a depositor in the bank, rather than a general creditor, and therefore accept a lower rate for the increased security.

Euro Commercial Paper

Commercial paper, which has been issued actively in the United States since the 1860s, first appeared in Europe in the early 1970s. It was aimed initially at U.S. corporations, which were required then by government regulations to finance all overseas investments with foreign borrowings, to provide a money-market alternative to bank borrowing. The effort was not successful. After commissions and set-up expenses, the cost of funds to the issuer was about the same as the cost of a comparable LIBOR-based bank loan. Euro investors were cautious; they were hesitant to buy the paper of companies that were not already well known and were unimpressed by the limited liquidity in the market. In 1974, the regulations requiring U.S. companies to finance overseas were repealed, and the market died away. The economics were simply not there—there was very little benefit of using the market at the time.

In the early 1980s, a new attempt was made to develop the ECP market. This time the initiative was aimed at banks that needed higher and safer returns on their money-market investments, and at corporate and institutional investors, which were increasingly concerned by the deterioration in bank credit ratings in the United States and wanted to diversify their cash management programmes into nonbank investments. Dealers, aware of these concerns, began to approach European money managers with proposals that they switch from ECDs or FRNs to ECP of top-name companies like AT&T and Exxon. They were earning only LIBID less 1/4 per cent from their bank deposits, but now they could diversify into higher grade paper, such as that issued by companies with AAA bond ratings, at a better rate, say, LIBID less 10 basic points. Or, if they were prepared to take corporate bond ratings of AA or A (with top grade U.S. commercial paper ratings of A1 and P1) they could look for an even higher rate, say, the mean between LIBID and LIBOR.

Treasury Securities

International money markets also include domestic short-term securities purchased by international investors. Mainly such investors are interested in government (Treasury) bills and notes because of their liquidity and high quality. These securities are available in all industrialised countries and in many less developed countries. Except during brief periods when foreign exchange markets are in turmoil pending a realignment, foreign investors rarely comprise more than a nominal percentage of the investment demand for domestic government securities. Even in the United States during the period 1984-87, when Japanese and other foreign investors (both central banks and private sector investors) were at their most active, all foreign holdings of U.S. Treasury securities never exceeded 7 per cent of the outstanding supply, of which perhaps half were official holdings of dollar reserves by foreign central banks. It is true, however, that foreign buying can be concentrated for a time on single auctions of newly issued paper, at which time the foreign demand can have a significant effect on the price of the paper being sold. Nonetheless, such concentrations of buying (or selling) power rarely last for long.

Investors acquire foreign treasury securities for essentially two reasons. One is to take a position in a liquid instrument that is subject to an expected price change because of changing interest or foreign exchange rates. Such investments are "uncovered," or unhedged positions. The investor *wants* the risk that the deutsche mark will increase in value relative to the dollar, and that foreign "speculators" will bid up the price of German Treasury securities. The other reason is to take a "covered" position, through which the investor might pick up several basic points of yield. If the investor can buy a six-month German Treasury bill, which, when swapped into dollars, yields more than six-month U.S. Treasury bills, he may be better off. A well-informed investor will scan the world's treasury and swap markets frequently looking for such opportunities. For a start, the investor can consult the daily posting in the *Financial Times* of world money rates, which are mainly reflections of secondary market prices for treasury bills in the various cities (i.e., countries) indicated.

Foreign Exchange Markets

Dealing in foreign exchange has become one of the most important activities for all international bankers and money-market investors. This is due to the continuous increase in world trade and cross-border financial flows in support of the real economy in a time of high volatility in foreign exchange markets. Customers of banks need assistance in managing and hedging their international cash flow, and banks have long been in the business of assisting them. In addition, funds flows in support of crossborder financial investments have increased substantially as a result of greater appreciation of international investment opportunities and easier mechanics through which to make them. The sums involved have been growing rapidly during the last several years and continue to do so. Investors need to fund these investments and to hedge them from time to time. Market-making by banks in foreign exchange has been an essential and profitable service to customers in both the manufacturing and financial sectors. Finally, banks and investment banks, and some investment funds, have found dealing for their own accounts to be an attractive source of potential profits. As in most trading markets, high volume and volatility make for an ideal environment for skillful participants.

Some years ago government officials, in discussing the foreign exchange markets, would refer to participants as "legitimate" commercial users, or as "speculators," presumably meaning that the latter group was something other than legitimate. This distinction, probably never very useful, is no longer used as market practices have become better understood.

For U.S. and U.K. investment banks, providing international advisory services has been a natural extension of providing the same services domestically. Increasingly today, whether the client is a buyer, a reluctant seller, or a willing target, tapping the international market for better terms than can be accessed domestically is often advisable and sometimes imperative. Banks with a strong local M&A team and an international presence—primarily U.S. investment houses—have been well positioned to take advantage of this aspect of globalisation.

To some extent the European and to a greater extent the Japanese environments have lacked the freely accessed capital markets and strict legal framework that have fostered the U.S. (and to a much lesser extent the U.K.) M&A business. As globalisation continues, however, a convergence of market conditions for M&As will occur. The evolving environment will have more of the transparent Anglo-Saxon characteristics than the continental European or Japanese.

As an activity generating substantial fees but requiring no direct commitment of the bank's capital, M&A and related advisory work has proved to be an irresistible attraction to many. Newcomers should be warned, however: M&A activities may not coexist easily with relationship banking in the same firm. Managing the M&A department is highly challenging. One must control the customer without alienating him and control the team without stifling it. One must maintain the delivery networks and the firm's image, knowing which deals to pursue and how to pursue them and which to decline. All demand skills specific to the M&A business increasingly projected into an international dimension.

The coming years will represent great challenges to most of the world's large financial service organisations. These firms will have to rethink their basic business strategies and attempt to reposition themselves so as to maximise their comparative advantages and minimise their weaknesses. Strategic repositioning, however, can be very difficult to execute, because the magnitude of internal change is so great. However, the key to succeeding in the new world financial order is adaptability.

CHAPTER 7

World Trading System

From World Trade Organisation (WTO) to General Agreement on Tariffs and Trade (GATT)

The World Trade Organisation (WTO) is an international organisation, established in 1995. It is responsible for administering multilateral trade agreements negotiated by its members, in particular the General Agreement on Tariffs and Trade (GATT), the General Agreement on Trade in Services (GATS), and the Agreement on Trade-Related Intellectual Property Rights (TRIPs). Total world trade in goods, services, and intellectual property stood at US $8 trillion in 2001, of which services and intellectual property accounted for over $1 trillion. The WTO's rules and principles establish a set of disciplines regarding the regulatory framework within which this exchange takes place.

The WTO builds upon the organisational structure that existed under GATT auspices as of the early 1990s. After its creation in 1947, the GATT progressively developed into a system of great complexity. Its reach expanded steadily in response to developments in the world economy and the interests of its signatories. Initially largely limited to a tariff agreement, the GATT increasingly came to incorporate negotiated disciplines on non-tariff trade policies, which increased in relative importance as average tariff levels fell. Its success was reflected in a steady expansion in the number of contracting parties. During the Uruguay round (1986-94), some 25 countries joined—bringing the total to 128 as of early 1995. To a large extent the GATT managed to fill the gap created by the stillborn International Trade Organisation (ITO) of 1948 and emerge as the world's *de facto* trade organisation. With the 1994 agreement to establish the WTO, the institution was formally transformed into an international organisation of equal standing to the International Monetary Fund (IMF) and the World Bank (as originally intended by the 1944 Bretton Woods conference where agreement was reached to create these bodies). The WTO itself does not embody substantive rules regarding government policies—it is simply a formal institutional structure under whose auspices members negotiate and implement trade agreements. The rules are contained in the treaties it oversees (GATT, GATS, TRIPs). The GATT therefore continues to exist as a substantive agreement, establishing a set of disciplines on the trade policies of its members. Indeed, its reach was greatly expanded by the Uruguay round. As trade in goods is by far the most important component of international trade, understanding what the GATT is and what it does (and does not do) is the key to understanding the WTO.

The basic underlying philosophy of the WTO is that open markets, nondiscrimination, and global competition in international trade are conducive to the national welfare of all countries. The underpinnings of the GATT and the WTO go back to the 1930s, a period when many countries pursued beggar-thy-neighbour policies including competitive devaluations and the imposition of high, discriminatory trade barriers. Such short-sighted, noncooperative behaviour was widely recognised to have constituted a very inferior policy in the aftermath of the Second World War. To a great extent the rationale for the creation of the GATT in 1947 was to prevent a repeat of the trade wars of the 1930s, not to mention the world war that followed. The collapse of world trade during the 1930s made a lasting impact on the generation that negotiated the GATT, as well as the International Monetary Fund (IMF) and the World Bank. The GATT became a forum for consultations and for recurring negotiations to extend multilateral liberalisation and co-operation on trade and related policies. It also acted as an institution that could act as a guarantor of domestic trade policy reform undertaken by governments desiring to dismantle barriers to imports.

The creation and success of the GATT constituted a striking example of international co-operation in an area where mercantilism was historically the norm. The basis of mercantilist policy was to maximise exports and minimise imports with a view to accumulating foreign exchange reserves (gold and silver). Mercantilism was driven by nationalism, the perception being that trade surpluses and political power were closely linked. Policy therefore tended to favour direct promotion of exports and restriction of imports through tariffs, taxes quotas, embargoes, and state monopolies. Despite arguments of major economists such as Adam Smith and David Ricardo that mercantilism constituted folly, few governments—Great Britain being a major exception—were convinced that free trade was a much preferable policy from a national welfare point of view. However, throughout much of the second half of the nineteenth century many countries negotiated bilateral trade agreements. The landmark that stands out in the commercial history of the nineteenth century is the Cobden-Chevalier Treaty of 1860, which liberalised trade between Great Britain and France, as well as throughout Europe. During 1862-7, France concluded a range of commercial treaties with every major trading nation in Europe (except Russia) and with the United States. As the treaties included a most-favoured-nation clause, and in each case the countries concerned also negotiated treaties with each other and with Great Britain, the trade concessions granted became general for all. As of the late 1860s, France was at the centre of an impressive network of trade agreements which substantially reduced protectionist trade barriers throughout Europe (Curzon, 1965).

As the US economy moved from recession into depression following the 1929 stock market crash, the US Congress adopted the infamous Smoot-Hawley Tariff Act, leading to a rise in average US tariffs from 38 to 52 per cent. This led US trading partners to impose retaliatory trade restrictions and engage in rounds of competitive devaluations. A domino effect occurred, as trade flows were diverted to relatively unprotected markets, resulting in lower prices, giving rise to protectionist pressure, and thus inducing higher trade barriers. The negative consequences of the trade wars and beggar-thy-neighbour policies of the early 1930s were still very vivid at the end of the Second World War. To a very significant extent they inspired the US willingness to pursue the type of international cooperation on trade that it had rejected in the 1920s and actively support multilateral liberalisation efforts (the GATT). The fear of a repeat also considerably hampered protectionist forces in the post-Second World War period.

While very successful in moving countries to liberalise trade and co-operate on trade policy-related matters, GATT rules and principles were frequently bent, if not broken, by its contracting parties. In instances where the choice was between risking serious conflict and attempting to enforce the letter of GATT disciplines—for example, on regional integration or on subsidies the contracting parties generally 'blinked' (Finger, 1993b; Hudec, 1993). In large part this reflects the nature of the institution, which is basically a club. The club has rules, but its members can decide to waive them, or pretend not to see violations. With the WTO, the institution has been strengthened, especially with regard to dispute-settlement and surveillance mechanisms. The WTO may therefore be somewhat less 'flexible' than the GATT was, which may in turn lead to greater pressures being put on the organisation if members decide to pursue the implementation of its rules more vigorously than in the past. This possibility is tempered by the fact that the WTO is a negotiating forum as well as a code of conduct. As under the GATT, bargaining and deal-making will remain at the heart of the WTO, as the organisation will continue to operate on the basis of consensus. Negotiating positions, the implementation of agreements, and the invocation of provisions allowing for the reimposition of protection are in turn all driven by internal political considerations in each WTO member, tempered by multilateral rules and expectations regarding the actions of other members of the club. The role of bargaining is probably the most striking dimension of the world trading system and perhaps the one that is most difficult for an outsider to grasp.

The focus is on the resulting rules of the game, not on the quantitative impact of the trade agreements (the effect on trade flows or the distribution of gains across countries). While such empirical issues are important, they are not particularly useful in understanding how the trading system functions.

Although economic theory suggests that countries should pursue liberal trade policies and exchange goods and services on the basis of their comparative advantage, in practice most nations actively intervene in international trade. Since 1947 the GATT has played a major role in constraining trade policies, in the process creating an ever more complex network of rights and obligations regulating international trade relations. Progress has sometimes been fitful, often involving two steps forward and one step back. None the less, recurring MTNs and the positive demonstration effects of the success of outward-oriented development strategies led to very significant declines in average levels of protection. GATT principles and mechanisms helped countries to grow by allowing firms to specialise and thereby fostering greater integration through trade. The trade flows involved are extensive. Global trade in goods and services equalled soms US $5 trillion (thousand billion) in the early 1990s. At $3.7 trillion, trade in goods accounted for the lion's share of global flows, followed by trade in services, which passed the $1 trillion mark in 1992. Much of the trade in merchandise involved OECD countries. Trade flows, intra-European trade accounted for over $1.2 trillion in 1992. Western European exchanges with the rest of the world accounted for another $450 billion. The dominance of trade was between and within the three major regions of the global economy: Europe, North America and Asia. Trade flows involving other parts of the globe are relatively small. Trade between these other regions is generally less than 0.5 per cent of world trade.

Although trade flows between developing country regions of the world are much smaller than those involving high-income regions, the volume and growth rate of global trade flows are important because international trade is an engine of growth. OECD markets provide developing countries with their most important export opportunities, while growth in developing countries generates imports of intermediate and capital goods as well as know-how. World trade growth has outstripped the growth of output consistently throughout most of the post-Second World War period, resulting in steady increase in trade openness ratios for most countries (the sum of exports and imports relative to gross domestic output). In the 1985-95 period, the growth of world trade was more than twice as high as the growth of global output (World Bank, 1995). This indicates that the world is becoming ever more integrated through trade. Rising trade openness ratios and integration in turn has significant positive impacts on total factor productivity—the portion of real output growth not accounted for by increasing inputs of labour and capital. This is because greater trade implies greater competition and therefore pressures to innovate and enhance productive efficiency, while at the same time allowing technological upgrading. By encouraging trade liberalisation, non-discrimination, and transparency of trade policies, the GATT supported the globalisation process.

Developing countries in particular have experienced very large increases in trade volumes and openness to the world economy. In the 1985-95 period they experienced real increases in trade flows that were on average 6 percentage points higher than real output growth (World Bank, 1995). This performance reflected to a great extent unilateral efforts by these countries to open their economies to foreign competition. As discussed at greater length below, developing countries traditionally refrained from full-fledged participation in GATT-based trade liberalisation efforts. With the establishment of the WTO, however, most developing countries signalled a greater willingness to abide by the rules of the game. The many reforms that have been taken unilaterally in the last decade by developing countries will lead to greater competitive pressure and concomitant dislocation costs in high-income countries. Although greatly outweighed by the gains associated with further integration of the world economy and economic growth of the developing world, fuller participation of developing economies and former centrally planned economies in global trade is likely to lead to friction. The creation of the WTO and the associated expansion of multilateral disciplines and strengthening of the institution therefore occurred at a propitious time. Indeed, the two developments were clearly linked. One of the major immediate challenges confronting the WTO will be to manage the process of integrating large economies such as China and Russia into the trading system. More generally, the system will be confronted with the continuing challenge of furthering the integration of the global economy.

WTO members face a different world from that existing in the immediate post-Second World War period. The US is no longer the hegemon of the world economy, willing to tolerate deviations from multilateral rules by trading partners. Many of the trade disputes and the recourse to NTBs in the 1980s were in part a reflection of what has been called the diminished giant syndrome of the USA (Bhagwati, 1991). The rising trade openness ratios alluded to earlier reflect the existence of a much more interdependent world than existed in the early 1950s. Instead of one hegemon (the US), there is a triad of powerful traders (the EU, Japan, and the USA). None of the three can be relied upon to take a leadership role. At the same time, the WTO as an international organisation has very few powers and at the end of the day what matters is the willingness of WTO members to invoke multilateral dispute-settlement procedures and play by the rules of the game. The absence of a hegemon can, in principle, prove beneficial in this regard, as all players have an interest in maintaining co-operation (or alternatively, enforcing the rules). Doubts can be and often have been expressed regarding the relevance of the rules for large players. The rise of creative forms of protectionism in the 1980s, such as voluntary export restraints, illustrates the difficulty of enforcing multilaterally negotiated rules. Time will tell how successful the WTO will be in maintaining and extending multilateral co-operation and preventing large countries such as the US from pursuing solutions to trade problems outside the system. The very act of creating the WTO gives some cause for optimism in this regard.

The World Trade Organisation

The WTO is entirely institutional and procedural; it draws upon the GATT and its Uruguay Round resolutions in its Annexes for compliance. The WTO is not a mere replacement or succession of the GATT. The WTO Agreement under the Uruguay Round of GATT Trade negotiations provides a 'common institutional framework for the conduct of trade relations among its members' (Article II of the Agreement). The new institution upgraded several working arrangements and rules with considerable clarity, as in the case of dispute resolution, adoption of resolutions and voiding veto powers for members. Some of the 'birth defects' of the GATT were modified in the WTO.

The WTO Charter XVI.1 states clearly that GATT's decisions, procedures and customary practices will be guiding principles to the extent feasible. The WTO budget was estimated (Blackhurst, 1998) at an equivalent of about 10 minutes of the value of the world merchandise trade in mid-1990s.

The WTO remains a rather unique intergovernmental institution governed mainly by a contract between its members. Unlike the GATT, the member countries are not simply 'contracting parties', and the organisation is governed by a treaty set up rather than as a 'provisional' organisation. The WTO does not describe itself as a 'free trade' institution. Rather, it prefers to be described as a 'system of rules dedicated to open, fair and undistorted competition'.

A brief history and salient features of the institutional innovation, implications of some of the provisions of the WTO Agreement, coexistence of the WTO with other international institutions like the World Bank and IMF, the role of environmental concerns within the multilateral trading regimes governed by the WTO are some of the issues for a brief summary in this chapter.

After about half a century of 'provisional' existence of the GATT, its replacement with the new and more comprehensive treaty-based member-driven institution WTO for the governance of multilateral trading systems is a reflection of the determination of the large number (135 at about the end of the twentieth century) of the countries that are members towards a strengthened global trade regime. The fact that about 30 more countries are waiting to join the WTO is a testimony to the functioning and efficacy of the new institution, shown by the results of the first five years. The charter of the organisation and the obligations of the members were formulated in the April 1994 Marrakesh Declaration 'The Results of the Uruguay Round of Multilateral Trade Negotiations'. This comprised 29 legal texts and an additional 28 Declarations/Understandings, leading to a total of 558 pages of statements and stipulations. Very few global agreements tend to be so clearly written and remain focused on the theme and relevant issues. The provision for cooperating with some of the international organisations (including nongovernmental organisations) 'that have responsibilities related to those of the WTO' was included in Article V.1 of the WTO Agreement. This is an improvement over the GATT framework which included only the IMF explicitly. The defining characteristic of the WTO is that it places more emphasis on contractual rules than on collective action, and it relies on the countries participating in the rules-based trade system to enforce the rules largely on the basis of individual initiative. Thus, the new institution is also called a 'contract' organisation. However, the participating countries are members and not simply 'contracting parties' as in the case of the GATT 1947.

The Legal Structure of the WTO

Whereas the GATT 1947 dealt with trade in goods, the WTO deals with those issues and also the governance of the General Agreement on Trade in Services (GATS), and Trade-Related Intellectual Property Rights (TRIPs), in addition to a well-defined Dispute Resolution Understanding (DRU). The WTO charter includes four Annexes 1 to 4, listed below (see also GATT, 1994 and WTO, 1995). Several additional details regarding these are given in Appendix I:

- Annex 1: Multilateral Trade Agreements. This contains most of the Uruguay Round resolutions and stipulates binding obligations on the members (unlike some or most of the loosely defined obligations under the GATT 1947), detailed below.
- Annex 1A: GATT 1994. This is the revised and comprehensive GATT which includes codes of standards and schedules of tariff concessions. The Agreement on the Application of Sanitary & Phytosanitary Measures deals with some semblance of environmental dimensions.
- Annex IB: GATS, with its Annexes and specific commitments.
- Annex 2: TRIPS, with its stipulations.
- Annex 3: Dispute Settlement Procedures.
- Annex 3A: TPRM, in existence since 1988 with an emphasis on transparency of trade policies at each individual country level.
- Annex 4: Deals with optional or plurilateral agreements in specific sectors or sub-sectors.

The new institution is unique in several respects, some of which are the following:

1. Specification of contractual obligations such as policy bindings on members.
2. Transparency and coherence in the enforcement of

trade policy mechanisms, dispute resolution mechanisms and their compliance.

3. One country-one vote mechanism of governance, providing sufficient voice for the developing countries to advance their viewpoints in trade and economic integration.
4. Time-bound completion of the stipulated methods of compliance of members to various policy agreements and dispute resolution mechanisms.
5. Well-defined time schedules for the governing council or other oversight groups to formulate/ implement required activities.
6. TPRM is now a permanent arrangement to integrate trade balance and development aspects of member countries.

Although the GATT progressively acquired many of the attributes of an international organisation, it was increasingly felt in the 1980s that it was not keeping up with the rapid changes in the global economy, and required strengthened dispute-settlement and transparency mechanisms. While this was reflected in the agenda of the Uruguay round, the Ministerial Declaration establishing the round's agenda did not call for the creation of a WTO. Instead, it was agreed that the round would be a 'single undertaking', with all its agreements applying to all GATT contracting parties. In principle, it was not necessary to create an international organisation to implement the results of the round, especially in so far as a common dispute-settlement mechanism was agreed to apply to all of the various agreements reached. The suggestion to establish a Multilateral Trade Organisation (MTO) by Canada in 1990—supported by the EU—was therefore something of a surprise. An important motivation to establish an MTO was to have a single institutional framework encompassing the modified GATT, its sister bodies on services (GATS) and intellectual property (TRIPs), and all other agreements and arrangements concluded under the auspices of the Uruguay round. The United States initially opposed the idea, but, after further negotiations on the substance of the new organisation, agreed to the framework that currently exists, including the name change. Although the US Congress remained suspicious of any limitations to its sovereign powers in trade policy, during the ratification debate it became clear that the establishment of the WTO would not do much to change the status quo as far as the infringement of sovereignty was concerned. The GATT-1947 was a binding international treaty, and most of the institutional aspects of the WTO already existed under the GATT.

None the less, the establishment of the WTO was a significant event. Attempts to put the GATT on a more secure organisational footing had been made periodically since the failure of the US Congress to ratify the ITO. During a 1955 meeting to review the GATT, a number of contracting parties proposed to establish an Organisation for Trade Co-operation (OTC). This proposal was much less elaborate than the ITO but it also failed to win the approval of the US Congress (Jackson, 1990). The issue of providing an institutional framework for international trade reappeared again in the Economic and Social Council (ECOSOC) of the UN in 1963. A group of experts called for the creation of a new UN agency with universal membership and substantial powers in the sphere of international trade (Kostecki, 1979). The idea was that this body would implement, inter alia, recommendations of UNCTAD as well as other relevant policy decisions taken by organs of the UN. The proposal envisaged that the GATT would become the agency's Committee on Tariffs. The proposal did not meet with much interest among the major trading nations. However, the 1964 UN General Assembly resolution establishing UNCTAD provided that it should be concerned with matters relating to the elaboration of a comprehensive trade organisation. Nothing concrete came of this—despite lengthy discussions about the need for a New International Economic Order during the 1970s—in large part because of the widely differing philosophies held by industrialised market economies and much of the developing world regarding the appropriate basis for international trade. With the creation of the WTO, an international trade organisation exists that is firmly based on GATT principles—reciprocity and non-discrimination.

Multilateral Trade Agreements, Trade in Goods

Economic theory suggests that trade policy is rarely the most efficient way of achieving a government's objective. Governments pursue trade policies for a variety of reasons, including as a means of raising revenue, to protect specific industries (whether 'infant', 'senile' or other), to shift the terms of trade, to attain certain foreign policy or security goals, or simply to restrict the consumption of specific goods. Whatever the underlying objective, an active trade policy redistributes income between segments of the population by protecting specific industries and the factors of production employed there, usually does so in an inefficient manner, and for that reason tends to be supported by interest-groups that lobby for import restrictions.

The GATT essentially regulates trade policies. It does not address the basic question whether governments should use domestic or trade policies to achieve particular objectives. That is, the issue of efficiency is not addressed directly. The implicit premiss is that inefficiency (i.e., the use of trade policy) must be accepted, and that the best that can be achieved is to discipline the use of different types of trade policies. Thus, while countries are free to use trade policies, they are generally encouraged to use measures that are the least trade restrictive. GATT rules are mostly consistent with what economic theory would recommend in many circumstances, but only in the sense of moving governments to use second-best rather than third-best instruments. The objective is in some sense to avoid the worst by accepting some bad in government intervention.

Three broad categories of trade-policy instruments can be distinguished: measures that affect quantities, restricting the volume or value of transactions; those that affect prices, involving the imposition of a monetary fee (tax) on foreign suppliers or have an equivalent effect; and those that may indirectly affect quantities and/or prices. Annex 4 provides a list of trade-policy instruments that are often used. Many of the specific policies mentioned are subject to GATT rules, while others are not. Virtually any policy or action by a government may have an effect on trade. As noted in Chapter 2, this is explicitly recognised in the GATT, in that dispute—settlement procedures allow for so-called non-violation complaints to be brought. Any policy—whether or not it is prohibited under GATT—can be contested if it acts to deny a benefit of the Agreement.

Dispute Resolution Mechanisms

Perhaps the most significant improvement of the WTO over the GATT 1947 is its dispute settlement understanding (DSU). The GATT clauses for trade disputes settlement were too vague and too brief: contained in three precious paragraphs. The DSU, spelled out in 40 pages, incorporates several new dimensions such as the role of rules that cannot be vetoed by a single member country, clear schedules and time-bound actions in processing disputes and their effective compliance, recognition of the role of customary international public law and provision of measures to compensate members for adverse impacts of any trade policy violation by one or more measures. The DSU was expected to contribute towards security and predictability to the multilateral trading systems.

During the first four years of existence of the new DSU, the complaints by developed country members added to 124 requests dealing with 96 different subjects. Complaints by developing country members during this period were 31 requests, dealing with 29 different subjects. There were 4 complaints by both developed and developing country members with 10 requests—these included three requests made by developed country members. The total number of consultation requests made by developing country members was 40; on the basis of distinct matters, the number was 32.

The role of the global trading institutions and specifically that of the WTO is critical as well in this context. The US has been the most active litigant, both in filing cases against other members and in defending various cases filed against it. Some of the cases are rather insignificant in the context of global trade volumes affected or potentially to be affected, but the dispute is one of compliance with agreed upon principles of trade and various rules evolved under the WTO Agreement. For example, five cases were filed a few months ago by the US against Belgium, France, Greece, Ireland and the Netherlands; all these relate to income tax subsidies, apparently in possible violation of the agreements on subsidies inhibiting competitiveness of exports. In the case against Belgium, this involved the provision of tax rules which enabled corporate tax payers to receive special tax exemption for recruiting personnel with export related work functions.

Developing Countries and the WTO

For a long time, the GATT was basically a club that was primarily of relevance to OECD countries. Developing countries did not participate fully. With the creation of the WTO this changed, significantly expanding the global significance of the organisation. Fuller participation on the part of developing countries constitutes both a challenge for the WTO and an opportunity. This chapter briefly reviews the history of developing countries' involvement in GATT.

Special and Differential Treatment

The terms of developing countries' participation in the multilateral trading system has oscillated over time. Three stages can be identified:

1. Small-scale membership of low-income countries in GATT based on a formal parity of obligations, although from the very start developing countries maintained that they should be granted special treatment (1947-64).
2. Substantial broadening of developing-country

membership based on the concept of 'more favourable and differential' treatment (1964-86).

3. Deepening integration of developing countries into the GATT-WTO system, with a return to reciprocal responsibilities (1986).

Although the initial premiss underlying GATT-1947 was essentially parity of obligations between rich and poor trading nations (Hudec, 1987), the concept of giving preferential treatment to developing countries existed from the start. It gained prominence in the mid-1950s, when a large number of colonies approached independence. Two types of preferential treatment can be distinguished. The first consisted of a request for preferential access to rich country markets through tariff preferences. Such preferences were already in effect, largely reflecting economic relationships built up by France and the UK with their colonies. A second form of preferential treatment consisted of exemptions from GATT rules and mechanisms. Preferences were justified in various ways. One argument was so-called export pessimism. The fear was that if developing countries relied upon exports for growth their supply of commodities would exceed what could be absorbed by the world.

GATT and Developing Countries

Date	*Event*
1947	Ten what would now be called low-income countries accede to the GATT on essentially the same terms as developed countries. An infant-industry protection clause (Article XVIII) is the main development-specific provision in GATT. Only one BOP Article existed: Article XII.
1954-55	Article XVIII is modified to include XVIII:b allowing for QRs to be used for BOP purposes whenever foreign-exchange reserves are below what is considered necessary for economic development. This vague test constitutes much weaker discipline

than Article XII. It has been invoked extensively (see Chapter 7).

1964 Establishment of UNCTAD. A committee for Trade and Development is created in the GATT to address development-related concerns; the International Trade Centre (ITC) is charged with assisting developing countries to promote exports.

1965 A new Part IV on Trade and Development is added to the GATT, which defined the notion of non-reciprocity for developing countries. However, Part IV contains no legally binding obligations.

1968 The USA accepts the Generalised System of Preferences (GSP) as called for by UNCTAD— under which industrialised countries were to grant tariff preferences to developing countries on a non-reciprocal basis. Tariff preferences were voluntary, not mandatory, and granted unilaterally. The ITC becomes a joint venture with UNCTAD.

1971 A GATT waiver is granted authorising tariff preferences under the GSP. Another waiver is adopted for the Protocol on Trade Negotiations among Developing Countries (Geneva Protocol).

1973-79 More than 70 developing countries participate in the Tokyo round. The enabling Clause is adopted which introduces the concept of 'special and differential treatment, (S&D) *inter alia* making the 1971 waivers permanent and including language on graduation. Most developing countries abstain from signing the various Tokyo round codes.

1986 Developing countries approve launching of the Uruguay round with a ministerial declaration that contains many references to S&D.

1994 All developing-country GATT contracting parties join the WTO, adopting the results of the Uruguay round as a Single Undertaking.

The resulting predicted decline in the terms of trade was considered to justify trade restrictions by developing countries —in effect, they had to impose an optimal tariff to improve their terms of trade (Prebisch, 1952; Bhagwati, 1988). Given their reliance on exports of commodities, export pessimism was complemented by the view—persuasively argued by Prebisch (1952)—that developing countries needed protection to achieve industrialisation and economic development, and that a new world trade order was required to break the 'vicious circle of underdevelopment'. Developing countries, it was argued, suffered from foreign-exchange shortages requiring protectionist policies to protect their balance of payments. International trade was also seen by some as an instrument of exploitation and self-sufficiency as beneficial. More generally, it was argued that development strategies required freedom to pursue import substitution policies.

The institutional expression of this line of thinking was embodied in the creation of UNCTAD in 1964, and the formation of a political bloc of developing countries in the UN called the 'Group of 77'. One year later, in 1965, developing-country demands for special status in the multilateral trading system led to the adoption of a new Part IV of the GATT. Part IV defined non-reciprocity for developing countries. To a large extent the inclusion of Part IV can be seen as a reaction of the GATT contracting parties to the creation of UNCTAD. As of that moment, special and differential treatment (S&D) for developing countries reigned supreme for the next 20 years. Developing countries were not expected to grant tariff concessions and bind tariffs, instead being granted the 'privilege' of free-riding through the operation of the MFN principle. However, these privileges were not formally embodied in the GATT, as the provisions of Part IV were of a best endeavour nature.

Developing nations successfully invoked the principle of non-reciprocity as cover for not engaging in reciprocal reductions of trade barriers. For example, the 1973 ministerial meeting that established the agenda of the Tokyo round stated that the MTN should secure additional benefits for developing countries in order to achieve a substantial increase in their foreign-exchange earnings, diversification of their exports, and an acceleration of the rate of growth of their trade. It confirmed that the developed countries should not expect reciprocal concessions from developing economies. The inconsistency between these goals and the policy of allowing developing countries to maintain protection and GATT-inconsistent trade regimes was not openly remarked upon. During the negotiations, developed countries repeatedly voiced their dissatisfaction with the reluctance of developing countries to accept GATT disciplines. This found its expression in the negotiation of codes on various issues in which membership was voluntary—voiding the veto that was likely by developing countries if an attempt was made to amend the GATT to include new obligations.

Trade Policy and Global Opportunities

There are many views as to the sources and characteristics of globalisation and the actors responsible for the shape it takes. Differing views over its merits and de-merits have led to many passionate debates in recent years. However, one common element permeates these debates: it is agreed that the process of globalisation is characterised by a greater degree of interdependence between nations. Equally well accepted is that international trade is an important feature of this interdependence. As trade in goods and services has been progressively liberalised over the past half-century, international trade has increased dramatically and so has the interdependence of nations and the process of globalisation. The rules that govern trade, and therefore the role of the World Trade Organisation in global governance, have proliferated accordingly.

The world spotlight was on the WTO at its third meeting of trade ministers in Seattle in December 1999. Many had hoped a new round of multilateral trade negotiations—the Millennium Round—would be launched at this meeting. Not only were the new negotiations not launched, but the meeting ended in disarray, with the WTO facing criticism from many quarters.

Conducting world trade according to multilaterally agreed rules has been a major contributor not only to the enormous expansion of the world economy over the half-century, but also to the avoidance of international conflict. Thus, if there is to be reform of the current trading system, it should be done with care in order to preserve the many strengths of the system while responding to legitimate concerns. Carefully guiding the process of globalisation-with-a-human-face is a challenging task. This, indeed, is one of the most important challenges facing policy makers at the international level today.

In the aftermath of Seattle, it became increasingly apparent that many varying views were held by prominent personalities regarding the current and future role of the WTO in international affairs. A number of these personalities represent bodies of the United Nations and other intergovernmental organisations, government ministries, and NGOs. Some present the views of private corporations, think tanks, and the press.

It is timely to bring together the views of a number of these prominent people in one volume. The intention is to provide an opportunity for contributors to state clearly their interests in a well-functioning WTO trading system and to offer suggestions about what the WTO can do to meet the challenges it faces in areas of particular interest to them. A clear statement of these concerns and proposed solutions should assist the debate to proceed in a positive manner.

Much of traditional economic theory presumes the infinite availability of ecological and environmental assets. This implicit assumption led to the focus on principles of comparative advantage as the single most important determinant of international trade. While this premise still has some merit, the empirical evidence shows that the role of a number of other important elements is rather dominant. These elements include national or geographic borders, transaction costs, institutional configurations like the RTAs, political economy of alternate forms of trade patterns, and the role of multilateral institutions (or endogenous institutional dynamics). Freer trade for its own sake is not a desirable end product; it should be integrated with broader issues of development, and sustainability.

The role of GATT and its impact during its half-a-century of provisional existence indicates its positive impact in reducing trade distortions and tariff barriers. The emergence of the new WTO with a full fledged charter structure and member participation portends much greater influence and impact on the global trade, economy and the environment will not be threatened by heightened international capital mobility. The truly representative consumer, if there is such a person, is a median worker with average skills and training whose wages are likely to fall in real terms, no matter how many imported consumer goods he or she buys.

Chronology

1944	Bretton Woods Conference on global economic arrangements.
1946	The International Bank for Reconstruction and Development (IBRD) and the International Monetary Fund (IMF) start activities.
1947	Drawing up of the institution of GATT.
1947	First Round of multilateral tariff reductions negotiated in Geneva.
1948	Adoption of the ITO charter by the International Conference on Trade and Employment in Havana.
1949	Second Round of multilateral tariff negotiations in Annecy.
1951	Third Round of multilateral tariff negotiations in Torquay.
1956	Fourth Round of multilateral trade negotiations in Geneva.
1957	Treaty of Rome establishes European Common Market.

1960-61	Fifth Round of tariff negotiations under the GATT: Dillon Round.
1964-67	Sixth Round of tariff negotiations—GATT: Kennedy Round.
1973-79	Seventh Round of negotiations—GATT: Tokyo Round.
1986-92	Eighth Round negotiations—GATT: Uruguay Round.
1989	Trade Policy Review Mechanism (TPRM) introduced in the GATT after mid-term review of the Uruguay Round.
Feb. 1992	Signing of the Treaty of Maastricht.
April 1994	Marrakesh Declaration—Final Act of the Uruguay Round resolutions and establishing the WTO.
Jan. 1995	Birth of the WTO.
Nov. 1996	Formal agreements regarding cooperation of the IBRD and the IMF with the WTO.
Dec. 1996	WTO First Ministerial Conference in Singapore.
May 1998	WTO Second Ministerial Conference in Geneva.
Mar. 1999	WTO High Level Conferences on Trade and Environment, and on Trade and Development in Geneva.
Dec. 1999	WTO Third Ministerial Conference in Seattle.

II. GATT 1994

1. The General Agreement on Tariffs and Trade 1994 ('GATT 1994') shall consist of:

   (a) the provisions in the General Agreement on Tariffs and Trade, dated 30 October 1947, annexed to the Final Act Adopted at the Conclusion of the Second Session of the Preparatory Committee of the United Nations Conference on Trade and Employment (excluding the Protocol of Provisional Application), as rectified, amended or modified by the terms of legal instruments which have entered into force before the date of entry into force of the WTO agreement;

(b) The provisions of the legal instruments set forth below that have entered into force under the GATT 1947 before the date of entry into force of the WTO Agreement:

"(i) protocols and certifications relating to tariff concessions;

(ii) protocols and accession (excluding the provisions (a) concerning provisional application and withdrawal of provisional application and (b) providing the Part II of GATT 1947 shall be applied provisionally to the fullest extent not inconsistent with legislation existing on the date of the Protocol);

(iii) decisions on waivers granted under Article XXV of GATT 1947 and still in force on the date of entry into force of the WTO Agreement;

(iv) other decisions of the CONTRACTING PARTIES to GAIT 1947;

The discussion of the Pacific rim surplus countries points out the subtleties involved in trying to disentangle structural and macroeconomic causes of trade imbalances. Since Japan, China, and Taiwan together account for roughly 80 per cent of the 1992 U.S. trade deficit, these three cases are clearly consequential to the aggregate outcome. In each case, it is possible to identify structural factors that contribute to large trade surpluses, including closed internal markets and highly competitive exports (Japan more in terms of rising technological sophistication and high product quality, China and Taiwan more in terms of low unit labour costs). Nevertheless, there are also macroeconomic factors at work, including undervalued currencies and insufficiently expansionary fiscal and monetary policies. In the cases of these countries, the structural and macroeconomic determinants of trade balances seem to be reinforcing each other in creating chronic surpluses, rather than offsetting each other and eliminating surplus tendencies. Macroeconomic correctives could be made but are impeded by political institutions and entrenched interests. Market forces alone do not automatically call forth such correctives.

As noted earlier, even allowing macroeconomic correctives to work can have its costs. Depreciating the dollar lowers the U.S. terms of trade and the purchasing power of domestic incomes. Slower income growth in the United States helps to keep the trade balance down but at tremendous social cost. For these reasons, it is imperative for the surplus countries to shoulder more of the burden of adjustment. Expansionary macro policies and market opening can both raise domestic living standards and cure external imbalances in surplus countries that are suppressing consumer welfare. This is the growth path, rather than the stagnation path, to restoring global trade balances.

In the end, this discussion shows that the structural and macroeconomic aspects of trade balances are closely intertwined. The structural characteristics (e.g., labour productivity, trade barriers, product quality, technological innovation) determine the parameters within which traditional macro policies (fiscal, monetary, and exchange rate) operate, while the latter determine the degree to which the structural factors are manifest in trade imbalances or in other variables. To ignore the macroeconomic relationships and policies would be naive and misleading. It is equally wrong to ignore the structural causes of trade imbalances, or to pretend that they are automatically and costlessly offset by macroeconomic adjustments. The precise way in which structural and macroeconomic factors interact will vary over time and between countries. Understanding the variety of ways in which they can interact and the full range of policy alternatives for dealing with imbalances when they arise is essential for sound policy formulation.

There is no single answer to the fundamental question of why nations grow at different rates, with diverse distributions of income and wealth. It is clear that policy must be tailored to the local situation and even to the particular conditions prevailing at the time.

This view contrasts with the Washington Consensus (WC) about how a relatively uniform policy package can be applied with beneficial results almost everywhere. For the record as well as for comparisons with counterpoints to be set out below, the WC embodies the following notions:

W1. The fiscal budget should be balanced, with a deficit of at most a few percentage points of GDP, tight spending controls, and broad-based taxation programmes with low marginal rates.

W2. Price reform should be aimed at positive (presumably moderate) real interest rates and a weak, stable exchange rate.

W3. Trade should be liberalised and direct foreign investment should be welcomed.

W4. State enterprises should be privatised.

W5. Markets should be deregulated, especially the labour market.

W6. There is a need for "sound" macroeconomic policy and at least a rudimentary social safety net.

W7. Accumulation of human capital has positive effects on growth and distribution.

W8. "Stabilisation" or removal of macroeconomically disabling balance of payments and fiscal gaps as well as inflation has to come before "adjustment" or creation of conditions for sustainable growth; together with institutional changes, stabilisation and adjustment are supposed to produce viable "reform."

W9. There is an implicit promise that pursuit of market-friendly policies will be supported by external donors, especially the World Bank and IMF.

Despite the appeal of these recommendations to the BWIs and the mainstream, "consensus" is too strong a word to apply to them. In particular, progressive (P) economists would on the whole agree with the following counterpoints to the WC:

P1. Fiscal equilibrium is desirable, but it can be devilishly difficult to attain. The fiscal, foreign exchange, and saving gaps are closely linked. Improvement in the first is not likely without gains for the other two as well. External support may well be required on all three fronts. It was certainly available in the (provisionally) successful reform cases of the 1980s. Reducing a fiscal deficit is always tricky in political terms; in some corners of the world, distributional conflicts make it well nigh inconceivable.

P2. Changing real macro prices, such as wage rates, exchange rates, and interest rates, is not easy. The required movements in their nominal counterparts may have to be large (tens of percentage points, or even more), with complicated, economy/wide effects and inflationary complications. Numerous orthodox programmes based upon such changes in nominal exchange and interest rates have resoundingly failed. Gains in allocative efficiency when real macro prices are revised can be trivial, while losses in production may be painfully large (recent experiences in Eastern Europe are obvious examples).

P3. External liberalisation programmes have fared no better than packages based on intelligent use of quotas and controls. The advantages of the latter include the possibility of using the threat of withdrawing protection to extract efficient production from the private sector without having to estimate and impose a whole set of allocatively "correct" prices. Direct foreign investment bolsters the balance of payments and may help with acquisition of technology, but home-based firms may be able to do a still better job of acquiring technology.

P4. Privatisation brings no obvious productivity gains, and if done in slapdash fashion it can adversely perturb saving, investment, and financial flows. The same observation applies to attempts to restructure a "repressed" financial system by raising interest rates and abdicating prudential control.

P5. Labour market deregulation may slash wage costs in the short run, presumably to some export advantage, but it may prove inimical to long-run socioeconomic development, and it can slow accumulation of productive human assets.

P6. Sound macroeconomic policy is always desirable, as are stable family relationships and apple pie. Whether it is feasible under LDC political and distributional conditions is another question. If "soundness" means austerity, it runs a grave risk of inducing secular stagnation.

P7. An increasingly educated, healthy, and well-paid population is necessary for long-run productivity growth. However, speeding up human capital accumulation is not a sufficient condition for raising actual or even potential output in the short run.

P8. Stabilisation before (or concurrent with) adjustment sounds sensible but does not always work out. Maybe basic improvements in fiscal or balance-of-payments positions are required before macroeconomic difficulties can be overcome. There are recent examples both ways.

P9. As the macroeconomic analysis and country vignettes in this chapter indicate, there is no certainty that external support will be forthcoming in exchange for pursuit of a WC policy package. Again, there are examples to support both possibilities.

P10. Indeed, there have been successes and failures of both orthodox and heterodox policy initiatives more generally. The problem is how to invent and sequence policy changes effective in each economy's historical and institutional context. A little bit is known about how such factors as the structure of the existing capital stock, the size of the population, and natural resource endowments put somewhat flexible boundary conditions on policies aimed at raising productive efficiency, but the general solution to this problem is neither known nor likely to be found.

Political Economy and Global Trade System

The World Trade Organisation (WTO) is an international organisation, established in 1995. It is responsible for administering multilateral trade agreements negotiated by its members, in particular the General Agreement on Tariffs and Trade (GATT), the General Agreement on Trade in Services (GATS), and the Agreement on Trade-Related Intellectual Property Rights (TRIPs). Total world trade in goods, services, and intellectual property stood at US $5 trillion in 1995, of which services and intellectual property accounted for over $1 trillion. The WTO's rules and principles establish a set of disciplines regarding the regulatory framework in which this exchange takes place.

The WTO builds upon the organisational structure that existed under GATT auspices as of the early 1990s. After its creation in 1947, the GATT progressively developed into a system of great complexity. Its reach expanded steadily in response to developments in the world economy and the interests of its signatories. Initially largely limited to a tariff agreement, the GATT increasingly came to incorporate negotiated disciplines on non-tariff trade policies, which increased in relative importance as average tariff levels fell. Its success was reflected in a steady expansion in the number of contracting parties. During the Uruguay round (1986-94), some 25 countries joined—bringing the total to 128 as of early 1995. To a large extent the GATT managed to fill the gap created by the stillborn International Trade Organisation (ITO) of 1948 and emerge as the world's *de facto* trade organisation. With the 1994 agreement to establish the WTO, the institution was formally transformed into an international organisation of equal standing to the International Monetary Fund (IMF) and the World Bank (as originally intended by the 1944 Bretton Woods conference where agreement was reached to create these bodies). The WTO itself does not embody substantive rules regarding government policies—it is simply a formal institutional structure under whose auspices members negotiate and implement trade agreements. The rules are contained in the treaties it oversees (GATT, GATS, TRIPs). The GATT therefore continues to exist as a substantive agreement, establishing a set of disciplines on the trade policies of its members. Indeed, its reach was greatly expanded by the Uruguay round. As trade in goods is by far the most important component of international trade, understanding what the GATT is and what it does (and does not do) is the key to understanding the WTO. Much of this volume therefore focuses on the GATT.

To a great extent the rationale for the creation of the GATT in 1947 was to prevent a repeat of the trade wars of the 1930s, not to mention the world war that followed. The collapse of world trade during the 1930s made a lasting impact on the generation that negotiated the GATT, as well as the International Monetary Fund and the World Bank. The GATT became a forum for consultations and for recurring negotiations to extend multilateral liberalisation and co-operation on trade and related policies. It also acted as an institution that could act as a guarantor of domestic trade policy reform undertaken by governments desiring to dismantle barriers to imports.

The creation and success of the GATT constituted a striking example of international co-operation in an area where mercantilism was historically the norm. The basis of mercantilist policy was to maximise exports and minimise imports with a view to accumulating foreign exchange reserves (gold and silver). Mercantilism was driven by nationalism, the perception being that trade surpluses and political power were closely linked. Policy therefore tended to favour direct promotion of exports and restriction of imports through tariffs, taxes, quotas, embargoes, and state monopolies. Despite arguments of major economists such as Adam Smith and David Ricardo that mercantilism constituted folly, few governments—Great Britain being a major exception—were convinced that free trade was a much preferable policy from a national welfare point of view. However, throughout much of the second half of the nineteenth century many countries negotiated bilateral trade agreements. The landmark that stands out in the commercial history of the nineteenth century is the Cobden-Chevalier Treaty of 1860, which liberalised trade between Great Britain and France, as well as throughout Europe. During 1862-67, France concluded a range of commercial treaties with every major trading nation in Europe (except Russia) and with the United States. As the treaties included a most-favoured-nation clause, and in each case the countries concerned also negotiated treaties with each other and with Great Britain, the trade concessions granted became general for all. As of the late 1860s, France was at the centre of an impressive network of trade agreements which substantially reduced protectionist trade barriers throughout Europe (Curzon, 1965).

Bibliography

Allen, D. (1979), "Tariff Games," in S. Brams, A. Schotter, and G. Schwoediauer (eds.), "Applied Game Theory" (Wuerzburg: Physica-Verlag).

Anderson, K. (1992), "Effects on the Environment and Welfare of Liberalizing World Trade: The Cases of Coal and Food," in K. Anderson and R. Blackhurst (eds.), *The Greening of World Trade Issues* (London: Harvester-Wheatsheaf).

——, (1993a), "Lobbying Incentives and the Pattern of Protection in Rich and Poor Countries," Discussion Paper no. 789 (London: Centre for Economic Policy Research).

——, (1993b), "US-EC Farm Trade Confrontation: An Outsider's View," Discussion Paper no. 849 (London: Centre for Economic Policy Research).

Anderson, K. and Norheim, H. (1993), "History, Geography and Regional Integration," in K. Anderson and R. Blackhurst (eds.), "Regional Integration and the Global Trading System". (London: Harvester-Wheatsheaf).

Angell, Norman (1929). *The Story of Money.* New York: Frederick A. Stokes Company.

Arayama, Yuko and Panos Mourdoukoutas (1999), *China against Herself: Innovation or Imitation in Global Business?* Westport, Conn.: Quorum.

Bagehot, Walter. *Lombard Street: A Description of the Money Market.* London: 1873.

Baillie, Richard T. and William P. Osterberg (1997), "Why Do Central Banks Intervene?" *Journal of International Money and Finance* 16, 6.

Baldwin, R. (1970), "Non-Tariff Distortions in International Trade" (Washington DC: Brookings Institution).

Baldwin, R. (1986), "Toward More Efficient Procedures for Multilateral Trade Negotiations," Aussenwirtschaft, 41: 379-94.

Baldwin, R. and Clarke R. (1987), "'Game Modelling the Tokyo Round of Tariff Negotiations," *Journal of Policy Modeling*, 9: 257-84.

Ballassa, Bella (1963), "An Empirical Demonstration of Classical Comparative Cost Theory." *Review of Economics and Statistics*.

Banks, G. (1983), "The Economics and Politics of Countertrade," *World Economy*, 6: 159-82.

Barker, David Knox (1995), *The K Wave: Profiting from the Cyclical Booms and Busts in the Global Economy* (New York: Irwin), p. 57.

Bartlett, C. and S. Ghoshal (1989), *Managing Across Borders: the Transnational Solution*, Boston: Harvard Business School Press.

Bennet, John and Maw James (June 1998), *Privatization and Market Structure in a Transition Economy. Working Paper* no. 175. Ann Arbor, Mich.: The William Davidson Institute.

——, *Privatization and Market Structure in a Transition Economy. Working Paper* no. 175. Ann Arbor, Mich.: The William Davidson Institute.

Bhagwati, J. (1971), "The Generalized Theory of Distortions and Welfare", in J. N. Bhagwati, R. Mundell, R. Jones, and J. Vanek (eds.), *Trade, Balance of Payments and Growth* (Amsterdam: North Holland).

——, (1984), "Splintering and Disembodiment of Services and Developing Nations," *World Economy*, 7: 133-44.

——, (1987), "Trade in Services and the Multilateral Trade Negotiations", *World Bank Economic Review*, 1: 549-69.

——, (1988), Protectionism (Cambridge, Mass: MIT Press).

——, (1991), "The World Trading System at Risk" (Princeton, NJ: Princeton University Press).

——, (1993), "Regionalism and Multilateralism: An Overview," in J. de Melo and A. Panagariya (eds.), *New Dimensions in Regional Integration* (Cambridge: Cambridge University Press).

Bhagwati, J. (1994a), *'Fair Trade,* "Reciprocity and Harmonisation: The New Challenge to the Theory and Policy of Free Trade," in A. Deardorff and R. Stern (eds.), *Analytical and Negotiating Issues in the Global Trading System* (Ann Arbor: University of Michigan Press).

——, (1994b), *'Labour Standards,* "Social Clause, and the WTO"', (New York: Columbia University, mimeo).

Bhagwati, J. and Irwin, D. (1987), "The Return of the Reciprocitarians: US Trade Policy Today", *World Economy,* 10: 109-30.

Bhagwati, J. and Jones, R. (1985), "World Trade and Payments: An Introduction." (Boston: Little, Brown).

Bhagwati, J. and Patrick H. (eds.) (1990), "Aggressive Unilateralism: America's 301 Trade Policy and the World Trading System" (Ann Arbor: University of Michigan Press).

Bhagwati, J. and Srinivasan T. N. (1994), *'Trade and the Environment: Does Environmental Diversity Detract From the Case for Free Trade?',* in J. Bhagwati and R. Hudec (eds.), *Harmonisation and Fair Trade: Prerequisite for Free Trade?* (Cambridge, Mass.: MIT Press).

Black, F. and M. Scholes. "The Pricing of Options and Corporate Liabilities." *Journal of Political Economy* 81 (May-June 1973).

Bovard, J. (1991), *The Fair Trade Fraud* (New York: St Martins Press).

Bradas, Josef C. (1998), *Behavior of Firms in Transition Economies.* Ann Arbor, Mich. The William Davidson Institute.

Brady, Rose (1999), *Kapitalizm: Russia's Struggle to Free Its Economy.* New Haven, Conn.: Yale University Press.

Braga, C. P. (1995), *'Trade-Related Intellectual Property Issues',* in W. Martin and A. Winters (eds.), "The Uruguay Round and the Developing Economies." (Washington DC: World Bank).

Branch, Melville C. (1962), *The Corporate Planning Process.* New York: American Management Association.

Brown, Lester R., Hal Kane, and Nicholas Lessen (1995), *Vital Signs 1995* (WorldWatch Institute) (New York: W.W. Norton), p. 71.

Brunetti, Aymo, Kisunko, Gregory and Weder Beatrice (1998), *How Businesses See Government*. Washington, D.C.: International Finance Corporation, The World Bank.

Burns, A. R. (1927), *Money and Monetary Policy in Early Times*. London.

Butler, Steven. "The Great Trade Wall." *U.S. News and World Report* (29 November 1999): 51-52.

Caves R. (1987), "Industrial Policy and Trade Policy: The Connections," in H. Kierzkowski (ed.), *Protection and Competition in International Trade* (London: Basil Blackwell).

Centre for Co-operation with the Economies in Transition (1997), *Privatization of Utilities and Infrastructure*. Paris: Organization for Economic Co-operation and Development.

——, *Privatization of Utilities and Infrastructure*. Paris: Organization for Economic Co-operation and Development.

Chan, K. (1985), "'The International Negotiation Game: Some Evidence from the Tokyo Round," *Review of Economics and Statistics*, 67: 456-64.

Choi, J. and John A. Doukas, (ed.), (1998), *Emerging Capital Markets*. Westport, Conn.: Quorum.

Clark, Ephraim, Michael Levasseur, and Patrick Rousseau (1993), *International Finance*. London: Charman & Hall.

Coca-Cola Annual Report, 1994.

Conybeare, J. (1987), *Trade Wars* (Princeton, NJ: Princeton University Press).

Cooper, R. (1988), *'Comment'* in L. Castle and C. Findlay (eds.), *Pacific Trade in Services* (London: Allen and Unwin).

Corden, W. M. (1974), "Trade Policy and Economic Welfare" (Oxford: Clarendon Press).

Culpan, Refik and Kumar, Brij Nino (1995), *Transformation Management in Postcommunist Countries: Organizational Requirements for a Market Economy*. Westport, Conn.: Quorum Books.

Curzon, G. (1965), *Multilateral Commercial Diplomacy* (London: Michael-Joseph).

Curzon, G. and Curzon, V. (1973), *'GATT: Traders' Club'*, in R. Cox and H. Jacobson (eds.), "The Anatomy of Influence: Decision Making in International Organisations" (New Haven, Conn.: Yale University Press).

Curzon-Price, V. (1991), "GATT's New Trade Policy Review Mechanism," *World Economy*, 14: 227-38.

Dam, K. (1970), *The GATT. Law and International Economic Organisation* (Chicago: University of Chicago Press).

Davies, S. and McGuiness A. (1982), "Dumping at less than Marginal Cost," *Journal of International Economics*, 12: 169-82.

Deardorff A. (1987), "Current Issues in Trade Policy: An Overview", in R. Stern (ed.), *US Trade Policies in a Changing World Economy* (Cambridge, Mass.: MIT Press).

——, (1987), "Safeguards Policy and the Conservative Social Welfare Function," in H. Kierzkowski (ed.) *Protection and Competition in International Trade.* (Oxford: Basil Blackwell).

Deardorff, A. (1992), "Third-Country Effects of a Nøndiscriminatory Tariff", Research Forum in International Economics, Discussion Paper no. 306 (Ann Arbor: University of Michigan).

Deardorff, A. and Stem, R. (1985), "Methods of Measurement of Non-Tariff Barriers" (Geneva: UNCTAD).

Donaldson, David J. and Wagle, Dileep M. (1995), *Privatization: Principles and Practice.* Washington, D.C.: The World Bank.

Dornbush, Rudiger (1997), "Brazil's Incomplete Stabilization and Reform" In *Brookings Papers on Economic Activity.* Washington, D.C.: Brookings Institution.

Downs, A. (1954), "An Economic Theory of Democracy" (New York: Harper & Row).

Doz, Yves L. and Hamel, Gary (1998), *Alliance Advantage: The Art of Creating Value Through Partnering.* Boston: Harvard Business School Press.

Economic and Social Commission for Western Asia (1997), *International Aspects of Privatization.* New York: United Nations.

Economic and Social Commission for Western Asia (1997), *Survey of Economic and Social Developments in the ESCWA Region 1996-1997*. New York: United Nations.

Economic Commission for Europe (1998), *Economic Survey of Europe*. Geneva: United Nations.

Edwards, S. and Savastano, M. (1989), "Latin America's Intra-Regional Trade: Evolution and Future", in D.T. Greenaway, T. Hyclak, and R. Thornton (eds.), *Economic Aspects of Regional Trading Arrangements* (New York: New York University Press).

Eggars, William D. and O'Leary, John. *Revolution at the Roots*. New York: The Free Press, 1995.

Eglin, R. (1987), *'Surveillance of Balance-of-Payments Measures in the GATT'*, *World Economy*, 10: 1-26.

Ehrenberg, R. (1994), " Labor Markets and Integrating National Economies" (Washington DC: Brookings Institution).

Eng, Maximo, Francis A. Lees, and Laurence J. Mauer (1998), *Global Finance*. New York: Addison-Wesley.

Esty, D. (1994), *Greening the GATT: Trade, Environment and the Future* (Washington DC: Institute for International Economics).

Ethier, W. (1982), *'Dumping'*, *Journal of Political Economy*, 90: 487-506.

European Bank for Reconstruction and Development (EBRD). (1998), *Transition Report 1998*. London.

Evans, J. W. (1972), "The Kennedy Round in American Trade Policy" (Cambridge: Harvard University Press).

Feinberg, R. and Kaplan, S. (1993), *'Fishing Downstream: The Political Economy of Effective Protection'*, *Canadian Journal of Economics*, 26: 150-58.

Feketekuty, G. (1988), *International Trade in Services: An Overview and Blueprint for Negotiations* (Cambridge Mass.: Ballinger Publications).

——, (1992), "The New Trade Agenda," Occasional Paper no. 40 (Washington DC: Group of Thirty).

Financial Times (1999), *Mastering Global Business*. London: Pitman Publishing.

Finch, D. and Michalopoulos, C. (1988), "Development, Trade, and International Organisations," in A. Krueger (ed.), *Development with Trade: LDCs and the International Economy* (San Francisco: Institute for Contemporary Studies).

Finger, J. M. (1974), "Tariff Concessions and the Exports of Developing Countries," *Economic Journal*, 335: 566-75.

——, (1982), "Incorporating the Gains from Trade into Policy", *World Economy*, 5: 367-77.

——, (1991), *'The GATT as International Discipline Over Trade Restrictions: A Public Choice Approach'*, in R. Vaubel and T. Willett (eds.), *The Political Economy of International Organisations: A Public Choice Approach* (Boulder, Colo.: Westview Press).

Finger, J. M. (ed.) (1993a), "Antidumping: How it Works and Who Gets Hurt" (Ann Arbor: University of Michigan Press).

Fitchett, D. (1987), "Agriculture", in J. M. Finger and A. Olechowski (eds.),. *The Uruguay Round: A Handbook on the Multilateral Trade Negotiations* (Washington DC: The World Bank).

Galbraith, John Kenneth. "Issues for the Millennium," *Finance and Development* 36, 4 (1999): 2-5.

Garrett, G. (1992), "International Cooperation and Institutional Choice: The European Community's Internal Market", *International Organisation*, 46: 543-60.

Garten, J. (1994), "New Challenges in the World Economy: The Antidumping Law and US Trade Policy", speech presented at the US Chamber of Commerce, Washington DC, 7 Apr.

GATT (1986), *The Text of the General Agreement* (Geneva: GATT).

——, (1988), *GATT Activities*, 1987 (Geneva: GATT).

——, (1989), *GATT Activities*, 1988 (Geneva: GATT).

——, (1994a), *The Results of the Uruguay Round of Multilateral Trade Negotiations: The Legal Texts* (Geneva: GATT Secretariat).

——, (1994b), *Analytical Index* (Geneva: GATT Secretariat).

GATT (1994c), "The Results of the Uruguay Round: Market Access for Goods and Services" (Geneva: GATT Secretariat).

——, (1995), *International Trade: Trends and Statistics* (Geneva: GATT).

——, (General Agreement on Tariffs and Trade) (1985), *Trade Policies for a Better Future: Proposals for Action*, Leutwiler Report (Geneva: GATT).

Gianaris, Nicholas V. (1993), *Contemporary Economic Systems: A Regional and Country Approach*. Westport, Conn.: Praeger.

Gianaris, William N. (1990-91), "Weighted Voting in the International Monetary Fund and the World Bank." *Fordham International Law Journal* 14, 4.

Giddy, Ian H. (1993), *Global Financial Markets*. Lexington, Mass.: D.C. Heath and Company.

Globerman, S. (1992), "North American Trade Liberalisation and Intra Industry Trade" 1, *Weltwirtschaftliches Archiv*, 128: 487-97.

Glover, Terrot (1942), *The Challenge of the Greeks and Other Essays*. New York: Macmillan.

Graham, E. M. and Richardson, J. D. (1994), *Summary of the Institute for International Economics Project on International Competition Policies* (Paris: OECD).

Grasso, Richard A. (1997), "Globalization of the Equity Market," *Fordham International Law Journal* 20, 4.

Gray, John (1999), *False Dawn: The Delusions of Globalism*. New York: The New Press.

Greenaway, D. (1987), "Intra-Industry Trade, Intra-Firm Trade and European Integration: Evidence, Gains and Policy Analysis," *Journal of Common Market Studies*, 26: 153-72.

Grose, Thomas K. "U.S. Shares Cross Border via Internet." *USA Today* (1 June 1999): IB.

Groupe MAC (1988), *Technical Barriers in the EC: An Illustration by Six Industries, Research on the Costs of Non-Europe*, vol. vi (Brussels: Commission of the European Communities).

Guislain, Pierre (1997), *The Privatization Challenge*. Washington, D.C. : The World Bank.

Haberler, Amacher and T. Willett (eds.), *Challenges to a Liberal International Economic Order* (Washington DC: American Enterprise Institute).

Haines, Walter W. (1961), *Money, Prices and Policy*. New York: McGraw-Hill.

Hamilton, C. and Whalley, J. (1989), "Coalitions in the Uruguay Round" 1, *Weltwirtschaftliches Archiv*, 125: 547-62.

Herin, J. (1986), *'Rules of Origin and Differences between Tariff Levels in EFTA and in the EC*, Occasional Paper no. 13 (Geneva: EFTA).

Hillman, A. and Moser, P. (1995), "Trade Liberalisation as Politically Optimal Exchange of Market Access"1, in M. Canzoneri, W. Ethier, and V. Grilli (eds.), *The New Transatlantic Economy* (New York: Cambridge University Press).

Hindley, B. (1987), "Different and more Favorable Treatment—and Graduation," in J. M. Finger and A. Olechowski (eds.), *The Uruguay Round: A Handbook for the Multilateral Trade Negotiations* (Washington DC: The World Bank).

——, (1994), "Safeguards, VERs and Anti-Dumping Action", in OECD, *The New World Trading System: Readings* (Paris: OECD).

Hindley, B. and Messerlin, P. (1993) "Guarantees of Market Access and Regionalism," in K. Anderson and R. Blackhurst (eds.), *Regionalism and the Global Trading System* (London: Harvester-Wheatsheaf).

Hippie, F. S. (1990), "The Measurement of International Trade Related to Multinational Companies." *American Economic Review*, 80: 1263-70.

Hirschman, A. (1969), *National Power and the Structure of Foreign Trade* (Berkeley: University of California Press).

——, (1981), "Three Uses of Political Economy in Analyzing European Integration," ch. 12 of id., *Essays in Trespassing* (London: Cambridge University Press).

Hoekman, B. (1992a), "Cascading Contingent Protection," *European Economic Review*, 36: 883-92.

——, (1992b), "Environmental Policy Formation in a Trading Economy: A Public Choice Perspective," in K. Anderson and R. Blackhurst (eds.), *The Greening of World Trade Issues* (London: Harvester-Wheatsheaf).

Hoekman, B. (1993), "Holes and Loopholes in Integration Agreements: History and Prospects," in K. Anderson and R. Blackhurst (eds.), *Regional Integration and the Global Trading System* (London: Harvester-Wheatsheaf).

——, (1993), "Multilateral Trade Negotiations and Coordination of Commercial Policies," in R. Stern (ed.), *The Multilateral Trading System: Analysis and Options for Change* (Ann Arbor: University of Michigan Press).

——, (1994b), "Antitrust-based Remedies and Dumping in International Trade," Discussion Paper no. 1010 (London: Centre for Economic Policy Research).

——, (1995), "The WTO's Government Procurement Agreement" 1, *Public Procurement Law Review*, 4: 63-79.

——, (1995a), "Tentative First Steps: An Assessment of the Uruguay Round Agreement on Services," in W. Martin and A. Winters (eds.), *The Uruguay Round and the Developing Economies* (Washington DC: World Bank).

——, (1995b), *Trade Laws and Institutions: Good Practices and the World Trade Organisation* (Washington DC: World Bank).

Hoekman, B. and Cremoux, P. (1993), "Perspectives for Multilateral Reductions in Agricultural Support Policies," in R. Stern (ed.), *The Multilateral Trading System* (Ann Arbor: University of Michigan Press).

Hoekman, B. and Leidy, M. (1990), "Policy Responses to Shifting Comparative Advantage: Designing a System of Emergency Protection," *Kyklos*, 43: 25-51.

Hoekman, B. and Mavroidis, P. C. (1994a), "Competition, Competition Policy and the GATT," *World Economy*, 17: 121-50.

Hopkirk, Peter (1992), *The Great Game*. New York: *Kodansha America*.

Hudec, R. (1987), *GATT and the Developing Countries* (Aldershot: Gower, for the Trade Policy Research Centre).

——, (1993), *Enforcing International Trade Law: The Evolution of the Modern GATT Legal System* (New York: Butterworth).

Iatrides, Demetreus S. (1998), *Privatization in Central and Eastern Europe.* Westport, Conn.: Quorum.

Institute for International Finance (1998), *Capital Flows to Emerging Market Economies.* Washington, D.C.

International Bank for Reconstruction and Development (1997), *Global Prospects and the Developing Countries.* Washington, D.C: The World Bank.

International Finance Corporation (1996), *Emerging Markets Stock Factbook 1996* (Washington D.C.: International Finance Corporation), p. 5.

International Monetary Fund (IMF) (1999), *International Capital Markets.* Washington, D.C: IMF.

Isard, Peter (1977), "How Far We Can Push the Law of One Price." *American Economic Review.*

Jackson, J. H. (1969), *World Trade and the Law of GATT* (Indianapolis: Bobbs-Merrill).

——, (1989), *The World Trading System: Law and Policy of International Economic Relations* (Cambridge, Mass.: MIT Press).

——, (1990), *Restructuring the GATT System* (London: Pinter Publishers). (1994), "The World Trade Organisation, Dispute Settlement, and Codes of Conduct,", in B. Bosworth and S. Collins (eds.), *The New GATT: Implications for the United States* (Washington DC: Brookings Institution).

Jacquemin, A. (1994), "Goals and Means of European Antitrust Policy After 1992," in H. Demsetz and A. Jacquemin (eds.), *Antitrust Economics: New Challenges for Competition Policy* (Lund: Lund University Press).

Jong, De H. (1968), "The Significance of Dumping in International Trade," 1, *Journal of World Trade Law,* 2: 162-88.

Kaplan, Robert D. "Could This Be the New World?" *New York Times* (27 December 1999): A23.

Kenen, Peter (1994), *The International Economy.* New York: Cambridge University Press.

Keynes, John M. (1930), *A Treatise on Money.* London.

Keynes, John Maynard, "Economic Possibilities for Our Grandchildren (1930)," in *Essays in Persuasion* (New York: W. W. Norton, 1963), p. 361.

Klitgaard, Robert (1991), *Adjusting to Reality Beyond State Versus Market in Economic Development*. San Francisco: ICS Press.

——, *Adjusting to Reality Beyond State Versus Market in Economic Development*. San Francisco: ICS Press.

Kozminski, Andrzej K. (1993), *Catching Up? Organizational and Management Change in the Ex-Socialist Block*. Albany, N.Y.

Krugman, Paul (1999), *The Return to Depression Economics*. New York: W.W. Norton.

Landes, David S. (1969), *The Unbound Prometheus: Technological Change and Industrial Development in Western Europe from 1750 to the Present* (Cambridge: Cambridge University Press), p. 5.

Laqueur Walter (1994), *The Dream That Failed: Reflections on the Soviet Union*. New York: Oxford University Press.

Lawrence, P. R. and J. W. Lorsch (1967), *Organization and Environment: Managing Differentiation and Integration*, Boston, MA: Harvard Business School.

Lenin, V.I., (1996), *Imperialism: The Highest State of Capitalism* (New York: Pluto Press), pp. 63-64.

Lews, Paul. "World Bank Says Poverty Is Increasing." *New York Times* (3 June 1999): C7.

Lieberman, Ira W. et al. (1995), *Mass Privatization in Central and Eastern Europe and the Soviet Union*. Washington, D.C: The World Bank.

Logue, Dennis E., (ed.) (1995), *The WG&L Handbook of International Finance*. Cincinnati, Ohio: South-Western.

Malkiel, Burton G. and J. P. Mei. "Hedge Funds: The New Barbarians at the Gate." *Wall Street Journal* (29 September 1998): A22.

Manser, Roger (1994), *Failed Transitions: The Eastern European Economy and Environment Since the Fall of Communism*. New York: The New Press.

Marks, Mitchell Lee and Mirvis, Philip H. (1998), *Joining Forces: Making One Plus One Equal Three in Mergers, Acquisitions, and Alliances*. San Francisco: Jossey-Bass.

Martinez, Gregory M. (1998), "Extracting Market Views from the Price of Options and Futures." *Journal of Futures and Markets* 18, 1.

McLindon Michael P. (1996), *Privatization and Capital Market Development: Strategies to Promote Economic Growth.* Westport, Conn.: Praeger.

McLindon Michael P. and Richard B. Samuelson, "One More Push: Sri Lanka's Bourse is Ripe for More Reform". *Far Eastern Economic Review,* 155 (February 13 1992).

——, "Privatization and Capital Markets in Developing Countries". Paper presented to the World Bank, Washington, D.C., 28 January 1991.

——, "Selling Thailand Inc," *Far Eastern Economic Review,* 152 (June 20 1991).

McLindon, Michael P. and Richard B. Samuelson. "Korea 1992: Foreign Perspective," *Business Korea* (July 1990).

McLindon, Michael P., Richard Downer, Richard Samuelson, David Levintow, and David Smith (1990), "Privatization in Thailand". Report prepared for the Centre for Privatization, Washington, D.C.

McLindon, Michael P., Richard Samuelson, Marianne Page, and Niall Shiner (1992), "Sri Lanka". In *The World's Emerging Stock Markets,* edited by Keith K. H. Park and Antoine van Agtmael. Chicago: Probus.

Megginson, William L., Robert C. Nash, and Matthias van Randenborgh (1995), "The Privatization Dividend: A Worldwide Analysis of the Financial and Operating Performance of Newly Privatised Firms". Public Policy for the Private Sector, Washington, D.C., The World Bank Group.

Mobius, Mark (1995), *The Investors' Guide to Emerging Markets.* New York: Irwin Professional Publishing.

Nankani, Helen (1988), *Selected Country Case Studies.* Vol. 2 of *Techniques of Privatization of State-Owned Enterprises.* Washington, D.C.: The World Bank.

New Dimensions in Regional Integration (Cambridge: Cambridge University Press).

Nohria, N. and S. Ghoshal (1997) *The Differentiated Network,* San Francisco, CA: Jossey-Bass.

Nonaka, I. and H. Takeuchi (1995) *The Knowledge-Creating Company,* New York, NY and Oxford: Oxford University Press.

Odle, Maurice (1993), *Foreign Direct Investment as Part of the Privatization Process. Transnational Corporations* 2.

Organization for Economic Co-operation and Development (1998), *Corporate Governance, State-Owned Enterprises and Privatization.* Paris.

Organization for Economic Co-operation and Development (OECD) (1995), *Mass Privatization: An Initial Assessment.* Paris: OECD.

——, *Financial Market Trends.* Paris: OECD.

Organization for Economic Co-operation and Development. *OECD Economic Outlook Number 64.* Paris, December 1998.

Panagariya A. (1994), "'Subsidies and Countervailing Measures and Anti-Dumping Agreements," in *The New World Trading System: Readings* (Paris: OECD).

——, (1995), "Legalized Backsliding: Safeguard Provisions in the GATT," in W. Martin and A. Winters (eds.), *The Uruguay Round and the Developing Economies* (Washington DC: The World Bank, forthcoming.

——, (ed.), *New Dimensions in Regional Integration* (Cambridge: Cambridge University Press).

Panagariya A. and Murray, T. (1990), "Policing Unfair Imports: The United States Example", *Journal of World Trade,* 24: 39-55.

Panagariya A. and Olechowski, A. (eds.) (1987), "The Uruguay Round: A Handbook for the Multilateral Trade Negotiations" (Washington DC: The World Bank).

Panagariya, A., Hall, H.K. and Nelson, D. (1982), "The Political Economy of Administered Protection," *American Economic Review,* 72: 452-66.

Pardy, Robert (1992), "Institutional Reform in Emerging Securities Markets". Working paper WPS 907, The World Bank, Washington, D.C.

Pardy, Robert, "Regulatory and Institutional Impacts of Securities Market Computerization". Working paper WPS 866, The World Bank, Washington, D.C.

Pinkham Richard (1996), "The Privatization of Port Kelang". Presentation at the training workshop, "Implementing BOO and BOT Projects," the Institute for Public-Private Partnerships, Washington, D.C.

Pohl, Gerhard et al. (1997), *Privatization and Restructuring in Central and Eastern Europe: Evidence and Policy Options.* Washington, D.C.: The World Bank.

Polanyi, Karl (1957), *The Great Transformation: The Political and Economic Origins of Our Time* (New York: Beacon Press).

Porter, Michael E. (1990), *The Competitive Advantage of Nations.* New York: The Free Press.

Privatisation International (1995), *Privatisation Yearbook* London: Privatisation International.

Prybyla Jan S. (1990), *Privatizing and Marketing Socialism.* Newbury Park, Calif.: Sage Publications.

Public-Private Partnerships in Infrastructure Development (1998), *Major Projects Survey, Public Works Financing.* Westfield, N.J.

Reason Foundation (1995), *Privatization 1995.* Los Angeles, Calif: The Reason Foundation.

Remnick, David (1997), *Resurrection: The Structure of a New Russia.* New York: Random House.

Ricks Thomas E. (1997), *Making the Corps.* New York: Scribner.

Roberts Paul Craig and La Follette Karen Araujo (1997), *The Capitalist Revolution in Latin America.* New York: Oxford University Press.

Rock, Milton L. and Rock Robert H. (1990), *Corporate Restructuring,* New York: McGraw Hill.

Rondinelli, Dennis A. (1994), *Privatization and Economic Reform in Central Europe.* Westport, Conn.: Quorum Books.

Sambunaris, Georgia A. (1995), "The Prospects for Multinational Banking in Mexico". Masters Thesis, Georgetown University, Washington, D.C.

Samuelson, Richard B. "Prospects for Investing in Korea". *Business Korea* (May 1988).

Sanchez, Manuel and Corona Rossana (1993), *Privatization in Latin America*. Washington, D.C.: The Inter-American Development Bank.

Savas, E.S. (1987), *Privatization: The Key to Better Government*. Chatham, N.J.: Chatham House.

Schonfield (ed.), *International Economic Relations of the Western World*, 1959-71 (London: Random House).

Segura, Jorge F. (1988), *Privatization of State-Owned Enterprises in Honduras*. Report prepared for the Centre for Privatization, Washington, D.C.

Shafik Nemat (1993), *Making a Market: Mass Privatization in the Czech and Slovak Republics*. Policy research working paper 1231. The World Bank, Washington, D.C..

Simon, Julian L. (1995), *The State of Humanity* (Cambridge: Blackwell Publishers), p. 649.

Skogstad Samuel (1995), "Policy Reform and the Transition from Command to Market Economy: A Conceptual Overview". Paper prepared for the Policy Research Centre, Georgia State University.

Smith, Hedrick (1990), *The New Russians*. New York: Random House.

Stanley, Marjorie T. (1995), *The Irwin Guide to Investing in Emerging Markets*. Chicago: Irwin.

Steinfeld, Edward S. (1998), *Forging Reform in China*. Cambridge: Cambridge University Press.

Stopford, J. M. and L. T. Wells, Jr. (1972), *Managing the Multinational Enterprise*, New York, NY: Basic Books.

Sudweeks, Brian L. (1989), *Equity Market Development in Developing Countries*. New York: Praeger.

The European Community, "Helping Eastern Europe Helps the West." *New York Times* (6 February 1990): A28.

——, "International Differences in Capital Output Ratios." *American Economic Review* 67 (June 1970): 465-477.

——, "Making It Progressive." *New York Times* (29 April 1993): A22.

——, (1993), *Eastern Europe and Russia*. Westport, Conn.: Praeger.

The European Community, (1996), *Geopolitical and Economic Changes in the Balkan Countries*. Westport, Conn.: Praeger.

——, (1996) *Modern Capitalism: Privatization, Employee Ownership, and Industrial Democracy*, Westport, Conn.: Praeger.

——, (1991), *The European Community and the United States: Economic Relations*, Westport, Conn.: Praeger.

——, (1998), *The North American Free Trade Agreement and the European Union*. Westport, Conn.: Praeger.

The Financial Silk Road (1995), *A Fifth Wave of Global Money: Cross Border Equity Flows 1995*, vol. I (New York: ING-Barings), p. 19.

The Financial Silk Road, p. 3. International Finance Corporation, p. 6. ING-Barings, *The Financial Silk Road*, p. 20.

The World Bank (1995), *Bureaucrats in Business—The Economics and Politics of Government Ownership*. New York: Oxford University Press.

The World Bank (1996), *Annual Report 1996* (New York: Oxford University Press), p. 98.

Toffler, Alvin, *The Third Wave* (New York: Bantam, 1980), p. 40.

Toso, Roberto (1990), "The Chilean Privatization Experience". Cambridge, Mass.: Paper prepared for Harvard University, Centre for International Affairs.

U.S. Central Intelligence Agency (1997), *Handbook of International Economic Statistics*. Washington, D.C.

Ullman, A. and Lewis, Alfred (1997), *Privatization and Entrepreneurship: The Managerial Challenge in Central and Eastern Europe*. New York: International Business Press.

United Nations (1998), *Foreign Investment in Latin America and the Caribbean*. Santiago, Chile.

Vernon, Raymond (1988), (ed.), The Promise of Privatization. New York: The Council on Foreign Relations.

Vittas Dimitri and Roland Michelitsch (1995), "Pension Funds in Central Europe and Russia: Their Prospects and Potential Role in Corporate Governance". Policy research working paper 1459, The World Bank, Washington, D.C.

Vittas, Dimitri (1992), "Contractual Savings and Emerging Securities Markets." Working paper WPS 858, The World Bank, Washington, D.C.

Vittas, Dimitri, and Augusto Iglesias (1992), "The Rationale and Performance of Personal Pension Plans in Chile". Working paper WPS 867, The World Bank, Washington, D.C..

Vuylsteke, Charles (1988), *Methods and Implementation*. Vol. 1 of *Techniques of Privatization of State-Owned Enterprises*. Washington, D.C.: The World Bank.

Wasserstein, Bruce (1998), *Big Deal: The Battle for Control of America's Leading Corporations* (New York: Warner Books).

Williamson, O. (1975), *Markets and Hierarchies: Analysis and Antitrust Implications: A Study in the Economics of Internal Organization*, New York, NY: Free Press.

Wint, Alvin G. (1995), *Corporate Management in Developing Countries: The Challenge of International Competitiveness*. Westport, Conn.: Quorum Books.

Yergin, Daniel and Stanislaw, Joseph (1998), *The Commanding Heights*. New York: Simon and Schuster.

Zloch-Christy Iliana, (ed.) (1995), *Privatization and Foreign Investments in Eastern Europe*, Westport, Conn.: Praeger.

Index

H

I